Not Just

A

Game

**Essays in
Canadian Sport Sociology**

Not Just

A

Game

Essays in
Canadian Sport Sociology

Edited by
Jean Harvey and Hart Cantelon

University of Ottawa Press

© University of Ottawa Press, 1988
Printed and bound in Canada
ISBN 0-7766-0115-6 (paper)
    0-7766-0189-X (cloth)

Canadian Cataloguing in Publication Data

Main entry under title:

Not just a game: essays in Canadian sport sociology

Issued also in French under title: Sport et pouvoir.
Bibliography: p.
ISBN 0-7766-0189-X (bound)
ISBN 0-7766-0115-6 (pbk.)

   1. Sports — Social aspects — Canada.   2. Sports — Social aspects —
Canada — History.   3. Sports and state — Canada.   I. Harvey, Jean,
1955-   . II. Cantelon, Hart, 1944-

GV585.N68 1988   306'.483'0971   C87-090332-2

Design by Gregory Gregory Limited, Ottawa
Set in Melior by Nancy Poirier Typesetting Ltd.
Printed by Friesen Printers, Altona, Manitoba

The University of Ottawa Press acknowledges the financial support of the
Government of Canada through the Canadian Studies Directorate of the
Department of the Secretary of State of Canada.

This book is available in a French-language edition entitled *Sport et
pouvoir : les enjeux sociaux au Canada.*

Table of Contents

Acknowledgements

This book is the culmination of the time and effort of many people. In a project of this magnitude, it would be impossible to mention all those who contributed to the final manuscript. However, there are some individuals who have provided valuable assistance to the editors.

We wish to thank Janet Shorten, Jean-Paul Morisset, and the staff of the University of Ottawa Press for their tireless enthusiasm for the project. We express our sincere appreciation to the contributors who worked diligently to meet our demands.

We also want to acknowledge those agencies that helped to finance the project either directly or indirectly. The Secretary of State of Canada generously funded the translation and co-ordination costs of the book. The essays of Donald Macintosh, Hart Cantelon, and Richard Gruneau grew out of research grants provided by the Social Sciences and Humanities Research Council of Canada, while Fitness Canada supported Suzanne Laberge's research.

Our respective universities, Ottawa and Queen's, provided necessary help and support. Finally, we want to acknowledge the external examiners and those colleagues who provided valuable comments on draft versions of the manuscript.

Notes on Contributors

Rob Beamish is jointly appointed to the Department of Sociology and the School of Physical and Health Education, Queen's University. He has taught the sociology of sport at the graduate and undergraduate levels for the past seven years. His research interests include social theory, the sociology of work, and the study of sport and the labour process.

Raymond Boulanger completed his master's degree in Leisure Studies at Trois-Rivières. His work has focused on the epistemology of the discourse and scientific practices of the Quebec milieu of leisure. He is currently studying for a Ph.D. in sociology at Université Laval. His major field of research is the study of voluntary associations.

Pierre Brodeur teaches physical education at St-Jean sur le Richelieu college. He is also a sessional lecturer in the political sociology of sport at the Université de Montréal. From 1978 to 1985 he was an active contributor to the journal *Le Desport* and more recently became a member of the Leisure-holidays committee of the C.S.N. (Confédération des syndicats nationaux du Québec).

Hart Cantelon is an associate professor in the School of Health and Physical Education at Queen's University. He is the joint editor of *Sport, Culture and The Modern State* (1982). He is presently investigating the history of Canadian and Soviet sport exchanges and policies.

Pierre J. Demers has been a sociologist at the Université de Sherbrooke since 1974. Professor Demers completed his Ph.D. at U.S.C. (1974) and has since analysed and published several sociological studies on physical education in Quebec society. He is currently working on a book which will present a new model of physical education based on health education.

Richard Gruneau teaches communication and cultural studies at Simon Fraser University. He is the author of *Class, Sports, and Social Development* (1983). His current research examines television and popular culture.

Jean Harvey teaches history and political sociology of sport at the School of Human Kinetics, University of Ottawa. He is now researching the evolution of sport policies and the development of the welfare state. He is also conducting research on health professions.

Bob Hollands has just completed his Ph.D. at the Centre for Contemporary Cultural Studies, University of Birmingham. Prior to moving to England, he was a research fellow in the Centre for Sport and Leisure Studies, Queen's University. His doctoral research deals with the British training and leisure schemes for unemployed youth.

Bruce Kidd is the Coordinator of Canadian Studies, University College, and an associate professor of Physical and Health Education at the University of Toronto. His books include *The Death of Hockey* (with John MacFarlane), *The Political Economy of Sport, Tom Longboat*, and *Athletes' Rights in Canada* (with Mary Eberts). He is also the Chair of the Olympic Studies Committee, Canadian Olympic Association, which conducts the annual Olympic Academy of Canada.

Suzanne Laberge is an anthropologist and professor of sociology of sport in the physical education department at the Université de Montréal. In addition to her work in women's studies, Professor Laberge has researched the somatic culture of marathoners, the application of economic models to the drop-out phenomenon in amateur sport, and the working conditions of coaches.

Donald Macintosh is a professor in the School of Physical and Health Education at Queen's University. His current research interests focus on government and sport and he is the principal author of the recently published book, *Sports and Politics in Canada* (1987).

Margaret MacNeill is a doctoral student in communication and cultural studies at Simon Fraser University, specializing in sport and leisure studies. She is presently researching CTV's television coverage of the 1988 Winter Olympic Games.

Ronald Melchers is an assistant professor in the Department of Criminology, University of Ottawa, and a member of the research group on the production of order (GREPO). His work deals mainly with the analysis of the systems of discipline.

Alan Metcalfe is a professor in the Faculty of Human Kinetics at the University of Windsor. His work has primarily focused on nineteenth-century Canadian and English sport history with a particular emphasis upon class and social stratification.

Roger Proulx is an associate professor in the School of Human Kinetics, University of Ottawa. His research interests are the qualification of manpower and facilities for physical fitness.

David Sankoff is a professor and senior researcher at the Centre de recherches mathématiques at the Université de Montréal. His interests are in statistics, computer science, and applied mathematical models for linguistics, biology, and several other domains.

General Introduction

Sport is primarily a social activity, and the sports problems that the media report on every day are essentially social problems. Sport is neither an idle flexing of the muscles without cause or consequence, nor merely a series of motor gestures devoid of social significance. It is a set of social structures and practices whose orientations and objectives have been adopted or challenged from the very beginning by various social agents.

Sport is also an economic phenomenon, a real industry that presents, in the form of entertainment events, "commodified" physical performance — physical activity offered as a consumer item. The sports industry also includes equipment manufacturing, which has been growing steadily since the boom in physical fitness started in the early 1970s. In Canada, the sports industry, especially professional sport, is linked with other major industrial and financial conglomerates.

Modern states — capitalist and socialist — are also influential agents in the area of sport. Major international sports events have become episodes of cold war propaganda for each of the two great political blocs, and at the same time symbolize the North's domination of the South.

The structure of sport encompasses more than might be imagined. For example, it includes physical education in the schools, which is not always the same thing as sports education; physical fitness clubs; the recent fad of physical fitness in business, encouraged by the Canadian state with heavy advertising; and all the activities related to sport which are engaged in by the middle classes. This multitude of forms has inspired a corresponding proliferation of labels seeking to identify the phenomenon: sport, physical activity, recreation, leisure, human movement, and so on.

Rather than trying to provide a precise definition of sport, the authors in the book have attempted to identify those social forces that produce and reproduce sporting practices, to outline the objectives pursued by the various social agents concerned with sport, and to describe the variations in sports participation which occur in our society.

Many objectives have guided our work on this book. We wanted first of all to make the country's two major language groups aware of the research that has been carried out across Canada in the sociology of sport. In a market in which American sports statistics and debates dominate, we believed it to be important to present original work by Canadian researchers. After all, sport has its own dynamic in Canada, even though it is heavily influenced by the United States. We also wanted the material to be written so that it would be understood by students unfamiliar with sociological analysis. Finally, we had to ensure that all the texts had a degree of theoretical unity. The varied approaches of the contributors have a common denominator — the perspective of critical sociology, used here in its broadest sense.

Like most Canadians, we have experienced the thrill of competitive sport. We have at times marvelled at the technical perfection with which certain skills are executed, and we have appreciated the accomplishments of high-performance athletes. But the emotional highs which are inspired by sport must not prevent us from maintaining a critical view: to understand a phenomenon, the analyst must recognize his or her personal feelings while maintaining a critical distance from the object he or she is studying. The challenge lies precisely in acknowledging the pleasure experienced in participation while, at the same time, recognizing that the forms of physical activity that we appreciate have emerged from struggles and developments peculiar to Canadian society. In specifically mentioning the idea of struggle, we are being implicitly critical, since the orientations of physical activity have always given rise to divergent views.

All the contributors have taken a critical view of sport, but this does not mean that their theoretical approach is a monolithic one. There has never been a theoretical framework that reflects, in itself, all facets of collective phenomena. We also had no intention of imposing a specific framework on our contributors. Consequently, each chapter will contain the necessary theoretical basis for understanding the analyses presented.

Besides the theoretical diversity that each paper demonstrates, the juxtaposition of anglophone and francophone points of view throughout the book will provide a general idea of the theoretical sources of inspiration prevailing in each community.

The unity of this book goes beyond the critical perspective on sport. Each chapter contains postulates that transcend the differences in the writers' approaches. One postulate is that sport is a social phenomenon linked to historical contingencies associated with a particular society. Simply put, the patterns of Canadian sports development are the result of historical circumstances. Another postulate holds that history is not a linear process, but rather a series of struggles regarding the very definition of sport, physical education, and recreation — a constant fight for control of organized sport.

The first part of this book deals with the historical determinants of contemporary sport. There is an emphasis on the major events and especially the historical forces that have shaped Canadian society as a whole and, as a consequence, sport itself. The other three parts of the book are devoted to modern sport. Here again, the approach is based on certain postulates. It is taken for granted that sport, having its own organizational structure as an element of Canadian society, also has its own dynamic and its own logic, which are partly consistent with those of society as a whole.

Like any institution, sport has a social philosophy, a set of symbols all its own, and takes on a precise meaning for some people. For those engaged in a sport, it can signify self-actualization, freedom from the constraints of daily existence. As an institution, sport reproduces the dominant ideas and goals of Canadian society and those who hold the reins of power. At the same time, this does not exclude challenging doctrines, which contain innovative ideological orientations.

We want to demonstrate that sport is more than a set of motor responses. It is a set of practices and a perspective of the body which is socially determined. We will not attempt to cover every aspect of the production and reproduction of sport in Canada. Nevertheless, those unfamiliar with the subject will find the ideas central to the study of sport in Canada. They will have an overview of contemporary trends in the critical sociology of sport, which will provide them with the essential background for in-depth theoretical discussions of Canadian sport. They will also be able to discern the similarities and differences between French- and English-Canadian sports research.

Finally, sports and physical activity professionals, as well as those responsible for developing policies and programs in the area of sport, will find in this book a wealth of useful information. They will see more clearly what is missing in government intervention, which is far from achieving its purported objectives; they will become aware of the forces and powers at work within organized sport. They will find specific information about the types of sports engaged in by Canadians, the social factors that, in part, determine them, and the possibilities for social change that sport carries with it. Finally, they will find avenues of discussion and proposals for reform.

Part One
The Historical Determinants of Contemporary Sport

The first part of this book examines the historical factors that have shaped Canadian sport. Collective phenomena such as sport are not static realities, because they are transformed by historical circumstances resulting from the actions of various social agents.

Marx, using materialism, the theory of history he tried to establish, revealed the essential links that exist between history and sociology. But he was not the only one: more recently, C. Wright Mills, in *The Sociological Imagination*, stated that "all sociology worthy of the name is 'historical sociology' [or] . . . an attempt to write 'the present as history' " (1959:146).

By postulating that sport is at once the product of contingent historical conditions and of the actions of social agents, this book explains the dialectical relations that exist between constraint and freedom, between structure and action, and between production and reproduction of society.

Every social system tends to reproduce itself. The mechanisms of social reproduction, like the means of socialization, ensure that the social norms are learned in such a way that everyone adheres to them. If their function is to perpetuate the minimum consensus necessary to collective living, they are also tools for the reproduction of the privileges of the dominant groups. They help legitimize the existing system, make it acceptable to everyone, and present it as an equitable arrangement despite the inequalities inherent in it. These mechanisms of social reproduction generally correspond to the structural aspect of society, that is, to constraint.

On the other hand, the domination of the dominated by the dominant is never complete, nor totally accepted: under constraining social conditions there persists an indeterminate zone from which free action may emerge. Constraint permits freedom up to a certain point, but a controlled freedom. Furthermore, since the mechanisms for reproducing the social order are not without flaws, there are, from time to time, challenges to the existing order and counter-models, which seek to institute new social rules. Hence freedom and action can be expressed in two ways: by taking advantage of the indeterminate zones that persist within the existing social constraints or by overthrowing the current system.

"Free" action and the appearance of counter-models constantly force the dominant groups to adjust whenever these pressures cast doubt on the balance of the social order and threaten its legitimacy. Thus the dominant order cannot remain static. It has its own dynamic, its objectives of perpetuating and increasing its domination. But to reproduce itself, it must make a series of adjustments in response to the incessant struggles in which the various social agents engage to institutionalize other possible models.

By explaining the changes that organized sport has undergone, it is possible to demonstrate in a theoretical and empirical manner its mechanisms of production and reproduction. Among the historical phenomena that have influenced the evolution of sport, industrialization and urbanization are often presented as the only determining factors. Approaches of this type, so common among sports historians, depict sport as the pale reflection of a linear evolution towards its contemporary forms. As a result, the influence of changes in the balance of power between the different social classes is pushed into the background, if not forgotten. However, these power relations and the social struggles they have created within sport, as in all areas of social life, have instead occupied a pivotal role in the evolution of the meaning, organization, and practices of sport. In the first chapter, which sets the tone for the rest of the book, Richard Gruneau tackles these epistemological questions, which are major issues in the social history of sport.

The notion of hegemony developed by Antonio Gramsci in the 1930s is an analytical tool that highlights the dominance exerted by a particular view of reality, that of a particular class or class segment. This notion also applies to the mechanisms for internalizing dominant values, since hegemony is in some sense the dominant representation of the social order in a particular society, a representation that holds the social order together by presenting it as the natural and only legitimate one.

The chapters by Gruneau and Alan Metcalfe are based on this notion. The latter, however, in focusing on the dominant forms of sport, does not include the history of specific groups such as women, francophones, or native people. For example, Metcalfe refers to the popularity of baseball among the working class. It is assumed that baseball attracts the members of this group because of the meaning they assign to it and not because of its intrinsic qualities. This case clearly shows the need for specific research on sport in the working class. There is also a desperate need for research on sexual inequalities in access to sport. What did working-class and middle-class women do in their leisure time? Were they only spectators?

Sport has not only served as entertainment for the middle class. Since the beginning of the twentieth century, it has been assigned utilitarian goals; capitalist entrepreneurs, for example, used recreational programs as an effective means of managing labour. The practices analysed by Ronald Melchers foreshadow modern physical fitness and recreation programs in industry.

Until quite recently, it was taken for granted in industrial capitalist societies that, as long as the necessities of war did not make it essential for women to work in factories, men would go out to work and women would stay home. For this reason, Melchers' data deal primarily with working-class men. Unfortunately, there are very few studies of the recreational activities of employed women and of the differences in experience between the unionized labour force and the non-unionized labour force. The evolution of management's ideology described by Melchers clearly shows that the organization of recreation in business never had any philanthropic intent, but was aimed at increasing productivity. Because Melchers is analysing only the strategies of the dominant classes, he does not take into account the pressures that may have been exerted by workers in favour of the establishment of recreational programs subsidized by business owners. In that connection, this chapter indicates the serious shortage of literature on the history of recreation among the working classes. It is also most informative about the social issues related to the setting up of sports programs in business.

Even though it has succeeded in imposing its domination on Canadian society, the industrial middle class has not been the only group to enjoy a degree of power. The Catholic clergy in Quebec, for example, was also quite powerful. Thanks to historical circumstances both threatening and favourable to it and its flock, it had considerable say in the perpetuation of French culture in North America. The clergy's purview was very wide, extending as far as sports and recreation, as Jean Harvey's paper shows in detail.

The society of modern sport thus bears the mark of its history, a history parallel to that of all Canadian society. Linguistic and cultural differences and conflicts between classes and class segments were at the root of the emergence of modern sport in Canada as they were in other areas.

Chapter One
Modernization or Hegemony: Two Views on Sport and Social Development

Richard S. Gruneau

Introduction

When Canadians consider the history of sport, they most often think about famous sports personalities from the past, changes in rules or styles of play, or the history of specific leagues, teams, and clubs. For a long time this was the only kind of sport history being written. Over the past twenty years, however, sociologists and historians have begun to write a different kind of sport history, one that focuses more broadly on the changing *social* aspects of sport in Canadian society.

The growing interest in the social history of sport in Canada has parallels in other western societies, and a substantial international literature has developed in the subject. This literature has provided considerable insight into how and why sport in western countries has developed in the ways it has. Most of these insights have been derived from a very simple idea: that the primary focus of any adequate social or cultural history of sport should be on relationships between sport and broader social determinants in the society at large.

Industrialization and urbanization are often singled out as the most notable of these social determinants. Modern sport has been widely viewed as a cultural by-product of the techno-logical and social changes associated with the development of an urban and industrial society (see, for example, Betts, 1974). These changes are said to have undermined the basis for older "pre-industrial" forms of sports practices while creating the conditions necessary for the emergence of modern sport.

Yet, beyond reference to technological pressures, few writers have been either specific enough or detailed enough about the precise ways in which industrialization and urbanization have transformed sport in western societies. As Adelman (1986) has noted, too often the concepts of industrialization and urbanization have been used merely as abstractions whose apparent influences on sport are treated as self-evident. Furthermore, there often seems to have been a confusion of cause and effect in discussions of industrial development, and the comparative impact of industrialization as opposed to urbanization is rarely sorted out. Adding up all the little bits of causation seemingly associated with the impact of industrialization and urbanization on sport can tell only part of the story. Any fully developed analysis of the social development of sport in western societies should be more broadly theorized.

A number of recent historians and sociologists have been sensitive to the need for a broader theoretical analysis of sport and social development (Dunning, 1973; Dunning and Sheard, 1979; Guttmann, 1978; Adelman, 1986). These writers all emphasize how the understanding of sport as a simple reflection of technological innovation, or of seemingly related changes in social organization, has proven to be extremely limiting. They offer a more complex analysis of sport in the context of the transformation of pre-industrial to industrial societies.

The ideas and theoretical arguments which have most influenced sociological and historical writing on the social development of western sport have an important coherence and a common origin. They are expressions of a "general theory of industrial society," many of whose assumptions and central concepts have been almost taken for granted in contemporary sociology and historiography. These assumptions and concepts need to be examined critically; as well, a complementary, and in some cases alternative, set of ideas from which to analyse the emergence of modern sport in western societies should be introduced.

Industrial Society and the "Modernization" of Sport: the Theory of Industrial Society

This general theory of industrial society is not a conception that can be tied to any one author. Rather, as Anthony Giddens (1977, 1982) has suggested, it is a composite of ideas stemming from many sources and expressed in quite different ways by various social theorists and historians. At the risk of excessive simplification, however, it is possible to characterize the model of social development associated with this "theory."

According to the theory, an older type of society existed prior to industrialization and its organizing structures and values were quite different from our own. Based primarily upon agrarian production, it featured a less specialized division of labour than that which exists today. This type of society could be termed "traditional society" because its social order was heavily based on tradition, superstition, and religious ritual. Family and community, labour, leisure, and religion were all highly interconnected features of localized cultural expression and it was often difficult to uncover any boundaries between them. The administration of social life was highly decentralized and tied to a clearly delineated and paternalistic social hierarchy. People were born into this hierarchy and rarely moved beyond their predetermined place within it. The dominant values in this social formation emphasized collective duties and obligations rather than individual "rights" and there was a tendency to view the existing order as a natural expression of how human beings should live.

Industrialization, the argument runs, emerged out of this context due to some combination of new ways of thinking about society, innovations in technology, and changes in the demographic composition of pre-industrial societies. Experimentation and the attempts to understand and control nature gave cultural support to a rational scepticism which helped to undermine the powers of religion and sacred ritual. The extension of this rational scepticism from the analysis of nature to the analysis of society helped pave the way for the idea that social order was made by humans rather than being something natural and inevitable. If it was possible to alter and control the natural world, then, presumably, it was possible for people to alter and control the social world as well. Innovations in technology and new, more secular religions helped to expand the continuing breakdown of tradition. New markets and trade routes were opened up as a result of technological improvements in transportation, production, and warfare; as well, a growing "middle" class of merchants, shopkeepers, and artisans began to emerge as a new social force.

The emergence of new occupations that were not tied to the land, coupled with new forms of technology in production, led to increased complexity and specialization in the division of labour and the beginnings of greater centralization of economic and administrative functions in towns. Related to this, the argument continues, people who had to earn their living by selling or making products began to resent the absence of individual rights in social and political life. New individualist philosophies which valued the free market began to emerge, and groups began campaigns to entrench individual "freedoms," such as the right to own property, freedom of speech, and freedom of representation, in the emerging structures of the modern liberal-democratic state. Meanwhile, the introduction of full-scale industrial production fuelled the expansion of new opportunities and initiated a generalized population movement from countryside to city. The developing urban-industrial society became less localized, more cosmopolitan, and the values of individual autonomy and achievement began to take precedence over, and ultimately came to replace, older values of social ascription. Industrial technology also produced unprecedented material affluence and created a separate and expanding sphere of "leisure time" in western societies.

Within this framework it has been possible to depict the social development of western sport as a manifestation of a broader transformation from "traditional" agrarian to "modern" industrial societies. Accompanying the movement from one type of society to another, the argument runs, has been a parallel movement between fundamentally different types of sports practices. As this has occurred, traditional sports practices in pre-industrial societies have been replaced by the new world of modern sport.

Social Characteristics of "Traditional" and "Modern" Sport

What are the allegedly typical characteristics of "traditional" and "modern" sport? In recent years, several extremely useful inventories have been compiled (see, for example, Dunning, 1973; Guttmann, 1978; Adelman, 1986). Different writers have emphasized some characteristics more than others, but overall there appears to be widespread agreement on the differing features of "traditional" versus "modern" sport.

Traditional sport, it is often said, tended to be periodic, unorganized, localized in specific communities, and governed by differing and often competing rules. There were no widely agreed upon ways of playing, no controlling organizational bodies, and little sense of sport as an institutionally distinct activity. Rather, traditional sport, as either a "folk" or "elite" recreational pastime, was closely interwoven with established conventions of ritual and social hierarchy (e.g., the social class structure and paternalistic authority) as well as the daily and seasonal rhythms of domestic and agrarian production, entertainment, and religious festivals.

"Modern" sport, by contrast, appears to be fundamentally different — a measure of its association with the broader social transformation of western societies. Modern sport is vastly more organized, highly structured, and regulated than was sport in the past. Unorganized, periodic, and localized forms of individual and community-based expressions of pleasure, entertainment, physical prowess, and ritual display have been replaced by an elaborate system of regionally, nationally, and internationally scheduled activities. As this has occurred, sport at the highest levels has become more specialized, bureaucratized, and oriented to the values of individual achievement expressed through the pursuit of "the record." Sports participation generally appears to have become more popularized and accessible as a form of leisure activity and it has developed an *institutional* character all its own. Related to this, modern sport has come to figure prominently in a vast array of contemporary social, political, and economic objectives such as education, health promotion, political image-making, and the pursuit of profits through mass entertainment.

The concept of institutionalization is not strictly limited to applications of the theory of industrial society and it is not always mentioned in conventional discussions of the "typical" characteristics of modern sport. However, the concept can be indirectly associated with many of the key features usually noted by writers in their discussions of the transition from "traditional" to "modern" sports forms and practices. Sport in the past was closely interwoven with other prominent features of social life, including other institutions. But the development of a distinct institutional character to sport itself, as a whole and seemingly coherent field of social and cultural practice, clearly appears to be a uniquely modern phenomenon.

Sociologists have used the word "institution" to refer to distinctive patterns and rules of conduct that persist in a recognizably similar form across wide spans of time and which represent established and widely accepted ways of doing things in society (see Giddens, 1982:10, and Gruneau, 1976b:20–21). The institutionalization of modern sport can be usefully understood as a process whereby one particular set of patterns and rules of conduct has gradually emerged to define and regulate our contemporary sense of *what* sport is and *how* it should legitimately be played. Over the past hundred years in particular, one dominant way of playing has tended to be seen as *the* way of playing, and certain recreational and contest activities have come to be defined as legitimate sport while others have not.

Three subprocesses are often noted as central features in the institutionalization of modern sport: codification, organization, and legitimation. Codification simply refers to the process whereby sports pastimes have gone from informal regulation by local and, in many cases, oral traditions, to a system based on written rules that have a more universal acceptance. The emergence of modern sport is often said to have been dependent on a movement from local variations in rules, games, and styles of play to more universal and widely accepted practices. Formal organizations, such as clubs, leagues, or national associations, have been the primary vehicles for this transformation. The codification of rules required the establishment of formal bodies that could act as the custodians of sports regulations and provide "proper" channels for their modification. It was also necessary for these organizations to legitimize particular practices in an attempt to build public support for particular ways of playing.

Modernization and the Forces of Rationalization

But *why* did all this occur? The answer to this question lies in the sources of change identified within the theory of industrial society as a whole. The emphasis here is on the combined role of ideas, attitudes, and technological innovation. Modern societies are only made possible in this theory by the *breakdown of tradition*. Pre-industrial social life based on ascription and backward-looking tradition can only be superseded by the development of a new "rational" industrial order based on achievement.

The clearest expression of these arguments in the sports literature can be found in Guttmann's highly influential book *From Ritual to Record: The Nature of Modern Sports* (1978). He argues that the transformation from traditional to modern sport can be viewed as one of many cultural expressions of the expansion of the scientific world view in western societies. According to Guttmann, this world view helped to undermine the ritualistic tie between sport and tradition. It also underlay the development of a new kind of rationality in sport — a rationality that culminated in the creation of sports organizations, and in the emergence of modern instrumentalities (politics, economics, etc.) in the field of sports practices.

Guttmann's analysis draws its strength from a perspective that looks beyond the immediate causal impact of technological innovations in production, and the accompanying growth of cities, on the social development of modern sport. Guttmann's reliance on a two-stage model of development between distinct social types, and the emergence of new forms of rationality in industrial societies, owes a debt to several classical social theorists, most notably the German sociologist Max Weber. But there is also a loose compatibility here with a number of other important assumptions often lodged in the cluster of ideas which make up the general theory of industrial society described earlier.

Background Assumptions and Contingent Arguments
These assumptions are usually linked to five major types of argument. Writers whose work can be related to the general theory of industrial society often advance at least some (but not necessarily all) of the following notions (this discussion adapts some of the ideas discussed in Giddens, 1982).

(1)   The transformation from pre-industrial to industrial, or traditional to modern, societies has been an essentially progressive movement in history and the "modernization" of sport can be understood in these terms. Despite numerous ongoing problems (e.g., violence, drug-taking), it is argued that modern sport has opened up many opportunities not previously available in pre-industrial societies (e.g., the best athletes are more skilled than ever before, sport has come to embody unprecedented degrees of international co-operation).

(2)   A continuing democratization of sport is widely noted as one of the most important consequences of the development of industrial societies based on values of individual achievement. The breakdown of social ascription in modern society at large has meant increased sports opportunities for poor people, women, and minority and ethnic groups. It is sometimes argued as well that upward mobility in sport (e.g., for black athletes) has actually contributed to the broader democratizing tendencies of modern life.

(3)   The social development of modern sports forms and practices tends to be viewed from this perspective as a "rational adaptation" made by voluntary actors, associations, and municipal governments to the stresses and strains associated with the broader transition from pre-industrial to industrial societies. Urban industrial society allegedly created new functional "needs" for the

rational organization of games — needs which were met by the emergence of sport as a modern institution.

(4) Major social conflicts in sport were simply a transitory feature in the emergence of fully modern sports forms and practices. Most of these early conflicts — for example, over the legitimacy of "blood sports" such as cockfighting or bear-baiting, or later, over amateurism and professionalism — were simply growing pains in the "maturation" of modern sport. These conflicts often had a notable social class element but in modern industrial societies where class conflicts are seen to have become effectively eliminated, sport no longer has relevance as a sphere of class conflict.

(5) Reliance on arguments associated with the general theory of industrial society tends to lead inevitably to the supposition that the fundamental characteristics of sport are basically similar throughout modern industrial societies.

One of the implications that stems from this last argument is the suggestion that variations in sport in different societies can be explained by the differing ways in which tradition and modernity are intermingled in social life. The most technically advanced societies, however, are generally depicted as the least "traditional," and it is in these societies, we are told, that one can find the most modernized or "developed" forms of sports expression. Modernization can easily be understood as equivalent to "westernization" in this formulation, and a contrast has often been drawn between "developed" western industrial societies and the so-called "underdeveloped" societies of the Third World. From this perspective, there has been a tendency to assume that the dominant structures and meanings of sport in technologically advanced societies will inevitably provide the model for sport in supposedly "underdeveloped" societies.

Limits and Problems of Industrial Society Theories

Descriptive, Cultural, and Evolutionary Biases

Sociologists and historians have used various concepts and ideas associated with this theory of industrialization in many different ways and with various levels of sophistication. Some of these concepts and ideas — the "rationalization" of sport, for example — have been extremely useful and have generated significant insights into the social development of modern sports forms and practices. Furthermore, individual research studies variously associated with this perspective (not always consciously) have provided invaluable historical detail on a broad range of issues and events.

Yet, it is not at the empirical level where the most caution needs to be exercised when assessing ideas and concepts commonly associated with the general theory of industrial society. Rather, the real problem lies in the underlying assumptions and explanatory categories of the theory itself. Many of these assumptions and categories are highly problematic. At best they can be said to have directed attention towards certain key research questions at the expense of other equally important ones. At worst they have tended to become fused with the most hollow of liberal clichés about the voluntary and consensual foundations of life in the west, the extent of social progress and equality, and the alleged problems of "underdevelopment" elsewhere in the world.

In order to discuss some of these problems, this chapter will focus initially upon the two-stage model of development from "traditional" to "modern" society that provides the descriptive core of the theory of industrial society. This model offers a description of social change by abstracting the seemingly definitive or dominant features of an earlier and quite different type of social formation, and contrasting these with the dominant characteristics of contemporary social life. As discussed earlier, the same strategy can usefully be employed with respect to the identification of fundamental differences in the characteristics of sport within these social formations. The virtue of this technique lies in its ability to focus attention upon major epochs or phases in human history and to convey the central organizing features of these phases in a simplified manner. It also allows the comparison of individual societies with the abstracted "ideal type" in order to determine, and then to explain, the amount of similarity or divergence between them.

But people often forget that they are simply working with an analytic model. The model tends to be taken at face value as an essentially "known" set of conditions. In such cases, all that remains is for historians and sociologists to track the passage of social development from the one apparently known state to the other — for example, from traditional to modern sport. This approach often lends itself to an overemphasis on the descriptive "mapping" of changes rather than their explanation. It may also result in overlooking extremely important differences *between* the characteristics of sport at varying moments in the history of specific societies and those of the abstract models of "traditional" and "modern" sport.

        To illustrate this, the example of sport in both Canada and
the United States as "typically" modern activities will be considered. One of the seemingly modern characteristics of sport in
each case is the prevalence of large bureaucratic organizations
that are often geared towards meeting political goals. But a focus
on the similarities between these organizations and goals may
result in overlooking their striking differences. For instance, Canadians have generally been much more willing to tolerate extensive government involvement in sport over the past thirty years
than have Americans. As a result, the types of bureaucratic
organizations in sport, and their formal connections to the state,
differ markedly in the two cases, as do the political goals that are
often in question.
        Even if these differences are recognized, the general
theory of industrial society explains them with respect to variations in degrees of "traditionalism" and "modernity" in each
country, or with respect to different cultural values. This is a
seriously inadequate view because it fails to identify the fundamental differences in the political and economic histories of each
country, especially with regard to Canada's cultural and economic
dependency on the United States (see Kidd, 1982). Canada's colonial history and dependent relation to more powerful economies
and cultures have always created pressures for high levels of state
involvement throughout various aspects of the society, and have
sometimes led to a perceived "underdevelopment" of certain features of Canadian cultural life. An emphasis on cultural and value
differences as an explanation of this is meaningless if taken out
of the context of shifting political/economic determinants.
        There is also a problem in that the language of moderni-
zation often harbours an implied evolutionary viewpoint — a subtle
historicism which blinds us to the recognition that fundamentally
alternative practices, new ways of playing, or new meanings for
sport always have the potential to develop within any society —
even modern ones. When considering a simple transition from "traditional" to "modern" sport it is easy to forget this. After all, what
is it in history that comes after "modern"? Some writers have proposed the idea of "postmodern" societies, but there is an absurd-
ity about this concept which largely undermines its usefulness
(however, see Featherstone, 1985). The point here is that industrial society theory too readily conveys the impression that the
development of sports practices in modern life is an essentially
completed phenomenon. All that might be expected in the future
are elaborations *within* the established and legitimated form.

Alternative Categories: the Emergent, Dominant, and Residual

The perception noted above is based on highly debatable premises. It greatly limits our capacity to conceive of *emergent*, perhaps even oppositional, ways of playing in modern societies, or to identify conflicts between *dominant* and emergent tendencies in modern sport. In some cases, it may also result in overlooking, or misconstruing, the importance of social and cultural continuities in sport. Modern societies still contain important *residual* sports practices, styles, and traditions. The term "residual" refers to sports practices, styles, and beliefs effectively formed in the past but which remain highly significant today. Some of these have largely become incorporated into more typically "modern" ways of playing (e.g., certain gambling and drinking practices and, more recently, older conceptions of "amateurism"). Others now exist only on the margins of the dominant institutionalized practices that define dominant conceptions of "legitimate" sport (e.g., "blood sports" such as cockfighting or pit-dog fighting).

Again, assuming that such residual practices are noticed at all, the temptation derived from the general theory of industrial society is to understand them simply as the lingering ghosts of tradition — archaic remnants of the "irrational" features of an older, more hedonistic, popular culture, or of a fading, more romantic approach to sports practices. With the continuing "maturation" of modern sport it is implied that these traditional remnants will slowly disappear. For example, such an argument could be invoked to explain how late nineteenth-century amateurism, with its romantic rejection of commercialism and its moral emphasis on gentlemanly behaviour, became transformed through sport's modernization in the twentieth century.

Yet, these arguments and observations would all be misleading with respect to the changing complexities of *power* in the social development of sport in industrial societies. Talk of abstract social or institutional "needs" has tended to confuse the needs and interests of specific groups of people with those of the whole society (cf., Gruneau, 1976a; Hargreaves, 1982b). Furthermore, the idea of certain sports remnants of traditional life fading naturally into disuse in the face of the long march of modernization has often led researchers to overlook the socially produced pressures and limits that have actively pushed these practices to the cultural periphery.

Sport, Power, and Cultural Struggle

Tradition, of course, *is* an important factor to consider. It is not completely inaccurate to view the residual sports practices still found throughout modern industrial societies as manifestations of more "traditional" forms of life. However, it is necessary to add an analysis of the changing meanings and uses of popular traditions by differing social groups in the history of modern industrial societies. This analysis should also take up the issue of the changing dynamics between dominant, residual, and emergent social and cultural forms and practices at any given historical moment.

When this is done, it becomes virtually impossible to conceive of the history of sport as a series of rational or functionally necessary adaptations to change, or as the consolidation of a consensus rooted in the changing "normative structure" of society, or even as the fully determined "product" of the relentless forces of rationalization. The history of modern sport, as in all areas of popular culture, is a history of cultural struggle. To paraphrase Hall (1981:227), it is a history where some cultural forms and practices are driven out of the centre of popular life, actively marginalized, so that something else can take their place. In sport, the focus of these struggles has been the monopolistic capacity to define the dominant forms and meanings of sports practices and the "legitimate" uses of time and the body (cf., Bourdieu, 1978; Gruneau, 1983; Donnelly [forthcoming]).

Perhaps the most notable of these was the attempt throughout western capitalist societies to actively police and to "reform" the cultural practices of the new urban working classes. In Canada, for example, the beginnings of notable urban growth in Upper and Lower Canada during the first half of the nineteenth century were accompanied by a whole set of regulations over drinking hours, and types, times, and spaces for "allowable" recreations. Play in the streets was made illegal, certain types of violent sports practices such as cockfighting and bear-baiting were banned, and game-playing on Sundays was prohibited. In addition to this, alternative forms of supposedly more "rational" recreation were developed in schools, clubs, and voluntary associations (see Gruneau, 1983:93–108).

Yet older sports forms and practices did not die out. In some cases, compromises were made, in others older traditions were clung to and often took on an oppositional character in the face of new forms of authority (see, for example, Palmer, 1979, and DeLottinville, 1981–82). However, by the late nineteenth century the *emerging institutionalized forms of sport* had become consolidated around the ideas of the moral usefulness of games, middle-class respectability, and gentlemanly propriety. Rational recreation had expanded to include a Victorian ideology of athleticism with its roots in the class-based traditions of the British public school. However, at the very moment that the amateur code established its dominance through a network of clubs and associations, it was itself challenged by a set of contradictory pressures and by emergent commercial sports forms which provided alternatives to the socially restrictive traditions of amateurism (for a discussion of contradictory pressures within amateurism, see Gruneau, 1983:108–123).

None of this occurred in any evolutionary way, nor did it simply turn on the emergence of new forms of rationality. The ongoing marginalization of certain traditional sports practices or their incorporation into more "respectable" and "useful" ways of playing, the constitution of the dominant forms and practices of sport around the concept of amateurism by the late nineteenth century, and the emergence of alternative commercial sports were all part of a broader process of cultural conflict and social change in Canadian society. Within this broader process, the specific struggles of men and women, social classes, and racial and ethnic groups, over different versions of how to live, how to work and play, and what to value, can be seen.

Capitalist Society, Hegemony, and the Commodification of Sport

The Social Context of Cultural Struggle: Capitalist Society vs. Industrial Society

Popular cultures have been an important arena in western societies within and through which various groups have actively constituted and reworked their relationships to each other, to "others," and to changing social conditions as a whole. But the most important point is that *the same resources have not been universally available in these negotiations and struggles*. In certain contexts, some groups have been *empowered* more than others and this has had implications for the creation of socially dominant cultural forms and practices and their preservation through the process of institutionalization.

This leads the argument back to the problem of power. Many writers whose work is influenced by the general theory of industrial society tend to say very little about power. When power is mentioned it is often used as a synonym for "influence" or "authority." For example, power in sports organizations, and in society as a whole, is seen to reside in, and be expressed through, established and legitimated structures of bureaucratic decision-making. Coercion is the obvious contrast to this rather benign view of power and can be defined simply as the exercise of power to get what one wants even if others resist. But this definition lends itself to simplistic dichotomies such as, for example, the powerful and the powerless. Social life is rarely so neatly packaged, and sometimes the "powerless" have many more resources at their disposal than is commonly realized.

A much better way to understand power is to view it as the capacity of a person or group of persons to employ resources of different types in order to secure outcomes (cf., Giddens, 1977:347). In sport, there are three notable measures of the "power" of different social groups: (a) the capacity to structure sport in preferred ways and to "institutionalize" these preferences in sports rules and organizations; (b) the capacity to establish selective sports traditions; and (c) the capacity to define the range of "legitimate" practices and meanings associated with dominant sports practices. The resources that have allowed particular groups to do this are socially produced. They are constituted in and through the logic and patterning of the formal and informal conventions which underlie broader structures of economic, political, and cultural life.

The primary disposition of power in industrial capitalist societies has often been understood with respect to differences between social classes. However, writers influenced by the theory of industrial society tend to talk less about class power than about socio-economic inequalities of opportunity and the process of "democratization" in sport. Class in modern industrial society is usually treated in this formulation only as a statistical abstraction; classes are said to have been replaced by a broader plurality of interest groups. That is why, the argument runs, the same kinds of class conflicts and inequalities are no longer being worked out in sport as in the early "transitional" years between pre-industrial and industrial social formations.

Yet, if "capitalist society" rather than "industrial" (or even "post-industrial") society is considered, it is possible to get a different view of this. Over a hundred years ago, Karl Marx argued that "capitalism" should be seen both as a form of economic enterprise and as a type of society involved in a distinctive process of development. Marx felt that capitalism was a distinct type of society because other institutions, and social and cultural practices, supported the basic forms of capitalist organization. Furthermore, as Anthony Giddens (1982:43) reminds us, Marx presumed that the origins of capitalism, as a type of economic enterprise, were established prior to industrial development and that certain emergent features of capitalist enterprise had provided the stimulus for industrialization.

From a Marxist perspective, it is impossible for class domination and inequality to disappear in the face of "modernization" because capitalism is an *inherently* class-divided type of society. Modern class structures may be complicated by residual class elements from the past — or seemingly intermediary "middle classes" — but there is a fundamental cleavage in capitalist societies between capital and labour. The owners of capital and their agents (e.g., managers, professionals) and the "working classes" define the essential character of the society as a whole by virtue of their unique social relationship. They depend on one another, but in a fundamentally unequal way.

Marxist writers emphasize that wage workers need to sell their labour to survive economically and that they have little say over the organization of work or the uses to which their labour power is applied. Their bargaining power is also said to be limited by the threat of unemployment, and the entire political system, it is theorized, is structured in a way which gives institutional support to the class structure (see Miliband, 1969).

Sport in Capitalist Society
Some critics, inspired by the Marxist tradition, have argued that modern sport should be seen both as a reflection of capitalist social processes and class relations, and as an expression of class power, social control, and the dominant ideology (see, for example, Hoch, 1972; Brohm, 1978; Rigauer, 1981). Some of the major ideas developed in this literature can be summarized briefly as follows:

(1) Marxist perspectives on sport emphasize how the dominant class that came into being with the advent of industrial capitalist production processes was able to extend its influence over all other areas of life. This not only included such areas as education, philosophy, politics, science, and the arts; it also included "leisure" activities such as games and sports. Members of the dominant class came to enjoy high levels of participation in certain "elite" sports, and often belonged to exclusive clubs.

However, it is also argued that they helped create, and eventually monopolized, national and international sports organizations. More notably, the dominant class was instrumental in the creation and control of highly commercialized team sports which were then "marketed" as spectacle to the new working classes.

(2) A related argument suggests that modern sport is actively involved in the *reproduction* of class power and unequal class relations. Attention is often directed towards the role of sport as a forum for exercising discipline and social control in schools and communities. Sport is also said to function as a vehicle for political socialization (learning particular ways of thinking and behaving) which reflects and reinforces the value preferences and beliefs of the dominant class. As a result of this socialization function, and because of its capacity to glorify state leaders and state policies, sport has become highly attractive to the capitalist state. State programs in sport, moreover, are seen to be generally representative of capitalist interests.

(3) Because of its role in social reproduction, sport is often viewed as a kind of ideological "product" of capitalist social relations (e.g., social classes) and productive forces (e.g., technology). As ideological forms, modern sport is seen to embody the values of hard work, discipline, and achievement demanded in a system of production geared to profit-making through the exploitation of mass markets. Modern sport currently dramatizes standards of hierarchy and success based on skill, celebrates commerce, and presents a false view of social progress based on the continuing assault on the record books. In a related way, it is argued, institutionalized sport reflects the rationalization process which has characterized the overall development of the capitalist labour process. Rationalization has transformed play into work and has created an artificial need for spectacle. As a result, it is argued, sports of all types are increasingly replete with the constraints characteristic of capitalist market operations: specialization, standardization, bureaucratic decision-making, over-reliance on technology, and the constant drive for efficiency and maximum production.

(4) Because of the reasons noted above, there has been a great emphasis on *alienation* in Marxist writing on sport. Although it is a complex concept, alienation can be loosely defined as an action or state of being in which a person, a group, or a whole society becomes alien (a) to the results or products of its own activity (and to the activity itself), and/or (b) to the natural world in which it lives, and/or to other human beings, and (in addition to any or all of the above) (c) to its own historically created human

possibilities. Sport in capitalist societies is often viewed both as an alienated activity on its own terms and as an overall manifestation of life in an alienated society. For example, it is often argued that, at the highest skill levels of sport, capitalist society has reduced athletic performances to simple objects of exchange value and commodity relations. Athletes are thus robbed of effective control over the expressive uses of their own bodies. At the same time, the excessive demand for (often violent) spectacle, and the obsessive pursuit of "leisure," can be viewed as a manifestation of a society where work has lost all meaning and the desire for political discourse has been replaced by the desire for escapist entertainment.

(5)   The solution to these problems is said to lie with the eradication of capitalist social relations through the collective ownership of the means of production and the creation of a culture not tied to the values of possessive individualism and capital accumulation. In such a society, it is argued, "modern" sport will differ markedly from sport in industrial capitalist societies. Some writers have made this case in evolutionary language: sports practices in feudal society became transformed with the advent of new productive forces and capitalist social relations. Capitalist sport will become transformed in a similar fashion in the transition to socialism. The key model of development here is not seen as a transition from "traditional" to "modern" sport; rather, it runs from feudal sport, through capitalist sport, to socialist sports practices. Other writers in the Marxist tradition are more pessimistic about the inevitability of such changes in sport. They argue that the capitalist "consciousness industry" has effectively undermined any real basis for an oppositional class politics.

Marx's writing has been interpreted in many ways and there are often striking differences between various "Marxisms" in western countries. These differences are in evidence in the sports literature and, in this chapter, they have not been drawn out in any detail nor has it been suggested which of the above arguments have the greatest force and which need to be revised or discarded.

Some attention to these issues, however, is unavoidable. As a first point, it should be emphasized that the great strength of the Marxist tradition of writing on sport lies in its emphasis on power and ideology in cultural analysis — *precisely those areas which are least developed, or are discussed in highly problematic ways, in the theory of industrial society*. Furthermore, many of the insights about the *continuing* class character of modern sport that are owed to the Marxist tradition have been an extremely important corrective to biases inherent in the modernization framework.

But in its evolutionary and most highly deterministic forms — or in versions which view culture in capitalist societies as *completely* co-opted by ideology — Marxist-inspired writing on sport has often proven to be one-dimensional and limiting. Consider just a few of these limitations. First, until just recently, there has been a tendency throughout Marxist writing on sport to employ one-sided and overly deterministic understandings of power and cultural practice. For example, the reduction of sports forms to simple economic or class determinations has led some writers to overlook the active and *meaningful* features of sport as cultural practices. Furthermore, Marxist writers have tended to pay so much attention to the appropriation of sport by the marketplace and to its containment by ideology and class interest that they have lost sight of the basis for its popular appeal. Many writers have also overlooked sport's role in various forms of resistance and opposition to capitalist processes and ideological discourses (cf., Hargreaves, 1982b; Gruneau, 1983).

It is not necessary to state the relationship between sport and class in capitalist society in such a reductionist manner. Sport is no more a passive reflection of capitalist social processes than it is of changes in technology or cultural values and beliefs. Rather, sport is better understood as shifting social and cultural practices which help to constitute particular ways of life. It is an expression of socially produced individual and collective wants, and choices of and capacities for entertainment, drama, excitement, or display, through competitive bodily practice. Sport signifies a great deal about ourselves and about different ways of living and in so doing contributes to the ongoing production of social life itself.

The Labour Process and Commodification

Despite the wide range of possible meanings in sport, it is important to understand how capitalist social relations have set limits and exerted powerful pressures on the constitutions of sport and society at varying historical moments. It may be too much to say that the dominant classes in capitalist societies have ever had a consistent or monolithic view of what sport is or ought to be (see the author's discussion of intra-class tensions in Chapter Three in Gruneau, 1983). Similarly, it seems a great exaggeration to suggest that these classes have been completely successful in adapting every aspect of modern sport to their own uses, or even that sport has become fully transformed into an appendage of the capitalist labour process. But it is not so far off the mark to argue that (a) capitalist forms of production (e.g., private ownership of property, wage labour) have bestowed differential advantages to some groups over others in the making of modern sport and that (b) these forms have created strong pressures on the structuring of modern sports practices.

Some examples will illustrate these ideas. Harvey (1973) has noted how the drive to expand the sphere of capital accumulation throughout the nineteenth century created significant pressures for the "rational" ordering (for capital) of urban space. He even goes so far as to argue that the most distinctive feature of the modern city in capitalist countries was that *space itself became a commodity*. It is for this reason, Harvey argues, that the struggle over the uses of space and the whole ordering of the modern urban experience cannot be disentangled from class conflicts and relationships. If Harvey's arguments are accepted, it becomes impossible to view the close relationships between urbanization and the emergence of modern sport as a product of *industrial* development. The struggle over space for recreational use and for profit-making in western societies has involved processes that are *specific to capitalism as a social formation*.

Struggles over "rational" recreation and over "amateurism" were also implicated in the social production of distinctly capitalist forms of social and cultural organization. For example, the emerging structures of capitalist societies were partly consolidated through the demands made by the new buyers of labour power for a reconstitution of traditional ways of life compatible with wage work and timed factory production. It was in this context that certain "traditional" leisure practices suddenly became a "problem" and were subjected to regulation and "reform." Rational work discipline demanded equally rational leisure discipline!

Capitalist production processes also had the effect of separating further the spheres of home and work, production and consumption, throughout the late nineteenth and early twentieth centuries. Leisure became the time when labour was replenished physically and culturally, and it continued to offer choices for entertainment outside the constraints of the workplace. Yet, the choices available to people during "leisure time" were themselves largely shaped by the degree to which the new forms of industrial work routine, cultural regulation, and urban living had destroyed more traditional forms of family and community life and their accompanying spaces, times, and opportunities for amusement. As a result, the time Canadians spent away from work became increasingly dependent on the marketplace as a source of personal gratification. This gave considerable impetus to the commodification of all forms of entertainment and popular cultural practice, and to the establishment of new hierarchies of consumption based on market position. Sport became one more site for capital accumulation and leisure expenditure. Facilities were increasingly provided by entrepreneurs for a fee, admission came to be charged for watching sports events, new labour markets for "professional" players opened up, and new markets were developed for sports equipment.

Hegemony and the Changing Social Definition of Modern Sport

As noted earlier, amateurism came to dominate the early institutional structure of modern sport in the late nineteenth century. The philosophy of amateurism was propagated from within these structures as the definition of what sport *ought* to be all about. It constituted a perception of sport as a form of respectable and "civilized" behaviour. Amateurism was also perceived to be useful as a cultural model for class conciliation. Males from the dominant and subordinate classes could supposedly be "brought together" as gentlemen on the playing field. Equally important here was the residual idea that true "gentlemen" were somehow above commercial considerations. Sport was an area where men might learn the lesson that "culture" was more important than commerce, fairness more noble than victory.

But this socially produced definition of sport was often at odds with people's real experiences. The ideology of class conciliation on the playing field could hardly dissolve real social divisions that were constituted through the capitalist labour process (cf., Cunningham, 1980; Gruneau, 1983). Furthermore, amateurism's emphasis on playing the game for its own sake, and its romantic denial of commercialism, were at odds with long-established commercial tendencies in popular culture and the relentless expansion of commodity production. The idea that there was something morally wrong with commercialized sports entertainment was simply unconvincing for large numbers of people.

Initiatives for leisure discipline, regulation, or reform have always had a contradictory character in capitalist societies. For every factory owner who bemoaned the lack of discipline at the workplace — or middle-class moral custodian who wanted to civilize the "rough" elements of the working classes — there seemed to be an entrepreneur prepared to market opportunities for pleasure, sociability, and escape. It is important to note here that most "consumers" were not prepared to accept excessively violent commercial recreations. The juxtaposition of a residual ideology of amateurism with the emerging structures of professional sport in Canada helped to secure an orderly audience for modern sports activities. Earlier forms of traditional gaming practice lost their rougher edges in their struggles and compromises with rational recreation and amateur traditions. Thus a new social definition of sport has become dominant within the institutional structures of sport in capitalist societies during the twentieth century. Sport has come to be widely understood as a completely open, achievement-based activity, conducted to further sports careers and reap economic reward. Also included is the notion that enjoyment in sport is tied to skill acquisition, that specialization is the basis of excellence, and that economic reward of some type or another is both justified and necessary at the highest levels.

This new dominant social definition of sports practice — and the full incorporation of professional sport as a part of sport's modern institutional structure — has become a constitutive part of the consolidation of capitalist *hegemony* in the modern world. The word hegemony refers to the whole range of processes through which dominant social groups extend their influence in such a way as to continually refashion their ways of life, and institutionalized modes of practice and belief, in order to win consent for the system and structure of social relations which sustain their dominant position (see Gramsci, 1971; Mouffe, 1979). Because no dominant social order ever completely exhausts or determines the range of possible available practices in cultural life, hegemony is an ongoing process. Social and cultural forms and practices, which are either residual or emergent, always pose a potential threat to dominant ones. So does the capacity to dream, to theorize, and to imagine a different world.

Dominant interests, however, tend to become centred in institutional life in ways that seek to *exclude* the full range of available human practice. This is what has happened with the institutional development of sport in western societies. "Modern" sport has emerged in its present form only through compromises and struggles. Sports practices first became legitimated for the emergent dominant classes in capitalist societies by virtue of their "rational" incorporation into educational and reform agencies, sports clubs, and associations. This legitimation was dependent, however, on the reconstitution of the dominant meanings of sport in a way that separated it from politically dangerous or economically disruptive practices.

Amateurism developed as an ideological focal point in nineteenth-century sport because it was represented as the most rational, useful, and "civilized" model for organizing human physical contests. Certain men were able to employ the social resources that came out of their backgrounds in commerce and the professions to integrate amateurism fully into sport's emergent institutional structure.

Opposition to amateurism occurred against the background of a growing hegemonic "crisis" brought on by overproduction throughout western capitalist societies during the late nineteenth century. New industrial technologies had saturated traditional markets, and new markets for new commodities were desperately being sought in order to stave off recession and high unemployment. This "crisis" was solved temporarily by the development of mass consumer markets centred on products for the home and on commercialized leisure and entertainment opportunities. These responses to the "crisis," however, have put tremendous pressure on amateurism throughout the twentieth century and have increasingly pushed it to the cultural periphery. The new dominant social definition of sport has developed as part of the emerging hegemony and vested interests of consumer capitalism.

Many people take this current dominant social definition of sport for granted. It seems "natural" and legitimate. Yet, contradictory pressures in sport have not completely disappeared. Play and leisure in capitalist societies have deep-rooted features that maintain a constant contrast to the pressures of wage work, duty, and routine. Consumer societies sell commercialized pleasure, but pleasure-seeking itself is always a potential threat to "responsibility." Furthermore, certain forms of community sports activities continue to emphasize a side of sport that seems desperately lacking in the world of big money games and international athletic competitions between nation states.

It is fair to say that "fun runs" and local leagues, for example, are often quickly incorporated into dominant sports structures and meanings. But the desires for sociability and enjoyment, which animate such practices, are never completely extinguished. Higher-level athletes are also often aware of the limits and possibilities of modern sport. A concern over athletes' "rights" or over forms of social inequality in sport demonstrates this awareness. Yet, one condition of hegemony is the great difficulty of co-ordinating such forms of opposition into any kind of coherent alternative to dominant structures and practices. It is far harder to talk about significant emergent tendencies in sport today than it was in the early or late nineteenth century. It is necessary to ask why this has happened and whether we are completely satisfied with the implications.

Conclusions

Much more could be said about different theoretical frameworks within which to analyse the emergence of "modern" sport. For example, the issue of patriarchy — the domination of women by men — has scarcely been touched in this chapter. Yet, clearly there is an important story to be told here. One cannot examine the social development of sport and not be struck by the centrality of hegemonic conceptions of masculinity throughout western sport. Indeed, there is a continuity to this masculine hegemony which cuts across other fundamental social transitions in economic and cultural life. There is little in the theory of industrial society to aid in the understanding of this continuity. And, while the Marxist tradition better alerts us to sources of domination and their continuity in social life, Marxist writing, with few exceptions, has tended to maintain a huge silence on the question of gender relations.

      Notwithstanding this and other limitations, work which maintains ties with the Marxist tradition has been highlighted in this chapter. It is not suggested that one should reject completely all of the concepts and ideas commonly associated with the theory of industrial society and its application to sport history. We are all compelled to some extent to talk about problems of "modernity."

      Yet "modernization," as described in this chapter, can very easily become an ideological concept. It offers a partial explanation of the social development of sport as if it were a whole and complete analysis. Furthermore, many of the concepts and assumptions associated with modernization — and industrial society theories more generally — are closely interwoven with the ideological tenets of modern liberalism. These concepts and assumptions often go unannounced and are presented as "objectivity." The purpose of this chapter has been to suggest why such arguments must be treated with considerable scepticism. But beyond this, and at the very least, the concepts of capital accumulation, unequal class relationships and powers, commodification, and hegemony need to be fully considered in any adequate analysis of the social development of modern sport.

Suggested Readings

Variations of industrial society theory as it applies to sport can be found in Allen Guttmann (1978), *From Ritual to Record: The Nature of Modern Sports*, New York, Columbia University Press, and in Melvin Adelman (1986), *A Sporting Time: New York City and the Rise of Modern Athletics*, Urbana, University of Illinois Press. For discussions of sport and hegemony, see John Hargreaves (1982), "Sport and Hegemony: Some Theoretical Problems," in Hart Cantelon and Richard S. Gruneau (Eds.) (1982), *Sport, Culture and the Modern State*, Toronto, University of Toronto Press; Richard S. Gruneau (1983), *Class, Sports, and Social Development*, Amherst, University of Massachusetts Press; John Hargreaves (1986), *Sport, Power and Culture*, New York, St. Martin's Press.

Chapter Two
The Growth of Organized Sport and the Development of Amateurism in Canada, 1807–1914

Alan Metcalfe

At the outbreak of the First World War, organized sport was being played and watched in villages, towns, and cities from Nova Scotia to British Columbia. It had penetrated the rural towns of francophone Quebec and the small hamlets on the North Thompson River, and had become a regular part of the activities of school-age Canadians across the country. This was a considerable change from the situation one hundred years earlier. The objective of this chapter is to provide an outline of the changes that occurred during this hundred-year period and to explain their significance. Is there anything that can provide some coherence to the history of the growth of organized sport? With respect to the forms and structures of sport and its particular Canadian pattern of development, the answer is yes. But in order to understand this pattern of development it is necessary to keep in mind that organized sport did not simply evolve by itself into the form we know today. Its growth was related to many factors that may be grouped under the structure/agency rubric, that is, organized sport, "as a distinct social practice [existing] in, and constitutive of, historically shifting limits and possibilities that specify the range of powers available to human agents at different historical moments" (Gruneau, 1983:140).

With the emergence of indigenous industrial capitalism in Canada, there was a reciprocal growth of capitalist social relations more in keeping with the new economic order. For organized sport, this meant that certain privileged ethnic and social groups could monopolize the scarce resources (e.g., leisure time and facilities) so that the resulting sports patterns bore the indelible print of their preferences.

This chapter, then, uses concrete historical scholarship to present a *particular* version of organized sport development. The evidence presented, both implicitly and explicitly, shows how the freedom of expression which could be demonstrated through organized sports participation for some (specifically white Anglo-Saxon males) limited the options for others (women, francophones, native Canadians, blacks). In other words, it is the history of struggle by the anglophone middle-class male to create sport in his image that provides the thread holding this history together.

Sports Organizations in the New Nation

The period from Confederation until the First World War can be considered the historical "moment" of struggle — the struggle of one class to expand its privilege and influence while limiting the opportunities of other classes to do likewise. It was a period critical to the affirmation and maintenance of a particular hegemony (to use Gramsci's term) in Canadian society. What results from hegemonic relations is a legitimation of social order, a predisposition to maintain the status quo. The implications for sport are enormous. Prior to Confederation, the colonial social order and way of life was little threatened by the emergent notions of class relations of an industrial capitalist state. However, by 1867, the residual notions of colonial British North America were challenged by the emergent ones of an increasingly industrialized Canada. In the case of sport, the victors won the opportunity to establish hegemonic control of future sport development; and since it was the colonial notions which lost out, perhaps it is best to establish the reasons for this loss.

Cricket: An Example of the Residual
In an 1836 *Toronto Patriot* editorial, cricket was identified as an undeniably British sport. Not only was it a delightful game, the writer observed, but it was a vehicle for developing those characteristics most in keeping with a British subject: unbending allegiance to the monarchy and acceptance of the strict (but necessary) dictates of a class society. It is not surprising, then, that cricket was the one game promoted and encouraged by the British colonial elite throughout English-speaking Canada in 1867.

In the small towns of Ontario and on the prairies the cricket clubs lasted only as long as the original immigrants remained active on the sports field, or until their numbers were surpassed by other ethnic groups. Halifax and Victoria remained outposts of the game because of the continuing English presence in the form of naval garrisons. The game took solid root in only one segment of society, that group which saw its particular view of society as the "correct" one, the colonial elite. As early as 1829, the year Upper Canada College was founded, cricket was adopted as the summer game of the private schools whose programs were based on those of the English public schools. It was in these institutions that the supply of cricketers was developed. Since the majority of political and economic leaders of British North America (and later Canada) were educated in these schools, cricket gained a prestige greater than its participatory base warranted. However, in the later years of the century, it experienced a significant decline. Only in the larger cities with a strong British tradition and numerous private schools did the game thrive.

What caused this decline? Certainly, the influx of immigrants from other countries resulted in a reduced British presence on the sports field. Nor was there much interest in the games of the British elite among francophones or working-class men who played sports. More important, however, was the rapidly changing economic climate. As industrial capitalism developed, the industrial bourgeoisie increased their wealth and influence. They were less interested in the social qualities which were allegedly gained from sports participation than they were in adapting or creating sports forms which more closely dramatized their own growing importance in post-Confederation Canada. How different their perspective was from that of the colonial elite can be seen in the organization, form, and philosophy of their sport.

The National Association: the Emergent Organization

Unlike the colonial elite who developed socially based clubs, the middle classes were interested in establishing regularly scheduled competition. Moreover, in keeping with their emerging nationalistic sentiments, they wanted the competition to culminate in a Canadian championship.

The year 1867 witnessed the first efforts to bring sports clubs together into a national association. With colleagues from the Montreal Lacrosse Club, George Beers called for a meeting of lacrosse clubs to be held in Kingston, Ontario, in September of that year. This resulted in the formation of the National Lacrosse Association (NLA), the first of many organizations formed to coordinate and promote sport.

The development of organized team sport (for this was most popular among the middle-class men) brought with it problems requiring solutions: the necessity for standardized rules, the emergence of player and spectator violence, the problem of fair play, and the entrance of new social groups onto the playing fields. Since it was considered necessary to have all parties playing by the same rules, sports leaders very soon created nationally based organizations to co-ordinate and control sport. These associations were the mechanisms by which the middle classes impressed their view of sport upon society as a whole. At the time, however, these "national" organizations symbolized little more than the growing sport rivalry between Montreal and Toronto. It is important to emphasize, therefore, the limited nature of these developments. It would not be until the first decade of the twentieth century that a sports culture, recognizable today, would emerge.

The Middle-Class Sports Form

Unlike British cricket, the games of the middle class were organized in ways which symbolized their middle-class way of life and growing sense of nationalism. The indigenous sports were promoted as representative of things Canadian and in opposition to things British or American. Lacrosse, Canadian football, and ice hockey were the games in which this nationalistic spirit took form. Given the popularity of ice hockey, it may be fruitful to look more closely at this sport to ascertain its middle-class roots.

Hockey was the brainchild of a few select young men of Montreal and it remained limited to the environs of that city until the early 1880s. Although games on ice had been played for many years, there is no doubt as to the origin of the modern version of the game, one played in a limited space and by a limited number of players and therefore compatible with the urban environment. The first ice hockey game was played at the Victoria Rink in Montreal, on March 3, 1875, by a group of university football players looking for off-season training. During the ensuing ten years it remained a game of the middle class, played with varying degrees of frequency. It was brought to the attention of a wider class audience in a demonstration given at the first Montreal Winter Carnival in 1882. From there ice hockey expanded into eastern Ontario, a prelude to the massive growth of the 1890s. Even in the moderate climate of the west coast, ice hockey began to flourish in 1911 and 1912 as a result of the construction of the first artificial ice rinks in Victoria and Vancouver. Thus, ice hockey was, by 1914, a truly national game. However, it still retained a class character in that the amateur game was administered and controlled by the middle classes while the semi-professional form provided a means of livelihood for many working-class athletes.

Baseball is another excellent example of the emergent trends in Canada during this period when there was a good deal of struggle over the dominant form of sport and its future direction. A visible American presence existed alongside those forms and structures which would establish clear links with British colonialism or Canadian nationalism. There had long been much social interaction between Canada and the United States, not the least of which took place through sport. In 1874, for example, McGill University students visited Harvard and played two football games, one by American rules, the other by Canadian. However, the strongest American presence was through the "great American pastime" — baseball (Humber, 1982).

It could be argued that baseball was considered a threat to the middle classes not only because it so symbolized the United States but because its popularity had spread beyond the middle-class anglophone community into French Canada and the working classes. Moreover, baseball had moved beyond the confines of the cities and towns into the rural areas of the country. By the mid-1870s, it was being played in Victoria, Winnipeg, and Halifax. Picnics and fairs on the prairies, in the Maritimes, and in Ontario frequently included a baseball game in the festivities. Montreal boasted the first French-Canadian team in 1872. Semi-professional baseball was extremely popular throughout Ontario. More than in any other sport, teams were created for specific occasions and then disbanded. In short, baseball, unlike the other team sports, was not the preserve of a specific social or ethnic group — it was available to all Canadians. By 1914 baseball was played across the length and breadth of Canada. It had become the summer counterpart of ice hockey.

Thus, from 1867 until 1914, the future direction of sport in Canada was greatly contested. Perhaps because of the growing sense of Canadian nationalism or the spread of liberal social and political sentiments, the middle-class approach to sport gained a foothold in Canadian society. Whatever the specific reasons, the particular philosophy of this class increasingly came to define the nature of sport. Since many features of contemporary sport had their beginnings in the philosophical debates prior to the First World War, it is wise to address some of these.

The Early Structure of Competition

Sport has always been predicated upon competition, the determining of a winner, but the emphasis placed on victory varies. In post-Confederation Canada it gained considerable importance. While this change eventually affected all sport, it will be examined here only in the context of lacrosse.

Prior to 1867, all lacrosse games were exhibition or challenge matches; thus they had no importance beyond the individual contest itself. This is not to say that the games could not be violent and that intense rivalries could not develop, but rather that, ultimately, the importance of the game lay in its playing. In 1866, a major change took place in the structure of competition: the Caughnawaga Indians played the Montreal Lacrosse Club for the first Championship of Canada. No longer did the meaning of the game terminate with the conclusion of the contest, as the winner remained the champion until challenged and defeated by another club. Thus the notion of victory, external to the game itself, became more meaningful than the playing of the game. During the ensuing twenty years the majority of teams played exhibition and challenge matches, but for a small group of senior clubs the Championship of Canada became the coveted prize. A definite shift towards an emphasis on winning emerged in these championship games.

Between 1870 and 1887, for example, the two Montreal-based clubs played 207 matches against various teams; 26 per cent contained violent behaviour. Of these matches 114 were exhibition games, only 14 per cent of which were violent. The 93 championship games, on the other hand, were replete with violence, 43 per cent containing unacceptable behaviour. What this suggests is that the structure of sport, while emphasizing victory, began to include the "win at any cost" philosophy. By 1884, in addition to the Canadian championship, there were District of Ontario and Quebec championships, local contests for area supremacy in southern, eastern, western, and central Ontario, western Quebec, Manitoba, and the Northwest Territories, and intermediate and junior championships. Thus, all games had an importance beyond the actual contests; the standing of the clubs at the end of the season depended upon results throughout the season.

By 1914, most of the team sports had adopted league competition, although there were significant differences in the degree of acceptance. For example, cricket, as a residual domain of the old colonial class, remained attached to exhibition games throughout this period. Baseball, while accepting league competition for some teams and areas as early as the 1880s, remained rooted in exhibition games and challenge fixtures until the First World War. Football and ice hockey soon adopted leagues. However, it is important to emphasize the variability in the acceptance of league competition; old ways died hard and certain groups appeared to deliberately reject league competition, for example, French-Canadian ice hockey in Montreal in the early 1900s. Theoretically, it could be said that the emergent notions of sport were still not fully incorporated as the dominant form.

Standardization of Rules

As sport spread across the country, and championships of cities, districts, provinces, and even the nation as a whole were promoted, teams from widely separated areas came into contact. This created problems for the middle-class organizers with regard to rules. Cricket, because of its roots in eighteenth-century England, had, under the aegis of the Marylebone Cricket Club, developed a set of rules that were accepted as the game; thus cricketers did not face a problem. During the 1850s and 1860s baseball was played by a variety of local rules, although an identifiable Canadian game, different in some respects from the American, emerged in Ontario. But in 1876, the major Ontario teams adopted the New York rules, and thus Canadian baseball was brought within the orbit of the United States, where it has remained to the present day. By the mid-1880s, the rules for the various Canadian games had become standardized to the extent that sportsmen moving from one part of the country to another could find similar rules in their new communities.

Organized Sport: Democratization versus Discrimination

Canadian industrial capitalism brought with it distinct patterns of domination and subordination — the domination of the large urban and industrial areas and the gradual subordination of the previously dominant rural areas — as well as class, ethnic, and gender differences. However, the dynamic nature of change, which includes both constraining and enabling aspects, makes it impossible to suggest definite dates in which one social phenomenon gains dominance over others, which are marginalized. In light of this, it would be unwise to suggest a date in which the middle-class sports form of a specific activity came to be seen as a logical and common-sense definition of the activity. Despite this, there is ample evidence to suggest that the middle-class hegemony of sport was well established by the end of the First World War. The favouring of a particular class can be seen not only in the structure of Canadian society generally but also in the constraints and possibilities applied to groups that were not identifiable as "sports men." What were some of these constraints and possibilities, which led to the particular definition of sport after the First World War?

Impact of Industrial Time on Sport

When industrial time established limits on the workday, it also suggested possibilities for activity *outside* rationalized work time. Organized sport was predicated upon the possibility of large numbers of people having regular free time. The growth of leagues, with the beginnings of emphasis on victory, required players with regular free time to practise and to play. Therefore, it was no accident that, in the 1880s, leagues developed in the urban-industrial centres of Montreal, Quebec, Toronto, Winnipeg, and Ottawa. As industrial expansion spread to other parts of the country, so did the conditions for league structure. This did not occur uniformly, however; certain games retained the traditional pre-industrial forms of competition, especially baseball. The large working-class participation in the sport was a major reason for this. Only when the working class organized collectively in trade unions were they able to win concessions from employers. Until the workers could bargain for a reduced work week (initially, half-day closing on Saturdays), there was little opportunity for a league structure in their sports. The constraints of a non-union work force limited the possibilities of league competition.

Commodification of Sport

In redefining sport in their terms, the bourgeoisie were emphasizing those qualities considered admirable, not only in sportsmen but citizens generally — a commitment to hard work and dedication to a rational and productive way of life. It is not surprising that many of these individuals found themselves in executive positions wherever the new clubs flourished. Yet in the entrepreneurial spirit of the day, these very qualities of dedication and hard work suggested to others that sport might become a means of livelihood. Thus, with the development of league competition and increased spectator interest came a concomitant emphasis on money — for an enterprising entrepreneur, the game could be sold to a consuming public. In fact, in the economic climate of Canada before the First World War, money was the central element, whether it was for the building of facilities, the renting of fields and rinks, travel expenses, or even to pay players to play. By the twentieth century the commodification of sport was a reality. The various ways in which money lay at the heart of the development of spectator sport can be illustrated in the case of ice hockey.

Ice hockey as a commodified spectator sport was related to two separate yet interrelated sets of events — the growth of amateur hockey and the development of the professional game. For the first decade after its formation in 1890, the Ontario Hockey Association (OHA) showed little interest in the profit-making potential of the game. The organization maintained itself with a yearly balance of approximately $200. It was not until 1902 that the annual report first mentioned the receipts for the final championship games ($517). The early 1900s witnessed a significant change in the financial status of the OHA, from less than $1000 in 1900 to nearly $7000 in 1914. Much of the increase was due to the receipts from the championship games ($2592 in 1914). Thus the financial viability and success of amateur hockey became inextricably linked with the generation of revenue from the high-profile championship games. The whole edifice of amateur hockey was becoming increasingly dependent upon profit, a paradoxical situation given the dichotomy between the amateur and professional games.

While amateur ice hockey had other sources of income and fewer expenditures, professional hockey relied heavily upon spectator support. Thus, some of the basic requirements for successful professional sport in Canada are demonstrated in the emergence of professional ice hockey. The first professional hockey league, the International Hockey League, 1904–1907, defied all the assumptions about the conditions necessary for professional sport. Located in three small northern Michigan towns, as well as Pittsburgh and Sault Ste Marie, Ontario, it teetered on the brink of financial collapse. It was not until 1910 and the formation of the National Hockey Association that professional hockey was placed on a relatively firm footing. In the early years, small towns such as Haileybury, Renfrew, Cobalt, Brantford, Berlin, Guelph, Halifax, Moncton, New Glasgow, Sydney, and Fort William flirted with the professional game. All succumbed to financial failure, due in large part to the lack of spectator potential. Only Montreal, Toronto, and Ottawa in the east and Victoria and Vancouver in the west achieved any degree of stability. Thus, ice hockey as a profit-making venture was, by force of circumstance, limited to the larger urban areas.

Sport and Discrimination

Throughout this chapter, the discussion has focused on limits and possibilities. One should not infer from this that the range of possibilities and the overcoming of limits remained completely within the realm of the individual. They clearly did not. One of the major reasons for the popularity of baseball among the francophone and working-class communities was that they were denied access to other sports. The middle classes and colonial elite were not interested only in more sports options for themselves: they also deliberately denied access to those they considered their social inferiors. This was a basic reality of Canadian society — institutionalized social discrimination.

Access to sport was severely circumscribed by those with greater access to economic and political power. Discrimination was based on wealth, education, religion, ethnicity, class, and gender.

In the select social sports clubs of 1914, social and gender discrimination was open and explicit. Many of the clubs in the larger urban centres had rigorous entrance requirements to ensure that only the most "desirable" gained access. And desirability included more than sports prowess, since many clubs recruited persons with a private education and Anglican Church affiliation. Indeed there was a hierarchy of exclusivity which paralleled the class system of the day. At the top were the hunt clubs that emerged after 1872 in Montreal, Ottawa, Quebec City, and Toronto. Unequivocally British in orientation, these clubs were closely tied to the colonial aristocracy. They remained isolated bastions of the old order in the central Canadian cities until the early 1900s when clubs in Victoria and Vancouver also came to be identified as "proper."

More broadly based but still selective in membership were the golf and curling clubs (Redmond, 1982). The first golf club in Canada was formed in Montreal (1873) and was followed by another in Quebec City the following year. As with many other sports, it was not until the 1890s that the game spread from coast to coast. More solidly rooted in the middle class was the other Scottish game — curling. Curling had a long history in Canada, but the 1870s and 1880s witnessed a significant expansion. By 1905, Canada boasted over 250 clubs in the cities and towns.

Finally, and by 1914 even more broadly based, there were the lawn tennis clubs. These were introduced into Canada from England in 1874. At first limited to the clubs of the social elite, tennis soon became popular amongst the middle classes from Sydney, Nova Scotia, to Victoria, British Columbia.

However, the degree of democratization did not filter much beyond those who could clearly demonstrate their middle-class origins. At all levels, these clubs were the preserve of the doctors, clergy, barristers, businessmen, and teachers. For the most part, the clubs were established with little pretence of equality, entrance being carefully monitored. The most exclusive clubs doubled as locations where the economic, commercial, and political elites met on common ground. However, their homogeneity and exclusiveness must not be overemphasized. Homogeneity was correlated with the size of the urban area. The larger the city or the more stable the class divisions, the clearer the dividing lines.

It was within the lawn tennis clubs that women began to struggle for representation in sport, first as spectators and later as participants. From the mid-1870s, women played tennis, albeit within severely circumscribed boundaries to "ensure" that their femininity would not be threatened. The possibility of participation was within the limitations of a restrictive social code.

Those women intent on contesting the male domination of sport did gain access to a limited number of activities. It was women from the upper levels of society (since they had the leisure time) who began to push for access to the golf courses, tennis courts, and curling rinks in the 1880s and 1890s. In a limited way, they moved beyond the spectator role at male competitions to that of active participants. By the early 1900s, women's golf had developed to the extent that a national championship was organized by the men's organization. In 1913 the Canadian Women's Golf Union was formed, again under the auspices of men. In addition to male domination, these early female events and organizations were also subject to class discrimination. These sports were limited to middle- and upper-class women. However, other events held the seeds of real change. A small number of professional women athletes competed in the pedestrian craze of 1879–1881 and the bicycling mania that occurred in the late 1880s. Admittedly, this was a small advance, but the fact that it happened is significant.

Perhaps more important was female involvement in a limited number of team sports — ice hockey, basketball, and baseball. For the most part this was restricted to the larger cities and, in particular, to the universities. However, by 1905, women were playing ice hockey in widely separate areas of the country. In all instances the games were played in male-controlled facilities. While it appears that subtle changes were taking place, these should not be overemphasized; the dominant ideology of the day clearly stated that a woman's place was in the home. Most Canadian males believed that women were physically, intellectually, and emotionally inferior, and could not provide any *real* competition in sport.

It was not only women who were demanding increased opportunity in sport. Greater male participation was also desired, particularly by those men working in low-paid white-collar jobs; as in the case of the women, the success rate varied. For those groups who were readily identifiable by race or colour, participation was restricted through legislative action. Thus, native Indians and black Canadians were specifically barred from amateur sport by legislative action in the 1880s and 1890s. Those workers, on the other hand, who were not visible by colour or race were denied access by the ideology of amateurism.

The Hegemony of Amateur Sport

If working men were to participate in regular, competitive sport, they had to be compensated for lost time, expenses, etc. The middle-class organizers of amateur sport used the prohibition on the payment of money as the defining characteristic of amateurism and thus attempted to keep working men out of sport. It was no accident that the period of greatest debate over amateurism (1895–1909) occurred at a time when workers were not only organizing in trade unions but also participating in sport in significant numbers. Although it is true that the working class, native Indians, and black Canadians were actively discouraged from participating in amateur sport, it would be erroneous to conclude that they did not participate. The fragmentary evidence suggests increasing involvement in amateur sport and the development of alternative systems focusing on the popular tournaments, picnics, and challenge matches. Within the limitations of the social and economic structure, the working class were creating possibilities for leisure participation. This was also true for French-Canadians.

Although French-Canadians were members of the Montreal Olympic Athletic Club in 1842, there is little evidence of widespread francophone involvement in anglophone-organized sport until the 1890s. In the next decade, French-Canadians, mainly college and university students, formed ice hockey, baseball, and lacrosse teams, often in conjunction with another minority ethnic group, the Irish Roman Catholics. Like the working classes generally, the French-Canadian organization maintained the challenge match system rather than league competition.

Sport in the Educational System

The recognition of sport as an integral element in the education of young male Canadians also served to legitimate the "correctness" of amateurism. In fact, it had been a part of the schooling of upper-class youth since 1829, when the headmaster of Upper Canada College incorporated cricket into school life. As new middle-class private schools emerged, they followed the Upper Canada College initiative. The sports, by and large, were team games, popular among the anglophone male population and introduced by members of the acknowledged middle-class profession of teaching. In short, school sport symbolized the form of middle-class activity as well as a particular ideology of life. The playing fields were perceived as a crucible in which the characters of young men were formed, developing characteristics that epitomized the values of the dominant middle class — perseverance, hard work, team co-operation, honesty, and fair play. Sport was not a frivolous diversion divorced from real life, but an integral component of the middle-class dominant hegemony and a most necessary means for inculcating desirable social characteristics.

Voluntary Associations and Sport

Two other institutions — the YMCA and the churches — played central roles in the development of amateur sport. In each instance, involvement was predicated upon the belief that, while sport itself was frivolous and ultimately unimportant, it could be used for the building of character and as an antidote to the evils of urban society.

Prior to 1884, all three institutions demonstrated a lack of concern about sport. If anything, the teachers, YMCA executives, and clergy were vociferous opponents. During the next thirty years, however, the leaders of these groups reassessed their positions. They started to get involved in the 1880s, and began to have a significant impact on sport in the early 1900s. By this time, these institutions were the most important avenue through which young male Canadians were introduced to sport. Therefore, the ideology promoted by the leaders was crucial. By 1914, with strong opposition to sport still being voiced, the leaders of all three institutions had, to some degree, accepted responsibility for the provision of physical recreation for their members. Sport was used for the inculcation of Christian values deemed important in middle-class Canada. Participation in various sports might be an enjoyable pursuit, but these leaders believed that it must culminate in some worthwhile goal. It was at this juncture that the ideology of the church paralleled that of amateurism. The Christian servant was the religious equivalent of the amateur gentleman.

The Hegemony of the Amateur Code

It is evident that the greatest organization (and hence control) of amateur sport rested with those individuals and clubs situated in the city of Montreal and the province of Ontario. This base of central Canadian domination increasingly came to be a contentious issue for participants and organizers in other parts of Canada. It well may have resulted in even more fragmentation and regionalism than actually existed but for the ideological link of the amateur code.

The ideology of amateurism provided a core of meanings that transcended geographical location and held middle-class Canadians together in their attempts to impose a particular view of sport on society. By 1914, they had achieved a remarkable degree of success through the earlier creation (1909) of the Amateur Athletic Union of Canada (AAUC). This body claimed jurisdiction over all amateur sport and established the authority to arbitrate questions pertaining to who was or was not an amateur (Lansley, 1971).

Prior to the 1880s, there was little concern over amateurism (the future direction of sport was still being debated, as discussed earlier). Yet the basic foundations had already been laid. Concern over amateurism first emerged in the 1870s in the two most popular middle-class male sports — lacrosse and rowing. In both cases, with victory being important, the middle-class participants could not guarantee consistent success against the working-class athletes or native Indians. The amateur code greatly increased the odds in favour of the middle-class athlete. In 1880, the NLA incorporated the word amateur in the title of the organization, thus excluding native Indians, who were legally prohibited from participation in amateur sport. More important to the future of amateurism was the formation of the Canadian Association of Amateur Oarsmen and its definition of an amateur. This definition

was used by the Amateur Athletic Association of Canada (AAAC)
on its formation in 1884. It stated:

> An amateur is one who has never competed for a money
> prize, or staked bet or with or against any professional
> for any prize, or who has never taught, pursued, or assist-
> ed in the practice of athletic exercises as a means of
> obtaining a livelihood. (*The Minute Book*, AAAC,
> April 11, 1884)

This was not only a definition, but a discriminatory system
based on money and/or occupation. It is difficult to escape the
conclusion that this was an explicitly class-based definition aimed
at keeping working men off the fields of amateur sport. Equally
discriminatory, but in an implicit way, was the notion that amateurs were men, not women. All definitions of amateurism prior
to 1909 simply added further exclusionary categories.

The AAAC definition of an amateur became the foundation stone of amateur organizations across Canada. What emerged
was a system of local, provincial, and eventually national organizations held together by a common ideology. At the same time,
each individual association and its executive jealously protected
its autonomy and resisted attempts to centralize authority. By the
early 1900s, amateur sport was held together only by a universal
commitment to amateurism; despite this consensus, however, the
growing regional dissatisfaction and individual sport autonomy
were creating chaos. It was only the threat of absolute chaos that
unified amateur sportsmen across Canada.

Those factors which led to the dénouement can only be
understood by examining the period 1895 to 1909, when the difficulties of amateurs and professionals were becoming acute. As
the acquisition of the regional or national championship became
increasingly important, teams at *all* levels of sport used induce-
ments to attract the best players. While theoretically amateur, all
sports departed from strict amateurism in practice. However, each
sport applied a different criterion. This had major implications,
since many players played two or three sports. Thus, while sanctioned as amateurs in one association, they were often considered
professionals in others, depending on how amateurism was
defined. As a result, amateur sport was in chaos.

This brought to centre stage a small group of individuals
representing approximately thirty clubs, predominantly from
Montreal and Toronto — the AAAC. The AAAC was formed at
the instigation of the Montreal Amateur Athletic Association
(MAAA), ostensibly to control track and field. From the outset its

executive claimed a more important mandate, the arbitration of disputes over the amateur status of all individual players. This function was also acknowledged by other sports. For example, in the early 1890s when lacrosse organizers were looking for an impartial group to arbitrate disputes over amateur status, they turned to the AAAC, thus legitimating the foundation of its power. As the problem of differentiating between amateurs and professionals escalated, the AAAC (renamed in 1902 the Canadian Amateur Athletic Union [CAAU]) became increasingly important. Its response to calls to solve very real problems was a rigid adherence to the most conservative definition of an amateur — no contact with money or professionals.

That this definition had no real support except at the executive level of the CAAU is evidenced by the departure of major sports associations from the parent body. By 1906, with its authority base rapidly eroding, the CAAU executive undertook a nation-wide campaign to attract membership. Their initiatives met with astounding success. In 1906 and 1907, membership rose from 36 to 465. Amateur sportsmen across the country opted for a strong national organization, thus temporarily putting aside individual sports and regional aspirations in order to solve the problem. This is not to suggest that the decision to have the CAAU represent Canadian amateur sport was unanimous. In fact, the organization was threatened by a breakaway of the Montreal and Quebec membership. The latter members had cause for concern because, in becoming the representative body for Canadian sport, the CAAU was also shifting its location and executive base to Toronto and Ontario. The Montreal and Quebec bid failed and on November 27, 1909, the Amateur Athletic Union of Canada (AAUC) was formed.

Representing over nine hundred organizations with a membership of over 60 000, it was the first truly national organization with provincial affiliates across the country. While it soon faced the problem of individual sport autonomy, it acquired, and until 1936 kept, its most important single jurisdiction — the definition of an amateur. In this it rigidly adhered to the most conservative definition of an amateur, one that equated any contact with money, no matter how small, or with professionals, even if unintentional, as sufficient to professionalize the individual and team. The executive also adopted as a basic principle one adopted by the OHA in 1905: once a professional, always a professional. No reinstatement of professionals was permitted. The middle-class conservatives of amateur sport reigned supreme with the institutionalization of a clear, class-based definition. Anyone wishing to play amateur sport must henceforth live by its dictates. The hegemony of the middle class was, for one brief moment, complete.

The AAUC symbolized the victory of a particular view of sport which specifically rejected alternative views. In effect, sport had to be an avocation, played for ends other than victory, and by a particular class of society. By defining an amateur in negative terms, the AAUC placed a class connotation upon amateur sport. Either consciously or subconsciously, the administrators of amateur sport failed to recognize the relationship between sport and the changes in the wider social context. They had recontextualized an ideology that was rooted in the lifestyles of the British landed aristocracy. The massive changes wrought by the emergence of urban-industrial society may have altered the form of sport, but the ideology remained little changed. Thus, for the CAAU executive, amateur sport was increasingly divorced from the realities of life faced by the majority of Canadians. Amateur sport remained, at the administrative level, within the purview of the middle classes; they controlled access to amateur sport through their dominance of middle-class institutions.

However, the real differences that underlay the chaos of the early 1900s did not disappear. Victory, particularly at the national championships, was of paramount importance. Recruitment of skilled performers continued, as did the more or less "liberal" interpretation of amateurism. This was the case particularly within those activities that had always attracted members from minority groups (soccer, baseball, lacrosse) and that recognized the realities of working-class/ethnic participation. Competing definitions of sport emerged within such activities. It is with the various systems of competition, the popularity of one-day tournaments, and the development of alternative organizations that different meanings of sport, a struggle against the dominant forms, can be found.

This struggle was particularly evident in those groups which suffered discrimination from the amateurs (francophone, black, native Canadian, women) and the struggles varied from one group to another. But for the males, the struggle was manifested in the gradual but steady legitimation of professionalized lacrosse, ice hockey, and football. From 1914 on, professional sportsmen and state-supported amateurs were appropriated as the legitimate examples of Canadian sport.

As subsequent chapters will demonstrate, sport in Canada became increasingly democratized as a consequence of a more liberal interpretation of amateurism and the legitimation of the professional athlete. But while these trends have enhanced the sporting activity of many Canadian males, for other groups in Canadian society inequality and limited sporting opportunities remain a fact of life.

Suggested Readings

A more complete analysis of the historical development of Canadian sport is contained in Alan Metcalfe (1987), *Canada Learns to Play: The Emergence of Canadian Sport, 1807–1914*, Toronto, McClelland and Stewart. For an in-depth examination of the structure and functioning of the powerful NAAAC, see Don Morrow (1981), "The Powerhouse of Canadian Sport: The Montreal and Amateur Athletic Association, Inception to 1909," in *Journal of Sport History*, VIII, 3. The impact of the British and the ideology of amateurism is examined in Morris Mott (1980), "The British Protestant Pioneers and the Establishment of Manly Sport in Manitoba, 1870–1886," in *Journal of Sport History*, VII, 3.

Chapter Three
Sports in the Workplace

Ronald Melchers

Recreational sports organizations set up by employers for workers developed rapidly during the first decade of this century in the largest industrial establishments in Canada. Before this method of managing workers attracted the attention of Canadian industrialists, it had already spread through industrial establishments in England, France, and the United States. This episode left its mark on organized sport; despite its limited impact in Canada, it cannot be dismissed as merely an historical curiosity.

This movement existed from the late nineteenth century to the early 1930s. In this period, the emergence of new relations within industrial society's system of production conferred a new role on the factory.

Two experiments which represent the high points in the development of recreation for workers will be discussed here: that of the railway companies, supported by the YMCA, and that of industrial establishments, encouraged by the Canadian Manufacturers Association.

The decline of employer intervention in the organization of sports and recreation for workers after the 1920s coincided with the rise of state intervention, chiefly by local governments.

Industrial Paternalism

Employers in Canada began to think about recreation for workers shortly after the beginning of the movement to limit the working day to eight hours without a reduction in pay.

In 1893, the *Moniteur du commerce* wondered what
would be done with this leisure time so eagerly demanded by
labour organizations:

> Would it be for rest, or for amusement, or for some other
> type of work — instruction, for example? If it is for rest,
> fine. For instruction, even better. But if it is for amuse-
> ment, we have our fears, for evil temptations are nu-
> merous for our youth and, apart from a handful of
> exceptions, the so-called honest means of distraction are
> of such a despairing monotony and generally of such in-
> sipidness as to touch the heart of even the most indif-
> ferent person. (Bliss, 1974:62)

Even worse than alcohol or games of chance — which
drained away the savings that could make an honest man out of
the savage who inhabited the factory — was the risk of seeing the
worker turn towards the infinitely greater evil of unionism. The
employers feared that a surplus of time outside work would encourage workers' associations that were hostile to "order." In a pamphlet distributed at the Universal Exposition in Chicago in 1893,
one member of the French employers' delegation assured his
counterparts in all countries:

> The worker must have something to distract himself, a
> change from his usual work. He has a certain amount
> of intellectual activity to use up, and he may use it well
> or not so well. Associations set up for economic, social,
> or moral purposes, or even to provide their members
> with honest entertainment, are the best nourishment one
> can provide for that activity. (Blanzy Mines, notice, 1893)

He persuaded his audience that the real problem was not
so much leisure as its setting. The speaker then listed the fifty-
nine associations which had taken on the task of responding to
his workers' spirit of initiative: musical bands, sports clubs, youth
clubs, and special-interest associations. Created with the active
participation of management and funded by it, these associations
were intended to exercise a positive influence on the worker's
mind.

As a result of the larger amount of time workers spent
outside the factory, employers established a range of institutions,
associations, and activities to structure the workers' time once
the working day was over. The labour community that grew up
around the factory — women, children, and the elderly — thus
benefitted from the employer's solicitude, which added the discipline of the industrial city to that of the workshop. The employers
regarded this set of institutions as their social responsibility, as

their social institutions. The workers called it paternalism, a term that would persist in labour history.

The advice to North American industrialists given by the head of the Blanzy Mines came a little late for a number of employers who had already taken action. At Lowell, Massachusetts, at Pullman and Dayton, Ohio, in the Carnegie plants at Pittsburgh, in the factories of International Harvester, in Rockefeller's various enterprises, and in the railway towns across the country, American employers provided workers not only with "honest entertainment," but also with housing, food supplies, care for the sick, injured and infirm, and education for the children. In 1887, the Pennsylvania Bureau of Industrial Statistics felt the need to undertake its first survey of social work by private industry (Brandes, 1970:17–18).

The motivation of employers was not limited to concerns of a practical nature. It was necessary to counter the pernicious effects of the better wages and greater free time than workers would have acquired on their own, which were the result of legislative interference and agitation by union organizers. It was also necessary to keep workers busy, to distract them from militancy, to anticipate their demands by giving them, even before they asked, the "small joys" of good workers, a cheap imitation of the "good life" that was not for those of their class. The social work of employers also helped discredit militants who were rebelling against paternalism, by making them look like anarchists whose sole ambition was destruction and general unhappiness. However, without losing sight of the immediate concrete advantages that their social work brought them, the employers were moved by a larger and more ambitious mission: as prophets of a new era, the avant-garde of the imminent industrial order, they intended to bring into being a new industrial man, who would be moderate, hard-working, provident, and docile.

For example, in a speech to the Montreal YMCA in 1894, George Hague, general manager of the Merchant Bank, announced that the ultimate aim of the social institutions created for workers was not only to provide distractions, but also "to reform the character of each individual" (Bliss, 1974:63). "The American phenomenon" was the expression used by Gramsci to describe "the greatest collective effort ever made to create, with incredible rapidity and an unprecedented awareness of the goal to be achieved, a new type of worker and man" (1957:351).

In this dream that pervaded employers' ideology, it was no longer merely their labour that workers were to place at the

disposal of capital, but their very existence. It would not happen
by submission, but by integration and internalization of new
norms, which would create a balance of divergent wills. Gramsci
wrote:

> This balance can be purely external and mechanical, but
> it may also be internalized if it is proposed by the worker
> himself and not imposed from without, if it is proposed
> by a new form of society, with appropriate and original
> means. (1957:352)

The social work of big industry heralded this new form of society,
from which the proletariat would emerge.

The Human Body as Machine

Capitalism was born when the bourgeoisie appropriated the
instruments of labour that were the proletariat's means of existence. But the ultimate instrument of labour, the worker's body,
would continue to escape the grip of capitalism for a long time.
Since simple appropriation — slavery — had proved to be a failure, the question became one of how to subject physical activity
to the imperative of capitalism.

   This was the axiom around which the first labour management policies of establishments in this emerging industrial civilization — paternalism and the Taylor system — were built. Both
of them essentially concerned physical effort, at work and in
recreation, which employers saw as an extension of and accessory
to productive activity.

> Man, as an instrument of work, can be compared to a
> machine powered by a driving force whose strength and
> endurance depend on the development of his organs and
> the amount of matter spent generating this force. (Dubois,
> 1855)

The author is obscure, the quotation trite. It shows, however, a
type of thinking that was commonplace in the eighteenth and nineteenth centuries. It was an extension of the thought of Diderot and
d'Alembert, who, in the illustrations of the *Encyclopédie*, depicted
the movements of workers in the same way as the tools and machines they operated. It also paved the way for a new science, the
physiology of work, which was used in industry by F. W. Taylor
in the last decades of the nineteenth century. Dubois continues:

> If this proposition is true, the question that follows from
> it is easy to ask and can be formulated in this way: What
> amount of useful work can be demanded of a man whose
> physical constitution and food intake are known? (1855)

Housing, company stores, schools, recreation, and assistance funds were among the measures used to increase the output of the worker-machine. Cities built near factories reduced the amount of energy the workers had to expend to get to their jobs. Food co-operatives provided constant supplies of low-cost fuel. Assistance funds reduced normal wear and tear and prevented breakdowns. Schools, for their part, provided a pool of spare parts for the factory, for what Gramsci called the collective worker, as the factory itself in some sense became an organism in which the individual workers were merely cells. *Industrial Canada*, the journal of the Canadian Manufacturers Association, stated:

> The intelligent manufacturer of today . . . knows that human beings, like machines, give best service, and require less time and expense for repair when carefully treated, and that good ventilation, wholesome food, and wise recreation are as necessary for the efficiency of the individuals in his employ as are oil and brush for the machinery. (*Industrial Canada*, 1909:424)

Other measures concerned the functioning of this collective worker, as well as the movements, activities, and abilities of its constituent workers. The first aspect was work. However, the labour force recruited did not seem to have the aptitudes necessary for industrial work. Mechanization itself was apparently seen as a solution to this problem. Another industrialist wrote:

> It takes time to train such men and they are trained by machines. A man ploughing with cattle thinks slowly, as he acts; he who works with steam power thinks quickly and acts quickly; and, to remain at the level of his task, to remain the master of his work, he makes himself stronger, faster, and more powerful than the machine that helps him. (Melchers, 1984:287)

These measures soon went beyond the workshop, spilling over into leisure time. As early as 1855, there were complaints that on-the-job training was no longer sufficient to change workers' physical movements. Thus it was that Dubois (1855) drew this lack of training to the attention of managers:

> When one watches your unskilled labourers work, one is struck by two things: first, their lack of energy; and second, their clumsiness, such extreme clumsiness that I have no doubt it is responsible for many of the accidents they suffer. Ask the average labourer to perform any but the most elementary movement of his arms and legs, and his clumsiness will betray itself at once, and at once it comes to mind that the workers need suitable physical training to help them develop and control their muscular strength.

The goal is specific: to resolve "the intimate conflict between 'verbal ideology' and 'animal' activity that prevents physical bodies from effectively acquiring new abilities" (Gramsci, 1957:348), in other words, to achieve the totalitarian mission of industrialization. Gramsci wrote about this process as follows:

> The history of industrialization has always been (and becomes so today in a more acute and rigorous form) a continuous struggle against the "animal" element in man, an uninterrupted process, often painful and bloody, of subjecting instincts (natural — that is, animal and primitive — instincts) to ever changing, ever more complex rules of collective life, the necessary consequences of industrialization. (1957:346)

The history of organized sport and that of industrialization are linked to this process.

The Railway YMCAs

The problem — or rather, the possibility — of integrating the worker within industrial establishments emerged late in North America. Before the second half of the nineteenth century, the centres in which a considerable proportion of the population was supported by wages earned from working in industrial establishments remained few and far between: public works projects, spinning mills, weaving mills set up by the British — the Montgomery mills in New England, for example. The situation changed rapidly when governments decided to encourage large-scale construction of railway networks throughout the continent, owing to the vast industrial mobilization necessary to supply labour and materials to business.

In the railway industry, the first formulation of the problem of constraining the body was related to the stabilization of the labour force and the struggle to keep it stable. Very early, the Young Men's Christian Association (YMCA) lent its support to business leaders (Ross, 1951; Brandes, 1970). In 1868, the association began accompanying Union Pacific Railway construction crews and, in 1872, it founded the first railway YMCA in Cleveland, funded entirely by Cornelius Vanderbilt, president of the New York Central Railway. In 1877, prior to the international congress of YMCAs in Cleveland, the permanent secretary explained the motives behind the railway companies' decision to finance the association's work among their employees: "Railway work pays dividends; Christian men do not make trouble, [and] association work is opposed to those who have nothing to lose and everything to gain by disturbance" (Ross, 1951:122).

The YMCA's efforts in favour of American railway workers expanded considerably after the strikes of 1877. Two years later, there were approximately thirty-nine railway-worker branches of the YMCA in North America (Brandes, 1970:14–15). These branches provided itinerant railway workers with shelter, meals, baths, and entertainment in the main switching yards of the railway network, just as the Sailors' Institutes, the Mission Houses, and the Settlement Houses did in the ports and the major cities. Initially, the entertainment offered was limited: reading rooms and concerts, and later, reading instruction and prayer meetings. It is easy to see that a gap separated the philanthropist from the railway worker; doubts leap to mind about the association's enthusiastic pronouncement, in a pamphlet distributed in 1882 to directors of Canadian railway companies, that "through its influence, men who formerly spent their leisure hours in saloons and variety theatres are now at home, or in reading rooms, or at social and religious meetings with their families, and influencing their companions to go with them" (Ross, 1951:122–123).

Despite vigorous propaganda from D. A. Budge and Thomas Radcliffe, secretaries of the railway workers' YMCA branches in Montreal and Toronto, Canadian companies long remained indifferent to the idea of founding a YMCA for travelling railway workers. When asked for funds, Sir William Van Horne replied that "the railwayman's morals are excellent" (Ross, 1951:234). This attitude may be due to the fact that there was a considerable difference between Canada and the United States in union activism and worker militancy: the prime motive of American companies was to counteract the influence of the socialist union movement of railway workers, led by Eugene Debs.

However, in 1901, Canadian Pacific's 5000 rail layers went on strike, and it took an act of Parliament, the Railway Labour Disputes Act, to end it. This strike was followed by other industrial actions, in 1903 and 1905, which affected all Canadian railway personnel (Jamieson, 1968). At the time, Ralph Smith, president of the Trades and Labour Congress, wrote to W. L. Mackenzie King, chairman of the Royal Commission set up to determine the causes of a strike by the United Brotherhood of Railway Employees and the Western Federation of Miners, which paralysed British Columbia in 1903: "Society is in danger of breaking itself into two armed camps, precisely as Marx has predicted" (Robin, 1968).

In 1904, Sir William Whyte, Canadian Pacific's director of operations for the western region, asked Budge to undertake a study of the living conditions of railway workers in the switching yards of western Canada. The following year, the YMCA established its first Canadian Pacific Railways (CPR) network centre at Revelstoke, British Columbia, financed by a CPR grant of one hundred dollars a month. After this experiment, the company maintained that "the YMCA made lambs out of the wild men of Revelstoke"; soon YMCAs were opened in Schreiber, Chapleau, Kenora, and other points along the network. In a pamphlet published by the company in 1909, it was stated that:

> This welfare or betterment work has done much to stamp out that spirit of discontent that once was prevalent among railway workers. It has generally raised the tone and character of the men, increasing their loyalty and efficiency, and helping them to realize that the success of the company that employs them means their own success and that these both depend upon each worker doing well his own part. (*Labour Gazette*, 1909:488–491)

The railway YMCA grew from six associations in 1900, only three of which were housed in separate buildings, to fifteen in 1910, eight of which were housed in buildings supplied by the companies. In 1920, nineteen associations received half a million dollars in annual grants from the companies to house, feed, educate, and entertain railway workers (Ross: 1951:236).

The companies soon realized the benefits to be gained from recreational and sports organizations set up for their employees; these organizations made up an important part of the companies' social services. They were set up either through the YMCA or directly by the companies' personnel services. The CPR stated in its 1909 pamphlet: "It has brought the men and the management into closer relationship. It has made the employees feel that the Company takes a sympathetic interest in their welfare" (*Labour Gazette*, 1909:488–491). The employers had recognized before the philanthropists of the YMCA that libraries and prayer meetings were not enough to keep the "wild men of Revelstoke" out of the "saloons and variety theatres" during the hours of waiting between train arrivals. They had greater success with sports activities: softball, baseball, horseshoe, and gardening competitions. Thus physical health was at least as important as moral health in the social work of the railways.

The YMCA's work was not limited to fighting unhealthy entertainment, or to struggling against alcohol, games of chance, and unionism, considered by employers to be the three major threats to the moral integrity of the railway worker. It was also intended to improve the rail worker, a project parallel to the improvement of the machines that regulated the work and determined the required abilities:

> The enormous increase in traffic and the many improvements in equipment have made railroading much more exacting in its requirements from the men engaged in it. The clearest heads, the steadiest nerves and the strongest muscles are demanded in the men operating the trains and manning the ships. How the men spend their spare hours is therefore of direct importance to the Company, even though it can exercise no immediate authority over its men when off work. Hence its willingness to help in providing its employees with healthful recreation and opportunities for mental and physical improvement. (*Labour Gazette*, 1909:488–491)

The extension of the employer's authority into the off-work hours was clearly seen as a means of revitalizing and developing the workforce. The same reasoning was applied to employee training: "The training of men for the service is especially important. . . . The training is progressive and includes the moral and physical as well as the mental side" (*Labour Gazette*, 1908:488–491). The organization within the industrial establishment of a closed system of reproduction of the workforce was a phase in the development of capitalism.

The Social Work of Industry

The concern for the moral and physical state of the worker and ways to improve it spread rapidly among large-scale industrial employers. As early as 1886, it assumed the characteristics of a real movement in the United States (Brandes, 1970). Carroll D. Wright, the head of the United States Labour Bureau, devoted numerous studies to it. This movement eventually attracted the attention of two American agencies, the Industrial Betterment Bureau of the American Institute of Social Service and the Welfare Work Committee of the National Civic Federation, which had a great influence on the Canadian Manufacturers Association and on several Canadian industrialists.

In 1898, Josiah Strong, secretary-general of the American Institute of Social Service, which was dominated by religious and philanthropic groups united under the banner of the Social Gospel, hired the engineer William Howe Tolman as director of industrial

improvement. Tolman, author of *Social Engineering* (1909), flooded American and Canadian industry with monographs, reports, and lectures. He put out a monthly bulletin on the improvement of working conditions and on the moral and physical development of workers. In 1906, the Chicago Institute of Social Sciences produced its first batch of specialists on industrial affairs; Yale University followed suit in 1908.

In 1901, Marcus Hanna created the National Civic Federation with the support of the most influential businessmen in the United States. He also had the support of Samuel Gomper, president of the American Federation of Labor, and of President Roosevelt, who was committed to promoting co-operation between capital and labour (Weinstein, 1968). In 1904, the American Federation of Labor created a service responsible for industrial social service under the direction of Gertrude Beeks Easley, fervent propagandist and apologist for the social mission of industry.

The YMCA, encouraged by its success with railway workers, also tried to play a role in proselytizing the new industrial and social order, but later and less successfully than in the case of the railways. In Canada, the first industrial secretary was appointed in Montreal in 1910. The most successful YMCA was set up in the industrial area west of Toronto. In 1919, five permanent secretaries looked after the recreation of Toronto workers with the support of local employers, including the Massey Harris Company. In several cities, permanent secretaries organized lunch-hour and evening sports events, evening courses, and film screenings for local factory workers. At Trenton, British Chemical provided the YMCA with office space, equipment, and funds for wages. In 1918, one thousand people participated in the athletic competition of the Brantford Industrial League before a crowd of 33 000 (Ross, 1951:239–241).

The majority of employers, however, preferred to take care of the social work in their businesses in a more direct fashion, although they provided grants to associations founded by employees, keeping them under strict supervision. Several businesses had already taken such initiatives before the turn of the century; after 1900, advertising made it possible to systematize and spread this trend.

Social action by employers was supposed to help solve the problem of controlling the workers. At the time, the Canadian Manufacturers Association saw it as the best way of preventing agitation: "You cannot make a socialist out of a man with a full stomach. It must be the work of employers to see that the just wants

of their employees are met, and in this direction lies the surest
safeguard against the more aggressive and more objectionable
demands of socialists and labor agitators" (*Industrial Canada*,
1909:669).

S. J. Williams, a shirtmaker in Berlin (now Kitchener),
Ontario, took a series of steps in 1902 to attract and keep workers,
and to reduce his staff conflicts. Assistance funds, rest areas, baths,
dining rooms, reception hall with cloakrooms, reading rooms, and
an athletic club, all run by staff committees, dispelled any yearn-
ings to form unions. The *Labour Gazette* (1907:892–894), the journal of the Department of Labour (one of whose directors was
W. L. Mackenzie King, the future Minister of Labour and future
Prime Minister of Canada), devoted several pages to the experiment. "Welfarism" would be the focus of Mackenzie King's 1918
book, *Industry and Humanity*.

In 1910, when the Canadian Manufacturers Association
set up a committee on labour affairs, with a secretary responsible
for industrial social service, the case of Williams, Greene and Rome
Company of Berlin, Ontario, was used as an example. This company encouraged the playing of several sports and provided its
employees with playing fields, equipment for football, baseball,
and tennis, a bowling alley, and a gymnasium:

> One of the most valuable contributions of psychology to
> the industrial world is the knowledge of the influence
> of the mind on the activities of the body . . . the working
> capacity of each worker in the average shop could be
> increased 40 per cent, without individual strain, by wise
> management and the inoculation of ambition and hope.
> (*Industrial Canada*, 1910:786–787)

Industrial Canada summed up the experiment this way:
"Under the present system, 430 people are doing ninety per cent
more work than did 522 under the old methods." It concluded
simply, "Welfare work has paid. Is this the cure for labor troubles?"
(*Industrial Canada*, 1907:778).

After the very bitter strikes of 1903, which gave Mackenzie
King a chance to build his reputation as a mediator, the Montreal
Cotton Company of Valleyfield, Quebec, initiated its own experi-
mental program. In 1907, the company placed bowling alleys, skat-
ing and curling rinks, and tennis courts at the disposal of sports
clubs organized for the workers (*Industrial Canada*, 1907:347). In
Ottawa, the welfare work of J. R. Booth earned him the nickname
"Carnegie of the Chaudière."

The number of experiments grew rapidly after 1910, following the invasion of American capital. Economic conditions —

a rise in tariffs, a drop in the value of industrial shares, and company mergers — caused an astonishingly rapid concentration of Canadian industry (Naylor, 1975). At the same time, the management of several companies was taken over by managers trained in American methods, including "welfare work." Among these companies were Dominion Foundries and Steel Company and International Harvester in Hamilton, British Empire Steel Company in Sydney, and Massey Harris and Lever Brothers in Toronto, which would all be the front-runners in the "welfare" industries. Dozens of articles praising the new methods appeared in employers' journals; the dawn of a new industrial age was announced in terms bordering on mysticism. The movement soon took over Labour Day, then a recently proclaimed holiday, in order to celebrate the union of classes through sport. Across the continent, the first weekend in September was a time for mass sports events. One such event, organized in 1909 by the Plymouth Cordage Company of Welland, was described in *Industrial Canada*:

> As early as five in the morning the employees leave their homes with wheelbarrows, little carts and arms filled with flowers, fruit and vegetables and fancy work (entries in the gardening and craftwork competitions). In a tent 220 feet by 60 feet these are exhibited. The fair is open on Labor Day from twelve to six and on the day following from 7 a.m. to 6 p.m. During the morning while articles are being arranged the people are gathering in the ball field, which has been laid out for the athletic contest scheduled to begin at 9 a.m. Last year, the ninth anniversary of the establishment of the fair, over six thousand assembled to enjoy the programme and it is estimated that eight thousand people at least were on the grounds. (*Industrial Canada*, 1909:424–427)

Party rooms, dances, concerts, plays, bowling alleys, billiard rooms, gymnasiums, playing fields, vegetable gardens for workers, holiday camps — in short, all the events and all the recreational equipment provided by business leaders for their employees — formed the developmental core of public recreation and began to play an important role in the emergence of labour culture in North America.

The Decline of Paternalism and the Birth of the Welfare State

In the mid-1920s, just as they were being enthusiastically received by the International Labour Organisation, the employer-established recreational and sports institutions seemed to disappear from North American industry. There were many reasons for this situation. First, some employers did not receive as enthusiastic a response as expected to innovations aimed at worker comfort. Others got only hostility and mistrust. Charges of paternalism and manipulation, levelled by unionists at business welfare efforts, rang true to workers, who were not much inclined to believe that their employers' actions were disinterested. For many, the collaboration between capital and labour seemed to be, to use Mussolini's words, "the collaboration of the hanged man with the rope" (de Grazia, 1978:244).

When a strike disturbed the harmony in relations within the model welfare business of S. J. Williams in Berlin, Ontario, *Industrial Canada* quickly published a warning about using the new methods. The failure was attributed to certain weaknesses in the methods:

> 1. An inherent spirit of superiority on the part of the employer, unexpressed, but none the less felt by the employees; an invidious distinction, based upon the character of the work done.
> 2. The exploitation of the welfare of the employees for financial returns from the employees.
> 3. The use of the benefactions to the employees as advertising capital.
> 4. Paternalism, giving gratuitous, unsolicited privileges.
> 5. An unwritten, unspoken law compelling the acceptance of conditions. (*Industrial Canada*, 1910:693–696)

The Canadian Manufacturers Association advised members who wished to see organizations for their workers spread further to keep their distance from the organizations so as not to arouse the workers' mistrust. For this reason, industrialists such as Carnegie and Ford created independent foundations to encourage the establishment of welfare institutions by municipalities and charitable organizations. Several business leaders followed this example by funding efforts that benefitted their businesses through charitable organizations. In 1912, the Canadian Manufacturers Association proposed a system under which charitable organizations would be approved by chambers of commerce in order to assist business leaders in the distribution of grants. In 1914, United Charities of Toronto, the predecessor of the United Way, followed up on this proposal. It was the Municipal Recreation Movement, however, that benefitted most from the employers' retreat from this field of intervention.

Errol and Tom Black (1983) have described how the union movement in Manitoba retreated into neighbourhoods and local communities following the failure of the general strike just after the First World War. Sennet (1980) covered the same subject in his studies of the neighbourhoods of that period in Chicago. Brandes (1970) attached particular importance to the scattering of much of the working class with the advent of the automobile, which modified recreational habits and doomed recreational activities associated with the factory. Brandes maintained that the stronghold of labour culture was no longer the city built near the factory, but rather the suburbs. Hence the community took over from the factory in the organization of social life.

There was another factor that may have contributed to a decline in employer enthusiasm for intervening in the social life of the workers: the about-face in union and social strategy regarding employer initiatives. After having long confined themselves to denouncing the recruitment of the working class, the activists came to realize that this contribution to social cohesion and the emergence of a class cultural identity could work both ways. They quickly appropriated sport as an ideological instrument: in the early 1930s, Communist Party and Workers' Unity League activists organized the Workers' Sport Association to compete with the employer associations and middle-class amateur sport. Bruce Kidd (1978) has described the opposition of the Workers' Sport Association to Canadian participation in the 1936 Berlin Olympics and the attempt made to organize a people's Olympic movement.

The adoption of the National Labor Relations Act (the Wagner Act) in the United States in 1935 marked the death of "welfarism." To win support for the New Deal from workers' associations, this statute instituted the system of contract negotiations that still characterizes the system of North American industrial relations today. The employee recreational and sports clubs were judged incompatible with the new system: "Good business, fair play, and good sportsmanship," explained a government spokesperson, "demand that the employer divorce from his recreational programs any attempt to interfere with the serious business of self-organization and collective bargaining" (Brandes, 1970:144). In some cases, the council responsible for administering the Act even obtained injunctions against employers who operated clubs with the aim of discouraging unionization. Order-in-Council PC 1003, which was enacted by the Canadian government in 1944 and laid the groundwork for the Canadian Industrial Relations Act of 1948, was based on the Wagner Act.

There were, however, other reasons for the decline of paternalism that were more directly related to the development of industry and to changes in labour management policies in the industrial world. The Taylor system already represented, in comparison with paternalism, a reorientation towards productive activity as such, one which aimed at encouraging employers to abandon their authoritarian desires to control workers' leisure time. Taylor ridiculed the idea that industrial progress hinged on the emergence of a new industrial man, stating that industrial man should not be just a "tame gorilla" whose every movement was determined down to the last detail by "the scientific organization of work." Little judgement and even less intelligence were required of him, only the automatic, machine-like execution of the movements he had been taught. Industrial progress was the result of the improvement of machines and the intensification of work. The worker, if he received a fair share of the benefits of progress, took care of his own needs within the factory (*Industrial Canada*, 1913:1105–1106, 1224–1225, 1349–1350). At the heart of Taylor's ideas lay the abolition of apprenticeship, the cornerstone of the paternalist system.

Ford fully understood Taylor's ideas when in 1914 in his factory he inaugurated the *assembly line*, where parts rather than the workers moved at a controlled speed and along a fixed course, to eliminate every false movement and every wasted gesture. He innovated once again when he announced that his workers would receive five dollars a day, double or even triple the wages of the time — the influx of workers allowed him to push the principle of worker selection to the limit. Even more importantly, he understood that the closed system of paternalism, which kept wages as low as possible while providing as extra benefits the essentials of a simple and mediocre life, could only lead to economic stagnation. On the other hand, the transformation of the worker into a consumer of his own product — through new marketing channels that were part of mass consumerism — started a new phase of capitalist accumulation.

"Fordism" — Gramsci's term — paved the way for mass production, leading to "a change in the relationship between social segments accumulating capital and a new relationship between the mode of productive consumption and that of rebuilding the labour force" (Coriat, 1979:142). It produced a new division of roles among agents in the system of production: the factory would produce the consumer goods, trade would distribute them, and the state would ensure that it all worked through interventionism, the

theoretical basis for which was provided by the economist
J. M. Keynes. The driving force of mass production would be mass
consumption. Gramsci wrote:

> Generally it can be said that Americanism and Fordism
> flow from the ever-present necessity to achieve the organ-
> ization of a planned economy, and the different prob-
> lems examined should constitute the links of a chain
> which mark precisely the shift from the old economic
> individualism to the planned economy. (1957:344)

If the decline of industrial institutions of recreation and
sport is considered in this light, it will be noted that the replacement of these institutions was assured by the same mechanisms
that led to the emergence of the welfare state — the state and commercial mechanisms of mass consumption — in the transition
between modes of capitalist accumulation. There was a movement
from constraint of the body — holding, mobilizing, and directing
it — to the winning of souls, from the management of a factory
to that of an entire society. The field of discipline shifted, the techniques became more refined. City space replaced factory space
in the governing of industrialized societies.

The welfare state provided the framework for this transition. It offered encouragement and funded the initiatives. The services, however, were organized at another level, the "local state,"
which is all too often ignored in studies of the subject (Cockburn,
1977; Magnussen, 1985). This expression has the advantage of not
being limited to municipal government, but of extending to all
institutions, public and private, at the local level, taking the place
of the factory in the organization of recreation for workers. But
this new space in human government was opened up by the factory
long before state intervention, and the local state will continue
to follow the lead of the factory for a long time to come.

Suggested Readings

Stuart Brandes' book (1970), *American Welfare Capitalism, 1880–1940*, Chicago, University of Chicago Press, provides an excellent overview of industrial paternalism in the United States. The bibliography presents a good
selection of titles on this subject. For a discussion of the Canadian scene
see the recent paper of Neil Tudiver (1987), "Forestalling the Welfare State:
The Establishment of Programs of Corporate Welfare," in Allan Moscovitch
and Jim Albert (Eds.), *The Benevolent State*, Toronto, Garamond. See also
Chapter Three of Michael Bliss (1974), *A Living Profit: Studies in the Social
History of Canadian Business, 1883–1911*, Toronto, McClelland and Stewart.

Murray G. Ross (1951), *The Y.M.C.A. in Canada: The Chronicle of a Century (1851–1951)*, Toronto, Ryerson, provides a useful source of historical data. The study of systems of discipline has been largely inspired by Michel Foucault's (1979) book, *Discipline and Punish: The Birth of the Prison*, New York, Vintage. Readers are also referred to No. 43 of *Recherches* edited by Alain Ehrenberg and entitled "Aimez-vous les stades?"

Chapter Four
Sport and the Quebec Clergy, 1930–1960

Jean Harvey

The Basis of Clerical Power and its Plan for Society

Until the Rebellion of 1837–38, the clergy had little authority over Quebec's francophone society. There were too few clergy to oversee adequately a population that was sparse and unwilling to submit to any authority at all. The liberal, anti-clerical ideas of the Rebellion leaders were bound to make the Catholic Church's already weak authority even more fragile. In addition, London initially wanted to make Anglicanism the state religion of Canada. In this context, the Catholic Church enjoyed neither conditions favourable to its expansion nor circumstances likely to help it exert any influence on society as a whole.

The Church's situation changed, however, after the upheaval of 1837–38. The British authorities regarded a strong clergy as a potentially effective instrument of social control, especially since senior members of the Quebec clergy had shown loyalty to the government by condemning the Rebellion. Thus, the authorities gave the Quebec clergy free rein and, initially, full legal recognition. The clergy then took a series of measures that assured its power over Quebec society. These measures benefitted from the advent of Confederation; the division of powers within the federal structure enhanced the Church's influence. "The areas under provincial jurisdiction are mainly those which interest the Church: public health, property, and civil law — in short, everything that touches the daily lives of the people" (Linteau et al., 1979:233). In Quebec, that meant effective control by the clergy over education, health, and social services in general.

Other factors besides the new structure of the Canadian state worked in favour of the clergy's plans. The administrative apparatus of the Catholic Church was well suited to an increase in power and to the preservation of that power over a long period. Based on a pyramid type of hierarchy, the Quebec Catholic Church, with its parishes grouped into dioceses, had at its disposal a powerful communications network, able to "operate in two directions, either centralizing or disseminating information as it chose. This was an important instrument of Church power" (Linteau et al., 1979:234). At that time, the social infrastructure, resting largely on an agrarian type of economy and a rural lifestyle, attached the greatest importance to the parish, the building block of the clerical institution. As head of the parish, the parish priest enjoyed the authority and prestige required to keep his flock under control.

Finally, political lobbying made the clergy highly influential in the Quebec state. The clergy used the electoral power of francophone Catholics in Quebec over members of Parliament for Quebec, most of whom were themselves Catholic. Nevertheless, as Bellefleur (1983, 1986) and Levasseur (1982) have pointed out, the clergy's prerogatives, though wide-ranging, gave it only limited power. Since it had no solid grip on the economic infrastructure of society, clerical power was primarily "cultural power," a power that depended largely on the persuasive force of its statements.

Sunday sermons were an excellent means of haranguing the faithful on all subjects of concern to the clergy. With respect to recreation specifically, the central co-ordinating agency of the clerical recreational organizations each year prepared a draft sermon outlining the services offered by these organizations. The priests were responsible for transmitting the message at Sunday mass, thus making it possible to recruit a large number of young people. The clergy made use as well of written propaganda.

Ideological persuasion was also facilitated by a set of strategies for educating the population. After the end of the Rebellion, the Catholic Church substantially increased its numerical strength, even making use of immigration. Many religious communities were established, either as branches of existing communities, such as the Dominicans and the Jesuits, or through new creations, such as the Société des Saints-Apôtres (Society of Holy Apostles) or the Moniales bénédictines du Précieux-Sang (Benedictine Sisters of the Precious Blood). Each community "had its own founder, traditions, constitution, subculture, and spirit" (Hamelin and Gagnon, 1984:136). This led to ideological stances that were sometimes very different, either between the communities themselves or between the communities and the lay clergy. The communities for women were probably less involved in debates of this nature, either because of their exclusion from positions of authority within the Catholic hierarchy (even though they far outnumbered their male counterparts), or because they tended to specialize in missionary work or in domestic service to the male communities.

Among the measures for educating the faithful, the Catholic Action (Action catholique) movement was unquestionably the most ambitious and most effective experiment. It was on the basis of this model and within the framework of Catholic Action that clerical recreational organizations were set up, beginning in the 1930s.

Catholic Action included specialized movements to ensure the adherence of lay members to the teachings of the Church hierarchy. Each movement was intended to penetrate a particular segment of the population — there were, for example, the Jeunesse ouvrière catholique (JOC) (Young Catholic Workers) and the Jeunesse étudiante catholique (JEC) (Young Catholic Students). These lay groups were dedicated to Christianizing society, under the direction of the clergy, of which they were in a way an extension.

The objectives of Catholic Action were stated as follows: "one *general* and *supreme* goal: to save souls for Jesus and to win back those who have strayed or who belong to Satan; *specific* goals, such as using the press, the family, schools, and enhanced morality, as powerful means for restoring Christ everywhere; and one *immediate* goal, the training of souls and leaders" (Caillé, 1941:68). In short, Catholic Action was a religious, moral, social, and apostolic training school.

The Quebec clergy wished to set up a solid bulwark against the assimilation that threatened French Canada, which was isolated within an Anglo-Protestant continent at a time when the industrialization of North America had begun and where, since the Conquest and especially since the Durham Report, forces were at work to destroy French Catholic civilization. The pre-Confederation constitutional negotiations, as well as certain laws (such as those which, at the beginning of the twentieth century, denied constitutional rights to francophones in Manitoba), had reinforced the clergy's convictions: it was defending a people under siege. For the sake of perpetuating the race and preserving French culture, the clergy took control of the destiny of its faithful.

For the clergy, salvation resided in the preservation of the rural, Catholic, and francophone character of Quebec and in its autonomous development apart from the rest of the country. It therefore exercised its cultural domination in the interest of defending Quebec against threats of assimilation. Sport would not escape this line of reasoning.

The Body: from the Root of All Evil to the Servant of the Soul

In his work on the history of horse racing, Guay (1973, 1985) provides an excellent example of the rapid spread of sports activities among the people of Quebec and of the particular attraction that some sports had exerted, since the first half of the nineteenth century, on the urban working classes. He demonstrates the problems of public morality, class conflict, and the danger to the social order of a sports institution that was controlled by the British but which French and English Canadians were attempting to take over.

It might be speculated that differences in interest with respect to sports activities — and also differences in access to them — were the result of the positions of individuals in the social structure. Thus the interest of the francophone working class in professional sports would have been the same as that of the anglophones of the same social level, while both the francophone and anglophone middle classes would have been promoting amateur sport. Such a hypothesis would explain in particular the great popularity of baseball and hockey among francophones, a popularity that Metcalfe (1983) has already discussed.

Having initially rejected sport, the francophone clergy went on to develop its own vision of the activity, while at the same time establishing its own network of sports organizations. The clergy thus seemed to be following its strategy of culturally isolating the people of Quebec by attempting to take over a movement that had until then been dominated by anglophones but that was attracting more and more francophones. Clerical publications on sport between 1910 and 1950, as well as more recent literature (Bellefleur, 1986; Levasseur, 1982; Pronovost, 1983), indicate that the Quebec clergy at first anathematized sport, as it did with every other new form of recreation such as cinema or theatre.

During the same period, however, several documents produced by the francophone clergy took a much more favourable attitude towards sport. Over time, particularly from the 1930s onwards, there emerged a genuine Catholic doctrine on sport, which helped guide the clergy's involvement. Soon the condemnations began to subside. Some contradictions in clerical thinking were due to a lack of unanimity within the clergy itself. In fact, there is every indication that the various factions of the Quebec clergy adopted different positions on the subject of sport. Some of the regular clergy, especially those orders heavily involved in social action, such as the order of Saint Vincent de Paul and the Jesuits, as well as some priests who were working in urban parishes or in seminaries, seemed to be sensitive to the wishes of their parishioners and to have rapidly sensed the formative qualities of sport. These priests set up and led the clerical sports organizations. The more detached orders, such as the Dominicans, who saw themselves as the guardians of Church doctrine, as well as the community superiors and the bishops, were much more reticent — and at times more aggressive — regarding the development of sport.

In the opinion of the clergy at the time, sport held many dangers for Catholic morality. In a paper on recreation for youth, Saint-Arnaud (1946:217) described these dangers:

> . . . an absolute obsession which negates concerns essential to the highest duty; primacy given to physical exercises over intellectual life; vulgarity in dress and language; the importance, so ridiculous that it may become almost immoral, of "champions," who are considered heroes. That which Andronicus calls the "science of etiquette in movement and comportment as well as understanding of specific social graces according to the circumstances" are totally laid aside.

The moral dangers of sport were thus emphasized in the general context of popular morality. In the first place, sports and physical education might upset the hierarchy of values by giving primacy to the body over the soul. The inevitable conclusion was not that physical education was dangerous, but only that it was not sufficient. Neglecting the simultaneous development of young people's moral, aesthetic, and religious activities would steer them towards a materialistic view of life. The end result might be a pagan cult of the body (Forest, 1936:349–350). The Church maintained cautious reservations about any excessive attention paid to the body, which was the refuge of instinct and the source of sin. Any search for pleasure might lead to hedonism, which contrasted with the virtue of temperance. The Sulpician Edouard Gagnon (1954:9), in an article in the magazine *Nos cours*, discussed the rules of temperance in the following way:

> The rule common to all kinds of temperance . . . is to use the goods of this world according to the dictates of reason, that is, with moderation, taking into account the purposes that God has for everything. . . . This rule applies

to sensual goods whose too powerful attraction would disturb the balance of our emotional faculties if the moderating influence of temperance were not exercised on them: the uncontrolled love of wealth, pleasure, or honour leads to evil and disordered acts.

In a 1934 address to the Ligue de Sécurité de Québec (Quebec Safety League), Cardinal Rodrigue Villeneuve set himself the task of preaching the austere morality of the Church in his own words. He stressed the faults in the modern view of life as he saw them in popular morality: "They reveal three dominant and exclusive concerns: physical strength, sensual pleasure, and the development of the human animal" (1934:13).

He also attacked licentiousness, which was particularly evident in the use of the female body for advertising in mass circulation magazines (a situation that unfortunately has not changed much since), and naturalistic science which had "worsened the disorder of the flesh." Sport was not the only activity condemned by the clergy because of its risks for public morality, especially for young people who were passing through the critical period of character formation. In short, any pastime in which the body was the focus of action was condemned by the clergy. Dancing and mixed bathing were on the list of prohibited activities. In this connection, certain regulations were supposed to prevent the contamination of souls. Cardinal Villeneuve's ordinance (1934) regarding morals on the beaches and in public baths is a good example of the moral rigour that the Church was attempting to impose.

Sport also constituted a risk of cultural contamination. In an article in which he attempted to find an acceptable perspective on sports participation and physical education, Forest, a Dominican friar, complained of the Americanization of French Canadians by sports. This tendency was due to the attraction of competitive sport, particularly professional sport. "This desire to do more and better than others has distorted the original intent of sport. Instead of being a diversion for those taking part, it has become a spectacle, a financial enterprise" (Forest, 1936:351). The pursuit of records and optimum performance also contravened the virtue of temperance, which required moderation in everything.

> Sport has thus ceased to be a harmonious diversion and has become harmful overexertion and an exhausting chore. Some hockey and baseball players have stated that they tire themselves excessively, that they nearly kill themselves playing. Physical exercise in this manner goes against its chief aim, which is the development of fitness. Others readily confuse fitness and muscular

strength with the *spirit of championship*. (Mercier, 1931:163)

The danger of cultural contamination, however, also stemmed from non-Catholic values. Certain sports organizations were seen as instruments for the spread of Protestantism. For this reason, the clergy attempted to keep Catholics away from organizations such as the YMCA and the YWCA. "The YMCA is primarily a Protestant institution, and all its activities, in whatever area, are organized for the Protestant cause. This shows up clearly in its origins, in the principles that guide its functioning, and in the official statements of its leaders" (Charland, 1941:261). In fact, for the francophone Catholic clergy, besides the fact that it had no control over these associations, the latter were shown to be particularly harmful in that

> . . . by benefit of their facilities and social, intellectual, and moral advantages, it [the YMCA] makes insidious propaganda for a non-Christian materialistic creed. To develop the mind and to shed light on religious problems, it preaches full and total freedom of thought about any dogmatic teaching.
>
> In contrast to Christ, who healed bodies to attract souls and give them the words of life, the YMCA provides an abundance of facilities of every kind, "which, in appearance, aim only at physical culture and intellectual and moral education, but in fact corrupt the integrity of the Catholic faith and tear children away from Mother Church." (Charland, 1941:263–265)

In sum, the Quebec clergy saw the development of sport, particularly professional sport, as a threat to the morality of its faithful. It felt that the abuses of modern sport overturned the hierarchy of values by setting up a cult of the body that could only lead to hedonism and neglect of the prerogatives of the soul. Sport was also seen as a product of Anglo-Saxon civilization and, as such, a threat to the survival of French-Canadian values.

From the 1930s onwards, a growing body of literature contrasted these abuses of sport with the practice of sport from a Christian perspective. Even some of the greatest detractors of professional sport at the time heartily endorsed the development of a sport that respected Catholic moral precepts. This concept began to take shape more clearly in the early 1930s (Bellefleur, 1983, 1986).

First, the true hierarchy, which ensured the primacy of the soul over the body, had to be reinstated:

> The body is the servant of the soul. Pulled in all directions by many real and artificial needs, the body cannot hope to impose its tyranny on the soul, whose role is precisely that of dominating matter, avoiding unnecessary servitude and developing in the greatest possible freedom, by embracing the will and cleaving to that which is good. (Racicot, 1949:226)

In a text on "the glory of the Christian body," the Jesuit Luigi d'Apollonia showed how the body should be used for higher purposes, as a vigorous servant of the mind, of the will, and finally of religion:

> It clearly seemed to us a heretical scruple to fear the body. The Church did not yield to such facile simplification: it abolished nothing but set everything right, did not condemn the flesh but strove like a mother to reduce it to service by bringing it back to its duty. Saint Paul had the right words for it: I have reduced my body to servitude. The body, more an instrument than a victim; an alert servant, and one essential to religion. To serve, truly the right words. (1941:206)

Pope Pius XII systematized clerical thought on the direction the practice of sport should take. In a speech to young Italian athletes in 1945, he urged the young to make their bodies temples of the Holy Spirit: "Praise God, glorify Him in His holy temple. About the human body it should also be said: 'Holy be Thy house, Lord.' It demands holiness; thus the dignity, harmony, and chaste beauty of this temple should be cherished and maintained: 'Lord, I love your home, the tabernacle in which your glory resides' " (Pius XII, 1945:15).

In the same document, Pius XII attributed certain values to sport: it could be an effective antidote to sloth and comfort, awaken a sense of order, train one to test and master oneself, and finally, develop natural virtues useful to spiritual ones. In this respect, it could teach loyalty, resolution, and universal brotherhood. Pius XII's approach seemed much more liberal — especially with respect to contacts between different communities — than that of the Quebec clergy who, in an effort to preserve French culture and the Catholic faith, practised strict segregation.

In a later document (1952), Pius XII suggested the purposes to which sport should be put. In his view, the immediate or primary purpose of sport was to train, develop, and strengthen the body. A less superficial purpose was for the soul to use the body in the development of a person's inner and outer life. Its profound purpose was to contribute to a person's perfection. Lastly, its supreme purpose was to bring man closer to God. Any sports practice consistent with this hierarchy of purposes was consequently considered legitimate; it would be in conformity with the precepts of revealed truth, of which the Church was the official guardian.

As in all things, the clergy maintained strict discrimination between the sexes, as much with respect to the practice of sport in general as to the choice of sport in particular and the objectives to be pursued. The requirements dictated by the nature of each sex could not be ignored. In this respect, women's activities had to be paid particular attention. Any demonstration of strength or excessive effort was to be avoided: these were incompatible with feminine grace. This grace excluded any form of perverse seductiveness, shown in particular by the wearing of certain clothes. "It has been correctly pointed out that, if some Christian women suspected the temptations and the falls from virtue that they caused men by their clothing and the routine things that they consider so unimportant, they would be appalled by their responsibility for it" (Saint-Arnaud, 1946:213). In his article on the Americanization of French Canadians by sport, Father Forest was concerned with women's participation in sport:

> That a woman should receive an appropriate physical education is a necessity for her as it is for a man. Real beauty is not a matter of powder and make-up, but of health. No one is offended if she takes part in gymnastics, skiing, golf, skating, or tennis. At most, we would find it ridiculous and unbecoming if she believed she had to imitate certain stars by appearing on a tennis court wearing shorts.
>
> Abuses only begin when she believes she has to participate in certain games that are suitable only for men, such as wrestling, boxing, baseball, or hockey. "The graceful sports," writes Lucien Dubech, "yes, the strength sports, no. It's ugly and foolish. It is ugliness without end. Look at the photos. A man with his face strained by effort is handsome, because the effort is manly, part of his nature. The face of a grimacing woman, her hair tousled and the rest of her body bouncing about, is ugly and foolish." (1936:361–362)

Hence, women's participation in sport appeared to be legitimate, as long as it was consistent with the social role assigned to women. In the clergy's view, women were the source of all temptation for men: a woman had to discipline herself so as not to provoke emotional outbursts for which she alone would be responsible.

From the clergy's perspective, sport ought to be a means of relaxation, a break from intellectual activities, a means of Christianization. Healthy participation in physical activity was even seen as a means of overcoming carnal instincts, as a "physical asceticism" for the elevation of the soul.

The Rise and Fall of the Clerical Recreational Apparatus

The precepts of the Church with respect to physical activity and sport did not have the success expected: this is the hypothesis put forward by Bellefleur (1983, 1986) and Levasseur (1983) to account for the fact that, in the 1930s, the Quebec clergy began developing an apparatus to intervene in the area of recreation which was not consolidated until after 1945. There is every indication that the clergy's condemnations had had little effect on the people of Quebec, who were increasingly attracted by sports, especially professional sports — whether as players or spectators.

A number of other reasons could have been behind the clergy's establishment of its own network of institutions. First of all, as Hamelin (1984) has pointed out, the clergy had initiated a far-reaching project of intervention at a time when the effects of industrial capitalism were increasingly being felt, particularly in the cities. As a result, the clergy felt that the traditional means of indoctrination had lost their effectiveness. It was during this period that Catholic Action was founded. The clergy's apparatus for intervening in sport and recreation was part of this movement. It might also be speculated that the first hints of intervention in sport by the municipalities and the federal state contributed to the clergy's decision to intervene in this area. The clergy's opposition to intervention by the federal state in an area it considered under its own jurisdiction became clear when the National Physical Fitness Act was proclaimed in 1943 (Trottier et al., 1967:13; Levasseur, 1982:61). Finally, the development of anglophone and Protestant recreation centres and sports associations probably played a role in the clergy's decision.

For any area identified by the clergy as being under its authority, Church social doctrine made provision for a hierarchy of responsibilities. Thus the first level of responsibility for organizing recreation belonged to the family, within which individuals should find the resources necessary for their recreation; furthermore, these recreational activities should be pursued primarily within the family. In this respect, the father held a substantial responsibility. Abbot Saint-Arnaud remarked that "if Adam had been looking after his wife's recreational activities, perhaps the serpent might not have so stupidly piqued Eve's idle curiosity as she wandered about Paradise. What a change that would have meant for the human family!" (1946:219). The second level of responsibility belonged to the parish. It was on this environment that the clergy concentrated its attention. As a community of families, the parish was the place where individuals could find what was lacking in the family. The third level of responsibility belonged to the authorities, who had greater material resources than did the Church. Nevertheless, the clergy, in keeping with its view of the state's role, believed that the state should supply it with the material resources it needed, but should never take the initiative in the organization of recreation.

As a result, the clerical recreational organizations were established. According to Bellefleur (1986), the main clerical recreational organizations were the patros, summer camps, the Oeuvre des terrains de jeux (OTJ) (Playgrounds Organization), recreation centres, and youth movements. Two of these organizations will be dealt with here very briefly: the patros, which promoted the exemplary aspect of physical activity, and the OTJs, which had a fundamental importance in the formation of the modern recreational apparatus in Quebec.

The patros — the Oeuvre des patronages (Youth Club Organization) — were certainly the first attempt to organize recreation for youth. Founded and directed by the order of Saint Vincent de Paul, the patros had originally developed in Belgium and were adapted to the Canadian situation; their general mission was to assist and educate the poor and working classes. The patros, which were both recreation centres and shelters for the poor and for apprentice tradesmen, were built in urban centres. They were actively involved in youth recreation, and it was mainly through them that the religious order performed its educational work among the working classes. A 1946 document, quoted by Bellefleur (1986:157), noted six characteristics of the patro:

> 1. It is essentially a local organization, even though it may be affiliated with a larger structure (for example, the Quebec Centrale des patros). It must be autonomous and have its own personality, which depends on the characteristics of the area it serves.
> 2. The patro is an enterprise for the moral and religious training of youth.
> 3. The fundamental means of this training is play.

4. The patro is a dominical organization dedicated to sanctifying Sundays.

5. The patro is a parish organization that carries out indoctrination complementary to that of the local clergy.

6. The patro is an auxiliary of Catholic Action, but is not specialized in the sense of being limited to a particular group such as workers or students. It declares itself open to all youth living in the area where it is located.

Organized activities within the patros varied from reading and prayer to physical activity, which apparently made up an important part of the program. Young people were divided up by age group; some patros were entirely for girls, others only for boys. Among all the activities, one is particularly interesting for our purpose: gymnastics. In 1924, the Lévis patro became the first to set up a gymnastics program. However, there is some evidence that gymnastics as such was practised in patros well before that, as shown by the program for the patro day, held on May 3, 1914, in Quebec City.

The short history of the gymnastics movement is outlined in a small magazine intended for patro gymnastics instructors. According to this history, in the earliest days of the movement, the military instructors of the Royal 22nd Regiment based in Quebec City were lent by the Department of National Defence to the Lévis patro to train gymnastics instructors. The patro sent the military packing as soon as the first group was trained: the instructors " . . . did not have sufficient comprehension to establish a 'patro' method of gymnastics." They had difficulty with French and their methods were too military for the taste of the monks responsible for the patros. According to the magazine, the success of the Lévis patro snowballed and in a few years, every patro had organized its own gymnastics movement.

But why organize gymnastics in the patros? The order of Saint Vincent de Paul saw it as a means of providing a complete education: "Everything that contributes to religious, intellectual, patriotic, social, and physical training is our responsibility." Most of all, it helped ensure better health for young people. "The soul inhabiting a vigorous and strong body achieves its goals more easily and has more freedom of action than one that is weighted down by a sick body that it has to support or drag along."

Also, gymnastics, particularly formative in itself, was seen as readily attracting young people, making them more receptive to education:

> . . . because experience shows that it is an attractive and
> formative element that can even keep in the patro those

children and young people who would otherwise escape the social and Christian influence of our organization. Attracted by the external glamour of gymnastics, the joy of wearing gym outfits, and the pleasure of gymnastic events and parades, these groups are more eager to join the patro; gymnastics becomes for them a springboard into their Christian life. This is the way it was seen by everyone — as the means that the patros use to achieve their goals. (*Le Moniteur*)

Finally, the organization of gymnastics teams, aside from making it possible to instruct a large number of young people at once, had the advantage of creating a community spirit among young people and allowing group gymnastic demonstrations, which spread a positive image of the patros. In addition, there were occasional parades through parish streets in gymnastics outfits.

As they were limited in number, the patros reached only some young people. OTJs were the agencies that had the greatest influence on organized sport in Quebec, if one excludes the sports federations, which were originally established by anglophones and gradually turned over to francophones as a result of the Quiet Revolution.

The OTJs were developed by members of the lay clergy who realized the difficulty young people were having in gaining access to certain types of recreation. The first playground was set up in 1929 by Abbot Arthur Ferland, in Parc Victoria, located in the "Basse-Ville" of Quebec City. With a view to social service and the protection of young people, several priests set up organized recreation, especially during the summer holidays. Out of school and without resources, young people had been left to their own devices:

In a city like Quebec City, where the number of children per family is high and housing is generally cramped, children spend a good part of their vacation time outside. And who would blame them?

Narrow streets, heavy traffic, and the examples that children too often have before them cause them many dangers, as much for the body as for the soul.

These dangers are countless. Traffic accidents and drownings are all too common when children are not sufficiently protected. The child is essentially an imitator. And what does he see around him? What does he hear which would lead him to virtue? The causes of perversion increase with each day of vacation: dangerous companions, scandal in the street, not to mention idleness and poverty, all of which offer very poor counsel. (Dion, 1943:11)

On the basis of this report, numerous summer camps and playgrounds were set up. Inspired by American and English-Canadian playgrounds, the OTJs pursued very specific objectives. According to its charter, the OTJ's mission was " . . . to bring together children, young boys and girls, for the purpose of recreation and fun, and to attend to their religious, moral, social, national, patriotic, charitable, scientific, artistic, vocational, athletic, and sports training" (Dion, 1943:16). Among the activities were games, physical tests, theatre, cinema, hobbies, swimming, and sports. Team sports were especially encouraged as they taught the children how to interact in a group and a respect for discipline. Baseball was unquestionably the sport played most often. Each OTJ had male and female baseball leagues. Sports, like all OTJ activities, were played from a Christian perspective: Levasseur (1982:60) points out, for example, that at the end of sports competitions trophies were awarded " . . . not to the team that had the most points, but to the one that had shown the best spirit." The children also engaged in athletics, but the clergy took great care to preserve the same values:

> Athletics is very much in vogue in the OTJ. In all the playgrounds, the various types of foot races, long jumping, high jumping, pole-vaulting, shot put, discus and javelin throwing, and even boxing are being practised.
>
> It must be said that here at the OTJ, there is no central preoccupation with training a few athletes to the detriment of the majority. Quite to the contrary, the aim of the athletic association is to create strong, fit young men, who engage in amateur sport to become vigorous, alert adults. (Dion, 1943:39)

In keeping with the reasons for its involvement, the clergy retained a structure in which the volunteer work of lay members assumed great importance with regard to physical organization, but the clergy kept control over the general policies followed by the OTJ and over its personnel management. Dion (1943) provided a table demonstrating the hierarchical structure of the Quebec City OTJ in 1943.

The OTJ formula was very successful. The prototype developed in Quebec City was copied across the province, which made the activities chosen very important. The OTJs were able to provide services almost all year round to both children and adults.

The expansion of OTJ activities and the activities of other clerical recreational organizations very soon created co-ordination problems, and then a province-wide planning agency — initially

Table 1
Hierarchy of the Quebec OTJ

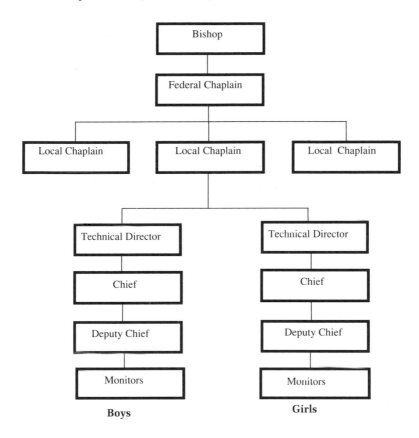

through the diocesan recreational federations, followed in 1946 by the Confédération otéjiste provinciale (COP) (Provincial OTJ Federation) (see Table 2).

> The creation of the COP fulfilled the following four objectives: (1) co-ordinate and unify all the recreational organizations at the different levels (local, religious, and provincial); (2) become the interlocutor and the agent for Quebec state intervention in recreation and thus obtain the grants necessary to accomplish its mission; (3) prevent the federal state from intervening in an area of provincial jurisdiction; (4) create a private agency sponsored by the Church to block any state initiative, either provincial or federal, in this new sector of activity. (Levasseur, 1982:68)

Table 2
Structure of the COP

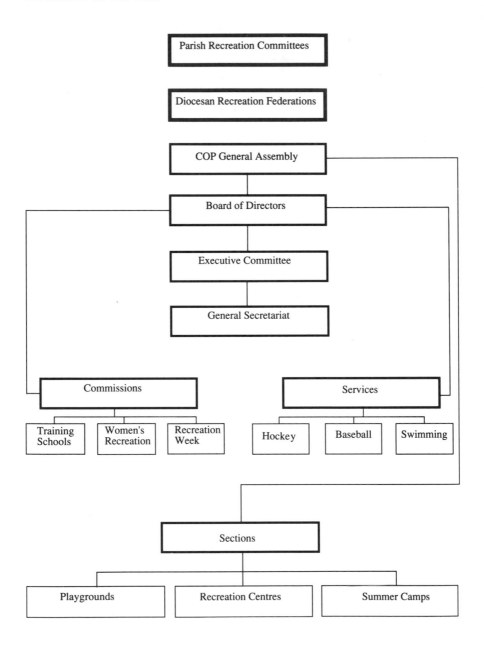

The COP's organization chart clearly shows the scale of the clerical recreational organizations in the late 1940s. In the services section, hockey, swimming, and baseball received particular attention. The swimming program, for example, was responsible for training lifeguards, since the clergy did not recognize certificates from the Red Cross, a Protestant organization. The hockey program maintained an amateur hockey organization that competed with the Quebec Amateur Hockey Association (QAHA). According to Meisel and Lemieux (1972), the hockey program was created primarily for two reasons: the QAHA was an anglophone agency within which francophones had no power, and it was too closely associated with professional hockey.

In the late 1950s, the clerical recreational organizations rapidly disappeared, as a result of both the financial burden and the emergence of new values in Quebec society. After a period of secularization, the different services and associations of the COP, as well as its co-ordinating structures, were slowly taken over by the state. The parish committees, gradually taken over by the municipalities, became municipal recreational services. The diocesan federations evolved into regional recreational councils, while almost all the recreation centres (except for the patros) and the summer camps passed into the hands of private non-profit organizations. Clerical authority in sport, as in all areas of social life, was sharply questioned during the 1950s. The decline in religious fervour slowly dried up the clergy's financial resources while its needs grew, and the state was becoming less willing to fund organizations it could not control. Moreover, a whole range of recreation and sports professionals, notably physical educators, questioned the competence of the clergy to administer recreational services and provide quality services with staff who had no technical qualifications. The winds of liberalism then blowing through Quebec brought a rejection of clerical morality in the practice of sport. The influence of the clergy was seriously weakened.

The Quiet Revolution was underway.

Conclusion

After the first emergence of sport, the Quebec clergy realized that the ideology of sport conveyed a set of values that were not always compatible with its own. In fact, the entire moral doctrine concerning the status of the body in relation to the soul was weakened by the appearance of sport. The growing importance attached to the body could lead to moral deviation. For the clergy, therefore, controlling the body and individuals' morals seemed an important part of its doctrinal structure. The many anathemas pronounced against sport slowed its progress until the clergy had no choice but to develop its own apparatus to regain control of its flock.

The clergy's attacks were aimed principally at professional sport — the form of sport most attractive to the dominated classes — which was then undergoing a process of commodification. It was professional sport that held the greatest attraction for the people of Quebec. The image of amateur sport as a middle-class activity, though much more acceptable to the clergy, nevertheless implied control by anglophone Protestant groups. For the clergy, this constituted a danger of cultural contamination of francophones and threatened its own cultural hegemony over the population of Quebec. Hence the clergy adopted a modified version of amateur sport, which it disseminated through its own associations. At times there were astonishing similarities between the condemnation of professional sport by the clergy and the disapproval voiced by the middle classes, which for their part were promoting amateur sport. Moreover, the clergy's intransigence, especially with respect to women's bathing suits, was reminiscent of Victorian moral precepts. This suggests that the clergy's primary goal was to protect French Canadians against the dangers of cultural contamination and to preserve moral values that it judged essential to the preservation of that culture.

There is a striking contrast between the moralizing discourse of social doctrine journals and the initiatives taken by certain sections of the clergy in the organization of sports activities. This is due to the fact that those sections whose mission brought them into close contact with the people were likely to have a certain awareness of popular tastes, which was not the case for the orders dedicated to meditation.

In addition, the criticisms of sport expressed by the clergy in the first half of the century are not unlike some modern criticisms. The headlong drive to win at the expense of certain educational values, and the commercialization of sport, which contrasts with the moral superiority of amateurism, are persistent issues in contemporary thinking on sport. What emerges most clearly from this study, however, is the fact that the clergy saw sport as an important cultural phenomenon. Committed as it was to preserving traditional Quebec culture, in sport as in all other cultural areas, the clergy became the leader of the resistance against what it perceived to be a means of assimilation.

Suggested Readings

For a detailed analysis of the problematic of leisure and the Quebec clergy, see Michel Bellefleur (1986), *L'Église et le loisir au Québec avant la revolution tranquille*, Sillery, Presses de l'Université du Québec, which provides the most extensive analysis of that topic. Everett C. Hugues (1963), *French Canada in Transition*, Chicago, University of Chicago Press, illustrates some of the changes in Quebec society that occurred after the Second World War. On the history of Quebec catholicism, see Jean Hamelin (1984), *Le catholicisme québécois: Le XXe siècle*, tome 2, *De 1940 à nos jours*, Montréal, Boréal Express.

Part Two
The Organizational Structure of Sport

Certain aspects of sport, such as the rules for engaging in it and the distinction between amateur and professional sport, have been the subject of negotiation throughout history. These problems have lost much importance today because they are considered definitively resolved. It would seem more useful to consider the way in which sport is organized.

The contemporary organizational structure is the end result of the transformation of sport, which has moved from chaos to the age of techno-bureaucratic organization. This organizational structure is itself historically specific, affected by the social currents that run through contemporary society. Thus the shift from the predominance of voluntary associations to the current power of the state's bureaucratic apparatus is not in itself progress towards greater rationality, but simply the result of the increased state role in advanced capitalist societies. In the same way, the organization of relations between employees and employers in professional sport is linked to the division of labour in these same societies. In addition, the structure of professional training in physical activity tends to produce agents who promote what has become the dominant model for participation in physical activity: competitive sport. In short, whether the modern techno-bureaucratic organization is rational or not depends on what the dominant model of sport defines as rational.

Two theoretical concerns underlie each of the four chapters dedicated to the dynamics of the organizational structure of sport: the distinction between civil society and political society, and the political economy of sport. Gouldner defines civil society as the organizational sphere of bourgeois society (Thériault, 1985:11). André Gorz, however, is more specific:

> Civil society refers to the fabric of social relations that individuals establish among themselves within groups or communities that owe their existence neither to state mediation nor to an institutional act of the state. They are relations based on reciprocity and voluntary work, not on law and legal obligation. (quoted in Levasseur, 1982:99)

Antonio Gramsci put forward the hypothesis that, in advanced capitalist societies, political society tended progressively to invade the areas controlled by civil society. Jean Harvey and Roger Proulx find exactly this trend with respect to sport and the state in Canada. However, contrary to Gramsci's theories, which hold that this is an exclusively capitalist process whose contradictions must be managed by the state, Harvey and Proulx point out that this process is also the product of pressures by social agents seeking some power against the determining role played by professional sport and the entire sports industry, as well as the result of the internal dynamic of the state apparatus.

Donald Macintosh shows how voluntary associations, which are part of civil society, have been progressively incorporated into the state, that is, political society. Albert Meister defines these associations as

> ... voluntary groupings that are somewhat or completely organized, more or less open to penetration by society at large, compatible among themselves, having only one unconditional constraint on their members, a democratic structure and collective ownership. (quoted in Levasseur, 1982:173)

The national sports federations analysed by Macintosh fit this type of definition. But, as sociologists who have studied associative phenomena have pointed out, these groups have relations with political society that are in constant flux. The trend uncovered by Harvey and Proulx and Macintosh suggests that the distinction between the area controlled by political society and the area controlled by civil society is becoming more and more blurred. The state has even initiated the establishment of agencies that, although based in principle on private association, are nonetheless extensions of its own apparatus. This applies to the Coaching Association of Canada, Hockey Canada, and Participaction.

The associative dynamic is also attributable to the social composition of the groups involved. Macintosh notes that volunteers are not recruited on a universal basis. The predominance of middle-class anglophone males in the senior positions in voluntary sports associations, previously pointed out by Metcalfe, apparently persists today. Macintosh shows the unequal representation of women and the dominated classes in the management positions of sports associations. Sport is also tied to the very foundations of the social infrastructure, the mode of production of the societies in which it has evolved.

This brings us to the second major theoretical concern in this part: the study of the political economy of sport. Political economy was defined by classical economists such as Adam Smith and David Ricardo as the study of the distribution of wealth among the different classes of society. The distribution of wealth does not only determine how things are produced (for example, by slavery rather than labour for pay) or whether the work will be done by sophisticated technology requiring little human labour rather than by labour-intensive technologies. It also has an influence on culture: on how all cultural activity must be organized in productive society, and also on areas of culture that are apparently less related, such as aesthetics and rational efficiency.

In his paper, Rob Beamish studies the political economy of professional sport. Starting with the concept of work, he attempts to account for the work process and the production relations in the professional sports industry. The concept of the work process is any process [or procedure] that transforms a particular object, a transformation performed by a specific human activity using specific work instruments (Harnecker, 1974:19). In professional sport, the work supplied by athletes is a sports performance, given in exchange for a salary and offered as an object of consumption, usually in the form of an event. The idea of relations of production refers to "the form in which the process of labour has been reified concretely in history" (Harnecker, 1974:19). Beamish examines the power relations between owners of the professional sports industry and the players. He also looks at the players' battles to improve their situation. The final part of his analysis shows how dominated social agents can take charge of their own situation and make their grievances known. In studying the "commodification" of sport by the sports event industry, Beamish exposes one of the least visible aspects of this industry. In general, studies of this industry deal only with the manufacture of sports equipment and the construction of sports facilities. Beamish shows the extent of the commodification of sport in contemporary society.

The study by Pierre Demers on the training of physical educators demonstrates that the educational system is organized in such a way as to propagate a dominant model of physical activity and how the training of physical activity professionals is biased towards turning out agents who will reproduce the dominant form. The reader will learn that the profession of physical educator sprang from the division of labour in industrialized societies, a division that led to increased specialization of tasks. This specialization is also linked to the specialization of knowledge within these societies.

Basing his study in part on the sociology of science, Demers examines the social impact of scientific activity. What is presented as neutral knowledge without values seems in fact to hold specific values linked to the dominant values of advanced capitalist societies. Demers also shows how the form of institutionalization of a new occupation determines the actions of those who are trained for it. Finally, Demers outlines a model that could be substituted for the dominant model.

The first part of this book described the struggle to find a particular form and significance for physical activity. This second part shows how the dominant model has been organized rationally and efficiently within the specific context of Canadian society and how the modern organization of sport and physical activity is linked to that of capitalist industrial society in general.

Chapter Five
Sport and the State in Canada

Jean Harvey and Roger Proulx

In advanced capitalist societies, organized sport has been marked, during the past three decades, by massive state intervention. Even though the myth of the separation of the two still persists, the state continues to strengthen its grip on sport. This intervention is becoming more pronounced and wide-ranging as the state imposes its particular policies on organized sport. Thus, according to Jamet (1980), political society has gradually taken control of a sector that until the 1960s had been part of civil society, that is, outside the direct control of the state.

The Motives for State Intervention in Sport

In his classic work on the political sociology of sport, Meynaud (1966) proposes a classification of the various motives that prompt states to intervene in the area of sport. The first of these motives is the safeguarding of public order. Improving the physical fitness of the population is the second major motive identified by Meynaud. Physical activity has long been fostered with a view to military preparedness. It is also encouraged by modern states to further the equilibrium and well-being of the population and to increase productivity. The third motive is the assertion of national prestige, which is probably the main reason for the massive intervention of modern states in elite sport. The competition for Olympic medals is not motivated solely by a desire for international prestige; it also allows individuals to increase their sense of national belonging. The television coverage of the Olympic Games is most revealing in this respect.

These factors have not arisen by accident. They are the result of historical conditions that broadly determine the extent and direction of government intervention in any area. State intervention in sport is consistent with the development of the state's role in every social context. Thus, to understand government intervention in sport, it is necessary to examine the role played by the state in the society in question and ascertain the historical forces that have governed its intervention in this area.

The Canadian state is not a neutral arbiter of the needs of each individual. Government actions fall within a network of ramifications arising from the economic system in which the state operates. In an economy in which the primacy of private property is a basic principle, the state apparatus cannot act against private property. This principle implies, broadly speaking, that the state should intervene in as few areas as possible. In the economy, it should intervene only in those cases where the natural play of market forces cannot solve the problems encountered.

According to Panitch (1977), the capitalist state has three functions. The first is the adoption of measures that permit the accumulation of capital: the state must act in such a way that the economic rules and conditions help businesses to grow, that is, indirectly promote the generation of as high profits as possible, with the consequent growth of capital — the increased wealth of the owners of these businesses. The tax clauses in the 1985 federal budget that allow a lifetime tax exemption of $500 000 on capital gains are a good illustration of this type of measure.

The second function of the capitalist state is the preservation of social harmony. This is achieved through measures likely to ease tensions created by conflicts of interest between the dominant and the dominated classes. According to Panitch, this second function is one of legitimation: it includes the means used to justify the social status quo. In societies that are based on the primacy of individual freedoms and the equality of all before the law, the state must at least give the illusion of being the guarantor of these principles. As Gruneau has pointed out, " . . . the effectiveness of state functioning is very much contingent upon widespread acceptance of the 'neutrality' of the state and this apparent neutrality cannot be manufactured if the state is too closely identified with the ruling class" (1982:16). Finally, Panitch suggests a third function, that of coercion, which involves the use of force to maintain social order.

There are other structural constraints that inform the role of the state. The constitutional framework defines the areas of governmental jurisdiction. In Canada's case, the federal system constitutes a particularly important structural framework owing to the respective jurisdictions of the different levels of government. The state's actions are also influenced by the parliamentary system, the electoral system, and the political parties.

The existence of these constraints does not mean that state action is merely a reflection of them. The state enjoys relative autonomy; it has its own dynamic and the capacity to act on its own. As well, it is not insensitive to the lobbying of pressure groups, nor to the diversity of opinion within the electorate. In short, the control of the dominant classes over the state is far from being complete. Moreover, the role of the state is not static.

In Canada, the initiatives of the state at the federal and provincial levels in the area of sport have been primarily linked to the development of policies of the so-called welfare state and to measures promoting nationalism. The strategies of the welfare state have been developed to influence market forces with a view to reducing social inequalities, notably through programs of income redistribution. Social assistance programs are an example.

These policies have had repercussions in sport and recreation since ad hoc programs of assistance to the unemployed were established during the Depression. In a predominantly descriptive article, Schrodt (1984) provides some evidence in support of this thesis. She states that the federal government first began intervening in the area of physical fitness around 1937; with the launching of programs to help the unemployed, programs were also set up to improve their fitness. It would seem, then, that sport has been a part of welfare state policies since their beginnings.

These programs were aimed at fitness or sports activities for all, not the development of elite performers. The same philosophy was behind the National Physical Fitness Act, passed in 1943. Federal intervention in the area of physical fitness was justified by the fact that many Canadians could not pass the physical fitness test required of those joining the Canadian armed forces. Under the National Physical Fitness Act, in effect until 1954, the federal government provided grants to participating provinces for the establishment of recreation and fitness services. Quebec, however, never participated in this program, regarding it as a federal intrusion into an area of provincial jurisdiction.

The Fitness and Amateur Sport Act of 1961, designed to reduce inequality of access to mass and elite sports, was also consistent, in part, with the philosophy of the welfare state. Since the mid-1970s — just as the Canadian welfare state entered a financial crisis — the state has shown growing concern about the physical fitness of Canadians, not only with the aim of improving their well-being, but also with a view to reducing the cost of health services.

While very little has been written about the relationship between the development of the welfare state and government intervention in the area of sport, there are a number of publications dealing with the relationship between nationalism and sport policies (Kidd, 1979; Macintosh et al., 1987; Gruneau, 1983).

During the decade following the Second World War, the provinces experienced substantial growth in their financial resources, with the result that they became more independent of the federal state. The latter, taking advantage of the unusual conditions prevailing during the war, had noticeably widened its area of intervention and fully intended to continue doing so after the war. Indeed, in the first few years of the postwar period, the federal government apparatus was greatly expanded with the development of welfare state policies. The federal government was involved in numerous cost-sharing programs and consequently tried to increase its control over the provinces.

The continentalization of the Canadian economy, due to the increasingly serious impact of the American economy, also played an important role in the emergence of new nationalist concerns in Canada. Moreover, as a number of writers have pointed out (Kidd, 1979; Gruneau, 1983), the internationalization of sports competition and its impact on the international image of nation-states also proved to be major factors in provoking an awareness of the Canadian state. Given these circumstances, Canada's prime ministers became the great champions of Canadian nationhood and took great interest in the possible benefits of the development of elite sports. As Meynaud's classification suggests (1966), it was a matter of using sport to assert national prestige and to promote among Canadians a sense of belonging.

Intervention in Sport by the Canadian State

Ideologies in the Federal State

There are two distinct periods in the development of federal government policy on recreation and amateur sport: the 1960s, a period of instability in policy-making; the 1970s and 1980s, a period in which the federal state has taken charge of virtually all amateur sport.

Health and fitness seemed equally legitimate in the political thought of the first period. But Canada's lamentable performance in international games was perhaps the main reason for the Canadian state's "re-involvement" in sport. It was believed that the vigour and power of a country could be measured by the international sports achievements of its athletes.

The mediocre showing of Canadian athletes in international games brought Canada's political parties together under the banner of national prestige. Thus, at the opening of the 24th Parliament in 1960, the Prime Minister announced that steps would be taken to encourage fitness and amateur sport. Bill C-131, which was introduced by the Minister of Health and Welfare, provided for the following: grants to sports agencies, institutions, and organizations; the launching of negotiations with the provinces for the payment of contributions to fitness and sports programs; the establishment of a National Advisory Council on Fitness and Amateur Sport; and an annual budget of five million dollars. The Minister did not see this program as a strictly federal undertaking; it would be developed on the basis of opinions and proposals from all interested parties.

This was the central government's response to the state of emergency perceived by various parties, who all felt that the situation was having a negative effect on Canada's image abroad. They were particularly sensitive to the losses suffered by the Canadian hockey team in international matches, as well as the poor performance of Canada's Olympic teams.

Armed with an Act whose provisions were, intentionally or otherwise, very vague, the state intended to encourage amateur sport and thereby to improve the physical fitness of Canadians. The general character of this Act helped the state, through the use of a cost-sharing program, to gain wider acceptance of its intrusion into an area which, historically, had been considered outside its jurisdiction. One might also speculate that the ambiguous clauses in the Act indicated the difficulty the state was having in developing the structure needed to achieve its stated objectives. The first priority was the building of adequate sports facilities; at the same time, the government bought itself enough time to work out a strategy that would enable it to attain another main objective — improving the quality of Canadian representation in international sports competitions. This situation created problems in the years after the Act was passed.

The assistance that the state provided to amateur sport, through the cost-sharing program to which the provinces contributed and through grants to national sports associations, satisfied neither the state nor the recipients. On the one hand, central government officials were pleased that the provinces were slow to get involved in the national project, merely receiving the grants without really taking any action. On the other hand, with provincial nationalism at its peak, federal officials felt that the government was not getting adequate recognition for its efforts; they also questioned the relevance of the programs set up by the national associations. Consequently, the agreements with the provinces ended after some ten years.

On this basis, we might surmise that the 1961 policy on fitness and amateur sport was launched without planning. Indeed, it was not until 1966 that the state asked national agencies to submit three-year development plans (Westland, 1979:22), a fact noted by the 1968 Royal Commission on Sport in Canada, set up by Prime Minister Trudeau.

In its report, the Commission, while recognizing the problems created by the country's physical size, pointed out that there had been a lack of co-operation and a duplication of effort, which had hampered progress. This may explain why, shortly after the report was tabled, a management consulting firm in Montreal was asked to review the national objectives and define the role of the federal government in meeting these objectives. Specifically, the programs and organization of the Fitness and Amateur Sport Branch came under scrutiny. As a result, a new policy on sport in Canada was proposed in 1970 by Health and Welfare Minister John Munro.

Bill C-131 had established the involvement of the Canadian government in both physical fitness and amateur sport. In reality, however, far greater resources were allocated to elite sport than to either recreation or fitness. The Minister himself admitted in 1971 that 80 per cent of the funding had gone to elite sport (Westland, 1979:108). This is hardly surprising in view of the nationalist motives behind the Bill. Nevertheless, the massive injection of funds into sport failed to satisfy those concerned with physical fitness and recreation. There were philosophical differences over what was meant by a "healthy" Canadian. Some people felt that elite sport would ultimately give rise to mass participation. Others believed that well co-ordinated participatory programs would inevitably lead to the development of an elite. It was the latter approach that the federal government eventually selected; that did not, however, prevent it from investing even more heavily in elite sport.

A gradual but systematic takeover of fitness and amateur sport by the federal government began in the early 1970s. This new approach by the state has been analysed in a number of documents, but *A Policy of Sport for Canada*, presented on March 20, 1970, is particularly important as it marks the state's ideological shift towards massive intervention. The government's policy was set out in the introduction to the document. In particular, it was stated that "the fact that we are proud of our country . . . shows another reason for a strong federal effort in the sport field: National Unity" (Munro, 1970:2).

The state saw sport as an effective means of bringing about national unity. Television, thanks to its phenomenal development, would shorten the distances between individuals and further "the new Canadian drive for the maximization of individual human potential" (Munro, 1970:3). In its effort to reduce inequalities, the state would pay "very special attention to the regions and to the least fortunate classes of individuals in our country" (Munro, 1970:3).

The ideology presented in the document revolved around three values attributed to physical activity: the development of physical fitness; the development of better mental health; and participation, particularly important as an antidote to the feeling of alienation created by industrialization and urbanization.

Sport would thus act as a stabilizer in an impersonal society, where the pressures generated by social conditions were often difficult for the individual to tolerate. Sport was seen as a means of preserving the status quo. The state's new approach represented, at least on the surface, a turning point for elite sport. As the Minister stated, "this new policy aims primarily at reinforcing and increasing the administrative strength of Canadian sports; . . . it seeks to change the focus of that administrative effort — chiefly by putting the pursuit of international excellence in its proper perspective, as a consequence and not as a goal of mass participation" (Munro, 1970:27–28). In effect, the state wanted sports organizations to increase the number of participants at the grass-roots level, which would enlarge the pool from which elite teams were selected. This pyramid idea was consistent with the hopes expressed by previous task forces, which saw well-organized mass sport as a means of enhancing the national image. At the same time, the state was tightening its control over sport; it set the objectives and proposed the courses of action.

The proposal set out in *A Policy of Sport for Canada* was intended to correct what the state had done since 1961. Federal involvement would now be more direct in that some national associations would be assigned an administrative director. It had been pointed out that the lack of significant improvement in Canada's representation was due in part to administrative amateurism in the national organizations and to their inability to set up programs capable of producing tangible results. This new policy marked the beginning, at least for amateur sport, of "rational" involvement by the state in this area. The state wanted more control of the management of the funds that it placed at the disposal of the national associations. Its right to oversee their policies was clearly established; these policies had to be in line with the goals set out in the new state policy.

With respect to health and recreation, government officials expected a policy change, one that was necessary because, in the past, "the lion's share of their [national sports associations] talents and energies [had been devoted] to the pursuit of excellence" (Munro, 1970:28). This expectation, though well supported in the state's policy statement, remained just an empty promise. "We are attempting to tailor our policies to assist the fulfilment of our overall goals of mass participation and social development" (Munro, 1970:43). At the same moment, the state terminated the cost-sharing agreements.

A New Perspective on Health for Canadians, published in 1974, presented a comprehensive look at health and some strategies for action. This overview was based on four factors: human biology, the environment, lifestyles, and the organization of health care. All sickness was caused by one of these factors or a combination of them, according to the Minister. He therefore proposed, to the extent permitted by law, strategies for improving the health of Canadians. The first strategy was the promotion of health. Various courses of action were suggested, among them an effort to promote physical exercise, increased assistance to sports programs with heavy public participation, securing of the co-operation of business and labour in setting up physical exercise programs, and the availability to the public of self-administered physical fitness tests.

This new strategy expressed concern about the excessive costs associated with the health of Canadians. The state was proposing an approach based on preventive care rather than cures. A healthy citizenry represented social progress and, at the same time, proof of good public administration. The proposed course of action suggested that the state would make a special effort to achieve this objective and that the Minister would put forward

a promotional strategy. Nevertheless, these intentions, the Minister stated, were not an "attempt to pre-judge jurisdictional and
financial issues nor to set priorities for other levels of government"
(Lalonde, 1974:73). One might have expected that budget priorities to implement the new strategy would have favoured Fitness
Canada or Recreation Canada. Such was not the case, however.
As in previous years, the level of funding given to these organizations was less than that received by Sport Canada, the body
responsible for the elite program.

      Immediately after the Olympic Games in 1976, government officials met with sports administrators and other interested
parties to dispel the confusion that existed between the areas of
health, physical fitness, sport, and recreation. The results were
to be used in developing a new national policy on sport. The confusion persisted, however. In the preface to the Green Paper entitled *Towards a National Policy on Amateur Sport*, the state
announced its intention to hold a series of similar consultations
on fitness and recreation. The main topic of these consultations
was elite sport. Yet because so little time was allowed for the consultations, because the subject under discussion was unclear,
because some athletes were "forgotten" in the process, and because
the field of elite sports was so narrow, the Green Paper failed to
meet the expectations of those concerned. Moreover, the results
were not used to make changes in the policies of Sport Canada.
According to Macintosh et al. (1987), the 1978 White Paper entitled *Together Towards Excellence* indicated the state's lack of
interest in fitness and recreation. While there was a general
concern throughout society about the situation of the elderly, the
handicapped, and native peoples, surprisingly little attention was
paid to them during these consultations. The state was in fact "concerned primarily with the development of a national sports policy
to meet the challenge of international competition" (Campagnolo,
1979a:6). In proposing this new order of priorities for services to
the public, the state explained that "the government does appreciate that sport can and does create jobs, and that the values
implanted by sport make a significant contribution to the betterment of Canadian society" (Campagnolo, 1979a:7). Sport thus
became a vehicle for improving the quality of life of Canadians.
This doctrine was distinctly reminiscent of the state's attitude in
the early 1960s.

      In the document entitled *Towards a National Policy on
Health and Recreation*, all parties concerned were invited to participate in a national discussion on health and physical recreation

in Canada: "Recreation in Canada is a patchwork quilt. . . . No one single level of government or private organization can claim primacy in the field of recreation" (Campagnolo, 1979b:3). In fact, the state had difficulty defining what physical recreation was and how it could encourage development in this area, which it continued to claim was part of its mandate under the law. This claimed mandate would be abandoned after the consultations.

The state's most recent official position paper, *Rising to the Challenge*, refers to two challenges facing the state in the 1980s: to push elite sport to new heights after the success of the 1976 Olympic Games and the 1978 Commonwealth Games, and to increase the number of people participating in physical activity (Regan, 1981:5). Realizing that this would not be easy owing to a drop in the economic growth rate, the Minister appealed to the public to take responsibility for their own fitness. Fitness Canada's new objective was "to raise the fitness level of Canadians by promoting increased participation in physical activity thereby encouraging healthy lifestyle behaviour" (Regan, 1981:17).

Individual responsibility for physical fitness became the state's official policy just as it was seeking to lower health costs (Brodeur, 1980; Crawford, 1981; Harvey, 1983).

The various position papers demonstrate the state's desire to rationalize its role as a provider of grants by demanding that the groups receiving support do a better job of managing the resources at their disposal. The state seemed to be having doubts about the cost-effectiveness of the assistance it was giving some groups and asked, at the same time, for a rational justification.

Intervention by the Federal State

In 1961, following the proclamation of the Fitness and Amateur Sport Act, the Fitness and Amateur Sport Branch began implementing its program. Grants were awarded to national organizations to encourage development of their programs of national and international activities. This assistance program still exists. In fact, most funds spent by the Branch since 1961 have been allotted to this program. Its budget went from $226 369 in the 1962–63 fiscal year to nearly $50 million in 1984–85. The majority of it was used by eighty-five national organizations to pay the salaries of their administrative directors and national coaches, to assist athletes in training, and to fund participation in national and international competitions. Grants were also given to the provinces to develop community activities.

In 1962, the state signed its first joint program agreement with the provinces and territories, except Quebec. Under the one-year agreement, grants were made available to the provinces and territories without their being required to match them dollar for dollar. In addition, the state gave the provinces a $250 000 grant for planning and organization; $15 000 was to be allocated to each province and territory, with the balance being apportioned on the basis of population. This formula was changed in 1963. The Canadian state would cover only 60 per cent of the costs of approved projects. After this, two additional three-year agreements were signed. The state terminated the program at the beginning of 1970. Between 1961 and 1970, the federal government attempted to work with the provinces, holding federal-provincial ministerial conferences, running cost-sharing programs, and so on. For the federal state, this addressed a concern about national unity, which was an issue in the 1968 election campaign. The drive for unity encountered roadblocks, notably Quebec's refusal to sign agreements until 1969. In fact, while accepting federal assistance in principle, Quebec wanted to set its own priorities. The development of Quebec nationalism paralleled the development of Canadian nationalism.

In 1962, the Branch set out to establish a health and sport information centre. Originally located at the University of Ottawa, it was merged with the Fitness and Amateur Sport Branch in 1968 and still exists today. With regard to research, agreements were signed in 1964 between the federal government and the Universities of Montreal, Toronto, and Alberta for the establishment of fitness research units. Under the agreements, which expired in 1969, universities across the country were able to equip themselves with research laboratories. As Westland (1979:78) notes, the majority of grants given out during this period went to a single field of research, the development of physical fitness programs, particularly the description of Canadians' physical and functional characteristics.

The promotional aspect of the program centred primarily on the preparation of teaching materials (films, pamphlets, and manuals) for participants. The Branch also contributed financially to the organization of national conferences on health, recreation, and amateur sport. The Montmorency conference on recreation in Canada (1969) is a good example. The policy studies and papers published in 1969 and 1970 preceded more direct state intervention, and this new policy reflected a number of the recommendations made in those reports. As noted by Broom and Baka

(1978), Hockey Canada is a case in point. This non-profit corporation was created eight days before the report of the Royal Commission on Sport in Canada was submitted to the Minister. One
of its major recommendations was that the government should
establish Hockey Canada, whose chief function was to develop,
promote, manage, and run the national team that would represent
Canada in international ice hockey competition. Domestically, it
was to encourage the development of hockey. Canadians had been
upset at the poor performance of the national team in international
matches. So the state and private enterprise got together to promote
Canadian nationalism.

In 1970, the National Sport and Recreation Centre opened
in Ottawa, ushering in a period of better communication on sports
issues across the country. At the same time, the government formed
the Coaching Association of Canada, one of whose objectives was
to improve the quality of coaching, which had been criticized by
the Royal Commission on Sport (Rea et al., 1969). The Coaching
Association later set up a national certification program for
coaches. Also in 1970, the Canadian Physical Proficiency Award
was launched. This program for students between the ages of six
and seventeen received the support of the provinces and was very
successful in schools across Canada. Now known as "Youth Fitness," it encourages young people to be physically fit. The program also provided the federal state with an excuse to go into the
schools, an area of provincial jurisdiction.

During the 1970s, the federal government's intervention
apparatus expanded considerably; at the same time, the state tight-
ened its grip on the area of sport. The Fitness and Amateur Sport
Branch underwent numerous administrative reorganizations. Its
current organization chart shows how elite sport and mass participation are separated.

In 1971–72, in order to slow down the "muscle drain" to
the United States, the state gave grants to student athletes to help
them continue their studies in Canada while pursuing excellence
in their particular sport. That same year, Sport Canada provided
additional assistance to potential Olympic medal winners. In 1973
this program became Game Plan, in anticipation of the Montreal
Olympics. The level of support provided to the athletes was to be
based on their performance in international competition. Sport
Canada's contribution was $4 890 000 in 1984–85 (*1984–85 Annual
Report*).

Looking ahead to the 1988 Olympics, the Canadian state
is once again striving to improve the ranking of the country's

Table 1

Organization Chart of Fitness and Amateur Sport Canada*

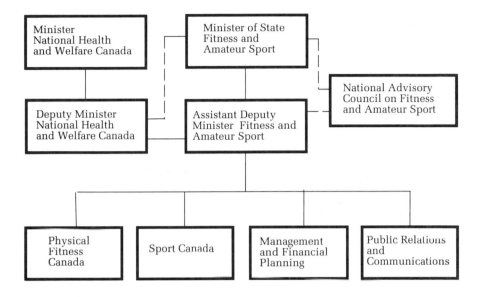

*Taken from the 1983-84 Annual Report of Fitness and Amateur Sport Canada

athletes. The "Better Than Ever" program was launched in 1983 for winter sports, and the four-year planning program for the Summer Games is the most ambitious long-term strategy ever undertaken in this area by the Canadian state. Under these programs, each sports federation is committed to produce a developmental plan for its particular sport, taking into account the directives prepared by a special team at Sport Canada. The state has allocated $25 million and $37.2 million per year, respectively, to these programs, to be added to the main sports budget for the 1988 Olympics.

In 1971, the Fitness and Amateur Sport Branch created a public information agency, Sport Participaction Canada. Its purpose was to make Canadians aware of the importance of physical activity — in practical terms, to market the idea of good physical fitness. Its operating budget rose from $200 000 in its first year to $861 000 in 1985–86. The government simultaneously set up a sports caravan to familiarize local sports leaders with new coaching methods and new equipment. The caravan's first tour took it through Ontario and Quebec. Also set up was a program of sports and recreation demonstrations to be given at community fairs across the country. This program, which later became Sport Action, continues to be supported by the Branch and is committed to making all Canadians aware of fitness and amateur sport.

Fitness testing has apparently always been a priority for the Branch. Besides the research units it had established, in 1973 the Branch took a leading role in the development of physical fitness programs for the workplace. Several federal departments introduced these programs at the time. In addition, tests were developed to measure physical fitness — Physitest, for example, which was placed on the market in 1975. Several surveys were also conducted with the support of the Branch, notably in 1976 and in 1981 (the Fitness Canada survey). The Branch also offered native peoples a program to help them fund their recreational activities. In addition, in 1985–86, Fitness Canada and Sport Canada earmarked $760 000 for the mentally and physically handicapped. These funds were distributed to national associations with the aim of supporting programs that provided the handicapped with an opportunity to engage in sports and selected recreational activities.

In 1980, the Branch set up a program to improve the status of women in physical fitness and sport in Canada. Under one segment of the program, retired elite female athletes were given training and experience in sports management. The program, which involved a great deal of on-the-job training, also involved women who had studied physical education and were planning a career in sports administration. This particular initiative was set up after it was reported that women were seriously under-represented in sports management positions. In 1984–85, the women's program was expanded to include funding to agencies that would encourage women to take upper management positions or to participate in sports activities, as well as continued assistance to national women's committees.

This brief overview of the federal state's doctrine and initiatives shows in detail how it has gone about taking control of sport and physical fitness since the early 1960s. The conservative tide of the 1980s and the accompanying reassessment of the welfare state have also had an impact on sport. The state is increasingly trying to persuade private enterprise to take over the funding of sports associations. Moreover, as we will see, the federal state is not the only level of government to have intervened in these areas.

Sport and the Quebec State

The Quebec state also began intervening in sport during the 1960s. In 1965, in the wake of the Quiet Revolution, during which the role and action of the Quebec state changed radically, the Bureau of Sport and Recreation, the predecessor of the current Ministry of Recreation, Hunting, and Fishing, was set up. This established the first Quebec government apparatus responsible for co-ordinating recreation and sport. More fundamentally, this period saw a change in the dominant force in these areas, specifically in the management of amateur sport. Private initiative, largely under church control in francophone areas, was replaced by state initiative.

The Quiet Revolution was characterized by a change in state action and the modernization of Quebec's institutions after new social groups, notably the intellectual and business middle class, came to power (Levasseur, 1983:167–168).

In place of the marginal role it played in the conservative ideology of the clergy, the state assumed the role of regulator and planner. The new Quebec state was based on the welfare state model, to which it would have to conform in order to raise Quebec to the level of a "post-industrial" society.

What distinguished the Quebec state from that of other provinces was the rapidity with which it introduced the new state apparatus, a drive to catch up with the other provinces that ultimately made the Quebec state much more interventionist than were those of most other provinces. This was connected to the weakness of economic development in Quebec at the beginning of the Quiet Revolution and the leading role played by the state in the development of a "national" economy. The rise and the transformation of Quebec nationalism, in which the state was used as a tool for the promotion of French culture in Quebec and North America, also had a major impact on the direction and extent of state intervention. The province took aggressive action to defend its areas of jurisdiction against federal incursions.

The Ideologies Behind Quebec State Intervention

Like every other area of Quebec social life that underwent changes as a result of the Quiet Revolution, recreation and sport have been the subject of intense ideological rhetoric, especially since the early 1960s. Briefs, Green and White papers, and reports of commissions of inquiry set up by the state mapped out suggestions for action. This ideological rhetoric also proved to be an effective tool for legitimizing the state's intervention plans.

The *Rapport du Comité d'étude sur les loisirs, l'éducation physique et les sports* (the Bélisle Report), published in 1964, was the first official document to have a major impact on the state's action in recreation and sport. The Bélisle Commission was composed almost exclusively of physical educators. Like other middle-class groups during the 1960s, physical educators wanted to increase their social and political status. To do so, they also needed the state's backing. This type of strategy is clearly reflected in the report of the Commission.

The Commission, having noted the difficult situation in which organized sport and recreation found itself, called on the government to neutralize the unpredictable forces of capitalism. With regard to professional sport, for example, the authors felt that " . . . while respecting private initiative, the state should regulate and control this sector in order to protect citizens against abuses" (1964:54). In both the Bélisle Report and subsequent reports, criticism of the dysfunctions of capitalism had a specific objective: to expose the tightening grip on mass recreation, and in particular that of professional sport on recreation and amateur sport, thus justifying massive state intervention in this sector.

The control of amateur sport by professional sport was only one of many problems, in the view of the Bélisle Commission. Organized sport generally was in a lamentable state owing to the lack of qualifications of its leaders and the lack of co-operation within it. Similarly, recreation in Quebec depended largely on voluntary organizations and personnel, which, without guidance or advice, could easily experience chaos. In the technocratic logic of the Bélisle Report, the good intentions of the volunteers were insufficient. This was an important theme in the report. Its authors insisted that the management of recreation and sport required qualified personnel, that is, university-trained specialists. Thus, with a view to acquiring power, professional physical educators advocated state intervention by arguing that it was important to provide quality services and improve the administrative efficiency of recreation and sports agencies.

The Bélisle Report and other documents laid the groundwork for public acceptance of massive state intervention in sport. In 1972, the state began playing a dominant role in recreation management, as grants were awarded on the basis of specific criteria and the government's contribution to the overall budgets of sports federations climbed well above 50 per cent (see Jamet,

1980:57). Based on a liberal definition of recreation, these reports promoted what Trottier et al. (1967) call the ideology of the right to recreation. Levasseur describes the parameters of this ideology, which he also refers to as a "professional culture": "The ideology of the right to recreation means the right of Quebeckers as individuals to participate in industrial civilization and its benefits, among them the civilization of recreation. The right to recreation has become a social right, like the rights to work, education, and health, which the modern state is supposed to guarantee" (1982:74). Levasseur then explains that, in line with state action in the area of recreation, increased democratization should occur, making "good" recreation available to all.

For people to develop through recreation, they could not be left to their own devices. They had to be introduced to officially sanctioned recreational activities in order to enjoy the benefits. This was the justification for the importance of specialized personnel in the ideology of the right to recreation, for these specialists were the mediators between scientific, professional knowledge acquired at university and the populace, who had to be taught the right choice and a taste for the legitimate practice of engaging in recreational activities (Levasseur, 1982; Harvey, 1983).

The victory of the Parti québécois in 1976 brought in a different ideological approach that built upon the previous one. This was the ideology of "cultural development" (Levasseur, 1982), whose formative ideas can be found in three documents published by the Parti québécois government between 1977 and 1979. In essence, recreation was no longer considered only as an area for personal development; it was also assigned a role in the cultural development of the "Québécois nation." Recreation became a place for collective emancipation.

Beyond these considerations of the philosophy of recreation, the very way in which recreation was viewed was the cornerstone on which the coming changes in state action were based. This view of recreation was developed in a White Paper on cultural development (Government of Quebec, 1978). Recreation was seen as a fundamental element of culture. It was no longer just an individual matter; it was also part of community life. In particular, it was a place for re-creating the fundamental solidarities destroyed by urban industrial society.

Accordingly, " . . . any policy on recreation must first recognize the right of individual and collective expression" (Government of Quebec, 1978:190). State intervention would no longer be confined to the provision of services to individuals. In fact, these services would only be offered to the extent that they were consistent with community interests. It was on this basis that the criteria for increased intervention were developed. The first criterion was that " . . . the state should, through its intervention and support, help hand over responsibility and freedom to individuals and groups" (Government of Quebec, 1978:197). The White Paper proposed that the state should establish planning resources and that it should participate in the development of recreational activities. In other words, "instead of reacting to the actions of other players and subsidizing a development process that it has had no part in defining, the government should participate directly in setting its course" (Government of Quebec, 1978:198).

The aim of the White Paper on cultural development was to take popular interests into account and not to define culture from an elitist point of view. One result of this was the government's marked interest in sport for all. This did not mean that support for elite sport was under attack. However, amateur sports organizations soon began worrying about the effects that this new interest by the state might have on the grants it was giving them.

In the White Paper on recreation (Charron, 1979), the state's position was made clear. Four basic categories were laid out: the citizen — the focal point and priority of recreation policy; the municipality — the supervisor of recreation development and organization; the state — the guardian and promoter of collective interests; and national and regional agencies — the partners of the municipalities and the state. In addition to these basic categories, state action would be guided by the following major national objectives: recovering health, developing creativity, exploiting nature, exploring the country.

The "recovering health" objective reflected the emphasis that the Parti québécois government intended to place on sport for all: " . . . it is imperative to make every effort to ensure that recreation is, for all Quebeckers, a special space in which to recover and maintain their health, their equilibrium, harmony with their bodies, all of which are the fruit of physical well-being that is a pleasure as well as a duty" (Charron, 1979:43). In the view of the Quebec state, engaging in physical activity was not mere play. It was above all utilitarian; it contributed to the maintenance of health. Only from this standpoint was physical recreation seen to be legitimate.

The Parti québécois' fierce opposition to intervention by the federal state in the area of recreation and sport was also a major theme in its thinking on the subject. Yet the nationalist motives

of the Quebec state in this area predate the election of the nationalist party in 1976. The authors of the earlier Bélisle Report pointed
out the extent of federal intervention and the resulting co-
ordination problems. Furthermore, as noted earlier, Quebec had
never participated in the grant programs set up by the federal
government under the National Physical Fitness Act of 1943. On
the other hand, as Gingras and Nevitte (1984:2) have pointed out,
it would be equally rash to claim that Quebec nationalism has
always followed a straight path. Nevertheless, the jealousy with
which the Quebec state, from its very beginnings, has guarded its
areas of jurisdiction (McRoberts and Postgate, 1980) is one of the
features that set it apart from the other provinces.

The Parti québécois government intended to pursue objectives that would further the individual and collective emancipation of the people of Quebec, who were considered to be oppressed
by the federal structure of the Canadian state. With regard to elite
sport, the following objectives were set out in the White Paper on
recreation: "Give priority to the development of a sports elite in
disciplines where there are genuine prospects for success at the
international level; support the development of a Quebec sports
elite up to the international elite level; and, where necessary, ensure
that Sport Canada respects the rights of Quebec athletes . . . "
(Charron, 1979:72).

In short, behind the shift in doctrine that occurred as one
political party succeeded another in power, there was an ongoing
trend towards increased intervention by the Quebec state in sport.

Changes in Quebec State Intervention Apparatus and Action

The Quebec state's action in the area of sport, as suggested
by Jamet's study (1980), can be divided into two distinct categories:
support and *guidance*. In general, *support* takes the form of grants
for the building or funding of the sports infrastructure, either equipment for public use (such as gymnasia and swimming pools) or
personnel (such as technical personnel for the sports federations
and support staff for sports facilities). *Guidance* relates chiefly to
the different types of planning introduced by the apparatus of state
intervention. As far as support is concerned, Quebec state action
between 1960 and 1985 can be summed up as steadily rising support expenditures until the early 1980s, followed by budgetary
restrictions. There are two distinct periods in guidance activities.
During the first period, from 1960 to 1972, the state left the initiative

to the voluntary recreational organizations. It was also during this period that the Quebec state gradually put in place its intervention apparatus. During the second period, from 1972 to 1985, guidance in the area of recreation and sport came under state control.

In the 1978 White Paper on recreation, the Parti québécois government would propose the creation of a ministry of recreation. But the government had long been under pressure to set up such intervention apparatus, notably by professionals such as physical educators and recreologists. The first intervention mechanism, established in 1968 — the Haut-Commissariat à la jeunesse, aux loisirs et aux sports (the High Commission for Youth, Recreation, and Sport) — was very similar to the one suggested in the Bélisle Report (1964).

In spite of its weakness, the state intervention apparatus was successful during the 1960s in completing the secularization of church-owned recreation facilities at the local, regional, and provincial levels. At the same time, government grants encouraged replacement of the OTJs (local sections of the Oeuvre des terrains de jeux) with municipal recreation services and the conversion of the diocesan recreation federations into Regional Recreation Councils. The Confédération otéjiste provinciale (COP) was also secularized, becoming the Confédération des loisirs du Québec (CLQ) (Quebec Recreation Federation) in 1965.

The creation of the latter umbrella agency, which was the result of a split within the COP, marked the beginning of the specialization of recreation associations, a trend which has continued. Between 1960 and 1972, state action was not much different from what it had been in previous years. In 1972, when the voluntary recreation associations were conspicuous by their number and size, the stage was set for the creation of a state intervention apparatus capable of "rationally" managing recreation and sport. From then on, the Quebec state handled sports development according to its own priorities.

The year 1972 remains a turning point. Several actions by the Parti québécois at that time demonstrate its intent to take charge of recreation. As Levasseur (1983) points out, the Quebec government in 1972 redefined the political and administrative framework of recreation. For the first time, political status was granted to the Haut-Commissariat à la jeunesse, aux loisirs et aux sports. One year later, the (Liberal) government assigned responsibility for this agency to a minister. In addition, the administrative bureaucracy for recreation has grown steadily in numbers and power since 1973.

Table 2
Organization Chart of the Quebec Ministry of Recreation, Hunting, and Fishing*

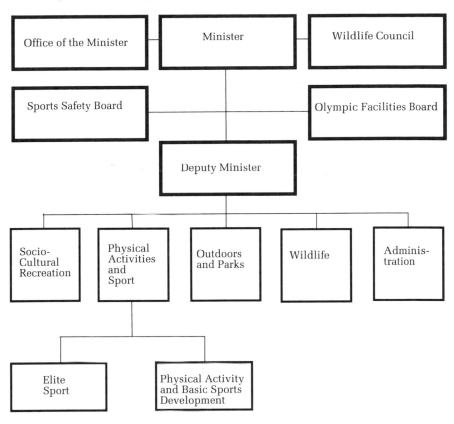

*Adapted from the 1982-83 Annual Report of the Quebec Ministry of Recreation, Hunting, and Fishing

In 1980, a number of state services were grouped together, for the purpose of rationalization, in the new Ministry of Recreation, Hunting, and Fishing. This ministry consolidated the Quebec state's grip on recreation and sport.

As shown in the organization chart, there are two boards and four branches. As its name indicates, the Régie des installations olympiques (Olympic Facilities Board) was concerned exclusively with the management of the Olympic facilities in the city of Montreal. For the purposes of this analysis, we will focus on the Physical Activities and Sport Branch.

The Direction de l'activité physique et du développement du sport de base (Physical Activity and Basic Sports Development Branch) managed two programs in 1982–83: the basic sports development program and the Kino-Quebec program. The former was consistent with the democratization of sports activities. Grants were provided in particular to the multisport sports federations (regional and scholastic), second-level sports clubs, and organizers of the Quebec Games. The latter were Quebec's answer to the Canada Games. They followed the same objective of promoting national unity, but the term "national unity" applied to a different geographic reality.

As recommended in the White Paper on recreation, the Kino-Quebec program, set up in 1978, became the Parti québécois government's key program in the area of sport for all. It was a particularly interesting program, as it was the Parti québécois government's response to federal intervention and the alliance between the state and the lower middle class (Harvey, 1982). Kino-Quebec was administered and controlled by the state, while physical educators were responsible for achieving the established objectives. The structure of Kino-Quebec was simple: a central organization (a team of five fitness advisers attached to the Physical Activity and Basic Sports Development Branch of the Ministry of Recreation, Hunting, and Fishing) and a network of about fifty Kino-Quebec modules, each covering part of Quebec. Each module had on staff a co-ordinator and a physical educator responsible for carrying out the main policies, called National Action Plans, set out by the central organization, as well as a plan drawn up locally (Harvey, 1982:90–91).

The establishment of this organization provided the Quebec state with a much more substantial basis for intervention than that of its federal counterpart, Participaction, which had been perceived as a federal intrusion into an area of Quebec jurisdiction. It was not until 1985, after the election of a Conservative federal government and the Parti québécois' ideological shift towards the "federalist challenge," that Kino-Quebec co-ordinated its own "physical activity week" with the federal one. Moreover, the setting up of this program probably contributed to the social democratic image that the Quebec government wanted. It also enabled the Parti québécois government to distance itself from the policies of the previous government, which favoured elite sport. In addition, the provincial state, like the federal state, was attracted to this program by the expected side-effect of reduced health-care expenses.

With regard to amateur elite sport, the growth of state intervention was achieved at the cost of incessant battles with the sports associations, which, while continually pushing for greater funding, strove to protect their independence from the state. The history of federated associations such as the CLQ, the Confédération des sports du Québec (CSQ) (Quebec Sports Federation), and the Fédération québécoise du plein air (FQPA) (Quebec Outdoor Federation) is replete with their never-ending struggles to gain a larger share of the resources allocated by the state to recreation and sport. To free themselves from this problem, government authorities, in accordance with the intentions announced in the White Paper, forced these associations to amalgamate into a single agency, the Regroupement des organismes nationaux de loisir du Québec (RONLQ) (Coalition of National Recreation Agencies of Quebec), which in 1985 became the Regroupement Loisir Québec (RLQ) (Quebec Recreation Coalition). This policy infuriated the sports world, which has since sought to rid itself of this organization.

The amateur sports federations had been trying for a long time to co-ordinate their efforts in order to produce a Quebec sports elite. But with the announcement that the Olympic Games would be held in Montreal in 1976, the Quebec state began to take charge of elite amateur sports planning. In 1972, the Mission Quebec 1976 was set up. Its objective was to see that Quebec athletes comprised 30 per cent of the Canadian Olympic team. The program became permanent when the provincial Liberal government created the Institut des sports du Québec (ISQ) (Quebec Sports Institute) in 1976. The Parti québécois contested the private status of this agency from the beginning. In the White Paper on recreation, it was proposed that the ISQ and the CSQ be merged to form the Société des sports du Québec (SSQ) (Quebec Sports Corporation), whose sole function would be to develop a Quebec sports elite. The SSQ was to prepare its own plan for the development of a sports elite that would then receive the approval of the state. The state, in turn, would provide the funding. In 1983, the SSQ published its development plan. Instead of approving the plan, however, the state in 1984 produced its own program, which it then undertook to impose on the sports world.

This new policy on elite sport was presented in *Le temps de l'excellence: un défi québécois* (1984). Four major approaches were set out: giving priority to the present and future needs of Quebec athletes; enlarging the pool of Quebec athletes; gradually narrowing and even eliminating the gap between the level of performance in Quebec and the international level; co-operation among the various parties in an effort to maintain consistency in interventions (Government of Quebec, 1984:49). This policy reflected the Quebec state's intent to take a firm hand in the development of a Quebec sports elite. What distinguished it from previous policies was that it instituted almost total state control over the development of the elite. Sports clubs were considered the building blocks for the development of elite sport and were to be funded directly by the state. In addition, it was announced that regional performance preparation centres would be established. The role of the SSQ was confined to that of a support and service agency for the national recreation agencies. Finally, it was announced that the Elite Sports Branch of the Ministry of Recreation, Hunting, and Fishing would be responsible for Quebec policy on the development of sports excellence. First and foremost, this policy was aimed at the power of the "sports bureaucracy." What remained of the ISQ's role after it was merged with the CSQ subsequently came under state control. Justifying its plan on the grounds that it had to make public spending as cost-effective as possible by ensuring that a larger part of the funds went to the intended recipients, the state centralized the management of elite sport in its own apparatus. The voluntary associations' bureaucracy was replaced by a state bureaucracy. Furthermore — and this is the point on which the state based its action — it was said that the policy would protect elite athletes. In this respect, the state proposed that a declaration of the rights and responsibilities of athletes should be adopted. The other facet of this policy statement, which was particularly unusual, revealed that the Parti québécois government intended to defend the rights of the state in this area.

The objective of the policy was clear: to produce in the near future an elite with the best possible chances of winning medals in the Canada Games and major international games. In view of the size of the challenge, it was proposed that disciplines should be classified according to various criteria for forecasting potential results and state expenditures divided accordingly. For example, only disciplines included in major international games would be listed in the classification. Another of the proposed criteria was social visibility of a particular discipline. Also, the right to participate in the Canada Games was confined to athletes under 21 years of age, which indicated the limits of the declaration of the rights and responsibilities of athletes. Thus, everything seemed to be arranged so that the Quebec sports elite would serve the interests of the state. From then on, every effort would be made to win as many medals as possible and to increase the elite's visibility, thereby improving Quebec's image.

Advocates of amateur sport "in the real sense of the word" had always seen professional sport as the root of all problems in organized sport and had frequently requested intervention in this area. Over the years, government authorities had partially given in to pressure from these groups, particularly physical educators. Nevertheless, these interventions were also affected by the attitude of the electorate, especially the middle class, towards the most blatant evils of spectator sports.

In 1975, for example, following yet another outbreak of violence in the Quebec Junior Hockey League, an outbreak fuelled by a sensationalist press, the Commission of Enquiry on Violence in Hockey was set up. The Néron Report (1975) gave a thorough account of the responsibility of the spectator sports industry, the mass media, and the state (particularly the judicial system) for perpetuating violence. The report concluded with a proposal to establish a quasi-judicial agency to ensure propriety in sport. This, of course, was well beyond the realm of hockey. Moreover, it applied to professional sport as well as amateur sport. As soon as the Commission started its work, open hostilities erupted between the Commission and physical educators on the one hand and the professional sports industry (at times assisted in its efforts by the sports press) on the other. The war of words broke out again after the Régie de la sécurité dans les sports du Québec (RSSQ) (the Sports Safety Board) was set up in 1979. This was a rather unusual part of the state intervention apparatus: the functions assigned to it by law substantially increased the potential for state intervention in sport, but so far, except for professional boxing, the Board has done nothing more than extend state control over amateur sport.

Conclusion

The Canadian and Quebec states have used increasingly forceful means of intervention. First, they used government expenditures, specifically larger and larger grants to the voluntary sports associations. In this connection, it is noteworthy that the increase in grants was accompanied by an increase in state control over the activities of the associations being funded. Taking control grew easier as the grants came to account for almost the entire budgets of most of the associations. Later, the states began using regulation. The RSSQ is the most obvious example of this type of intervention, but the rules on drug use and drug testing in sport proposed by Sport Canada in 1983 could also be included. Finally, with the establishment of Hockey Canada, a combined Crown/ private corporation, the Canadian state used public ownership as an instrument of intervention, just as it had done in setting up Participaction. Even though it calls itself a private company and tries to associate itself with the private sector, Hockey Canada is heavily supported by federal funds. Over the years, the services provided directly by the state have expanded considerably, from merely distributing pamphlets to providing a full range of services such as those offered by Kino-Quebec. Thus, all the evidence suggests that the Canadian and Quebec states are engaged in a take-over of organized sport and recreation. This process is not confined to associations; it also involves individuals, whose recreational activities the states are attempting to circumscribe. For example, promotional campaigns and services have been used to encourage Canadians to take part in physical activities, not for the fun of it, but to improve their physical fitness.

To conclude the analysis, it may be worth considering, now that the welfare state is in crisis and state intervention is increasingly being questioned, whether or not we are on the verge of a retreat by the state, at the threshold of the "liberation" of sport from the "pernicious" interventions by the state. The available evidence indicates that state spending will decline or at least level off while, at the same time, the state will encourage private enterprise to help fund sports and recreational programs, to become a full partner in state enterprises. If this trend materializes, we may see increased emphasis in state programs on the "practical" aspects (such as lower health-care expenditures and higher productivity) of engaging in physical activities. We may also see continued interest by the state in elite sport, in view of its value in the promotion of national unity.

As far as Quebec specifically is concerned, the government seems to be moving towards greater co-ordination of federal and provincial policies. The trend towards a retreat by the state, begun by right-wing governments, will not necessarily result in less interventionism. For example, the fact that the government of Quebec is considering abolishing the RSSQ and handing over its functions to the Ministry of Recreation, Hunting, and Fishing could be the beginning of a move to concentrate state decision-making. The state's supposed retreat would thus be merely a new form of extending its interventions, which would be carried out with a more modest apparatus.

Suggested Readings

Donald Macintosh et al. (1987), *Sport and Politics in Canada*, Montreal and Kingston, McGill-Queen's University Press, provides a more detailed analysis of the Canadian federal government involvement in sport. For Quebec, see Michel Jamet (1980), *Les sports et l'État au Québec*, Montréal, Éditions coopératives Albert Saint-Martin, and Roger Levasseur (1982), *Loisir et culture au Québec*, Montréal, Boréal Express. For an in-depth discussion on the role of the contemporary state, see Leo Panitch (Ed.) (1977), *The Canadian State: Political Economy and Political Power*, Toronto, University of Toronto Press. See also Claus Offe (1984), *Contradictions of the Welfare State*, Cambridge, MIT. Hart Cantelon and Richard S. Gruneau (Eds.) (1982), *Sport, Culture and the Modern State*, Toronto, University of Toronto Press, contains theoretical and case-study essays of the interrelations between sport and the state.

Chapter Six
The Federal Government and Voluntary Sports Associations

Donald Macintosh

Introduction

Recent federal government intervention in the promotion of high-performance sport has had a dramatic impact on voluntary national sports associations. As a result of this intervention, which began some fifteen years ago, associations have enjoyed expanded technical and administrative capacities and enlarged financial resources, provided mainly by the federal government. As well, they have adopted a rationalized approach to program goals and outcomes. But, at the same time, national associations have experienced a diminution of autonomy and have been unable to develop any united strategy to counterbalance the growing federal government presence in high-performance sport. This transformation can best be understood in the framework of two themes: the changing motives for government involvement in sport, and the political and administrative structure put in place by government to achieve its goals.

Voluntary Sports Associations and Bill C-131

Bill C-131 (the Fitness and Amateur Sport Act), which created the National Fitness and Amateur Sport Advisory Council (NAC), was passed by Parliament in 1961. Its passage has often been attributed to concern about Canada's international stature in hockey and to the Duke of Edinburgh's speech in 1959 to the Canadian Medical Association (CMA) in which he urged the CMA to take steps to rectify the poor state of physical fitness in this country. However, the Bill's passage was more likely due to the atmosphere in Canadian society at the time, which was one of more general change. Social, political, and economic changes expanded the boundaries of generally acceptable government activity during the 1950s to a point where fitness and amateur sport legislation became possible. At the same time, resistance to state intervention by sports organizations waned.

The autonomy of sports organizations had been a feature of their structure from the late nineteenth century (Wise, 1974:100). For example, the outcry against government control of sport, which greeted the announcement in 1945 that the National Physical Fitness Council would serve as a link between Canadian sports associations and government, was strong evidence that sports organizations were still zealous about their independence and autonomy (Broom and Baka, 1978:4; Kidd, 1981:241). This position was supported by the belief that the state had no business regulating the voluntary activity of Canadians (Cantelon and Gruneau, 1982:19–20). But the financial problems faced by these groups in staging national championships and sending teams to international events in the 1950s, and the lack of success by Canadian teams in these events, resulted in a growing acceptance of the idea that the federal government did have a supportive role to play in sport.

Bill C-131 received unanimous support in the House of Commons in the fall of 1961 (HC *Debates*, September 25, 1961:883F). It can be safely said that the Act was uncontentious, non-partisan, and widely supported, but at the same time, apparently of no great importance in certain governmental and other circles.

The Canadian Sports Advisory Council (CSAC) believed (incorrectly) that it would be responsible for co-ordinating and directing government funds earmarked for sport. However, the primary advisory role it perceived for itself was usurped by the NAC which, because it assumed the role of recommending sport policy to the federal government, became the unofficial voice of sport in the 1960s.

The creation of the National Fitness and Amateur Sport Advisory Council, to advise the Minister of Health and Welfare, was a compromise between pressures from interest groups and some politicians to create an independent agency similar in nature and function to the Canada Council *and* the federal government's reluctance to take direct responsibility for implementing the provisions of the Act by establishing a regular division and bureaucracy within a federal government department. In establishing a National Advisory Council, the federal government created a buffer group which would protect it from criticism from sports advocates and, at the same time, would allow it to gather information from various regions and from different program biases (see Macintosh and Franks [1982] for a lengthier account of the forces and events leading to the Fitness and Amateur Sport Act). The NAC, with its wide geographic representation and variety of views on sport policy, allowed some balance between high-performance sports advocates and those favouring participatory sports and fitness programs.

The Early Years (1960s)

In the first few years following the enactment of Bill C-131, federal government involvement was indirect and consisted mainly of distributing funds to national sports and recreation associations and to the provinces through federal-provincial cost-sharing arrangements. In this latter domain, policies and directions were determined by the Minister of Health and Welfare, the Hon. Waldo Monteith. In the other major areas of the program, the Minister relied upon the NAC's advice in the formulation of policies (FASD Files, PAC, RG 29, Vol. 1353). Thus, the NAC established a detailed set of criteria for making grants to national sports associations (NAC *Summary of Policy Statements and Decisions*, 1967:6.1–6.6).

The monies distributed through these grants did allow for greater participation in national and international sports competitions (FASD Files, PAC, RG 29, Vol. 1331), and modest improvements at the international level were realized (FASD *Annual Report*, 1965, 66:1–2). But the period from 1961 to 1968 was more noted for exposing the barriers to further gains. The sports associations, for the most part, did not have the organizational skills or leadership necessary to implement the improvements which would lead to better athletic performance; the NAC became convinced that full-time professional staff was required and urged the Minister to make administrative grants to national sports and recreation associations.

Amateur sports officials and the federal sports bureaucrats also perceived that the sporadic and unco-ordinated offering of clinics was not effective in developing coaches for elite athletes. In addition, poor levels of officiating in most sports and the almost complete lack of a sports medicine component to amateur sport were identified as barriers to further progress. It became clear as well that high-performance athletes would need to spend more time in training and competing in top-level events if significant improvements in international performance were to be attained. In order to accomplish these ends, a growing number of sports officials, sports writers and reporters, and politicians advocated direct financial assistance for high-performance athletes.

Anticipated opposition to federal government sport involvement by the sports organizations and agencies in the early 1960s did not materialize. On the contrary, demands for federal support in the form of submissions for financial assistance escalated (FASD Files, PAC, RG 29, Vol. 1331). The introduction of administrative grants to sports associations in 1966 was one of the first manifestations of this changing attitude. This precedent proved to be the forerunner of the establishment of the National Sport and Recreation Centre in 1970. The growing influence of the federal government on the national sports associations also helped shape future sport direction in Canada.

Two alternative strategies to rectify shortcomings previously mentioned became apparent in the late 1960s. The federal government could increase its financial support to the national sports associations, depending on them to upgrade coaching and stimulate elite sport, or it could opt for the development of its own agencies and bodies and deal more directly with athletes and coaches. In its new policy statement in 1970, the government opted largely for the second course of action.

Government Intervention (1970s)

Certain political forces in the late 1960s, in tandem with the growing importance and attraction of sport, caused the federal government to become interested in sport as an instrument that could be used as a national unity symbol. (A full account of these developments is given in Chapter 4 of *Sport and Politics in Canada*, Macintosh et al., 1987.) The federal government established a Task Force on Sport late in 1968, thus fulfilling Prime Minister Pierre Trudeau's election promise. On the basis of many of the Task Force's recommendations, the federal government embarked on a course of direct, aggressive promotion of the development of elite athletes. Attempts to promote mass sports and fitness programs in the 1960s had been frustrated by federal-provincial jurisdictional disputes and by the magnitude of this task relative to the resources available. In contrast, success in high-performance sport was not only attainable with a substantially smaller outlay of money, but could be easily verified in quantitative terms. Because of its high visibility, elite sport also had the potential for a much more attractive political payoff than did mass sports and fitness programs. But for sport to be an effective unity symbol, greatly improved performances by Canadian athletes in international events were necessary.

The most important legacy of the Task Force's report and John Munro's tenure as Minister with responsibilities for Fitness and Amateur Sport was the creation of four arm's-length agencies: the National Sport and Recreation Centre, the Coaching Association of Canada, Hockey Canada, and Participaction Canada. These agencies provided the support structure for both government and national sports associations and were central to the sport delivery system in the 1970s (Hallett, 1981:779). Although these organizations all received, at one level or another, funds from the federal government, they were not considered part of the government bureaucracy. Their employees were not public servants and they were responsible in theory to their respective Boards of Directors.

Two of these organizations, the National Sport and Recreation Centre and the Coaching Association of Canada, have particular relevance for the sports associations. In 1968, only six or seven national sports associations had the financial resources to hire full-time administrators (Cliff, 1981:1). Most administrators continued to run their associations "off the kitchen table" (the *Task Force Report*, 1969). It is not surprising, then, that John Munro moved quickly to create the National Sport and Recreation Centre.

The Centre commenced operations in Ottawa in temporary quarters in September of 1970 and moved to its new location in May of 1971. Some sports associations objected to the Ottawa location because they already had a national office located elsewhere. But thirty-three national associations became resident occupants of the new Centre, with some thirty-six additional associations receiving financial support as non-resident members. The initial budget allocation from the federal government was $430 976. By 1978–79, the number of resident associations had risen to fifty-seven and the budget to almost $3 million. Resident associations were provided with office space, and secretarial and other support services. As well, financial aid came directly from the budget of Sport Canada, which was set up in May 1971 as a government department with the Fitness and Amateur Sport

Directorate. This aid included monies to pay full-time professional staff hired by the national sports associations and to support travel for associations' national executive meetings.

The *Task Force Report* also recommended that a body be established to provide technical support to sports organizations. Accordingly, in December of 1970, a National Coaches' Association was formed which subsequently became the Coaching Association of Canada (CAC). The CAC mandate was to develop a national coaching certification program, which it commenced in 1972. By the early 1980s, some 100 000 persons across Canada, excluding those in the hockey certification program, had participated in at least one level of the program (Macintosh, 1984).

The Centre and the CAC have contributed substantially to the present level of sophistication of many national sports and recreation organizations and to the improved level of performances by Canadian athletes in international sports events in the 1970s and 1980s. However, these key agencies also created new problems.

The avowed purpose of the creation of arm's-length support agencies was to prevent a federal takeover of amateur sport in Canada (Campagnolo, 1977:5). But these key arm's-length organizations were funded largely by the federal government. Thus, the professional staff which was responsible for their operation, located in Ottawa and paid largely from federal coffers, had at best divided loyalties between the Fitness and Amateur Sport Branch and the sports organizations that they served. As the financial support grew, these organizations lost their autonomy. More and more, the acceptance of government funding brought with it the requirement to meet specific performance conditions in international sport as established by Sport Canada (Kidd, 1981). When the NAC was established as an arm's-length agency in 1961, it provided a buffer between the federal government and sports advocates. However, the relegation of the NAC to a purely advisory and long-range planning role at the start of the 1970s eliminated an important independent voice, one which had striven to maintain a balance between elite sport and mass participation programs.

For its part, the Canadian Olympic Association (COA) received scathing criticism in the *Task Force Report*; it was accused of symbolizing all that was weak and ineffective in the voluntary sports associations. The COA responded immediately to this criticism by commissioning a study of its purposes and operations which confirmed most of the Task Force's criticisms. One of the COA's major thrusts was the establishment in 1970 of the

Olympic Trust in an effort to raise funds in the private sector to support the costs of sending Canadian athletes to the Olympic and Pan-American Games. This was one of the most far-sighted steps ever taken by the COA. As a consequence, the COA was able to maintain an arm's-length relationship with the federal government, something that other sports associations were unable to do because they gradually became more dependent on the federal government for financial and other resource support.

Another fortuitous step taken by the COA was to remain in Montreal rather than move to the National Sport and Recreation Centre in Ottawa. The COA had just moved into Olympic House in Montreal, but it received considerable pressure in 1970 from the federal government to move. Although the COA relinquished many of the financial rewards it would have received from being housed in Ottawa, its decision to stay in Montreal was an additional factor in maintaining independence from the federal government.

One important development which contributed to further government control of sport was financial aid to Canada's elite athletes. This step had its origins at the National Conference on Olympic '76 Development, held in Ottawa in October of 1971. Game Plan '76 was initiated by the COA in conjunction with its fund-raising arm, the Olympic Trust. The two basic assumptions of Game Plan '76 were: (1) responsibility for developing excellence must lie with the individual sport federation; and (2) the Plan must not impinge upon, or distort, the overall long-range development of the sport, but complement and extend it (COA *Minutes*, November 1972). These pious hopes were to be dashed in the years to come.

A 1974 change in the International Olympic Committee eligibility regulations allowing competitors to receive lost-income compensation brought a quick reaction from Canadian athletes. In April 1975, the COA received a delegation of athletes representing all sports requesting such assistance. Lost-time income compensation was immediately introduced by the COA and subsequently the co-operative funding of Game Plan '76 between Sport Canada and the COA was modified. The COA and the Olympic Trust took over the lost-time compensation payments and some other direct-aid programs. The federal government assumed financial responsibility for the original Game Plan operations (COA, *Quadrennial Report 72–76*, 1977). The athlete assistance plan was ultimately taken over by Sport Canada in early 1976 because neither the COA nor the national sports associations had the money or staff to run the program effectively. This allowed the federal government direct access to Canada's elite athletes and represented a further loss of autonomy for the national sports associations (see Chapter Fifteen of this book).

The Transition to a Unified Voice for Sport

The lack of a unified voice for sport in Canada was a persistent issue in the 1970s and the COA made a number of attempts to rectify this shortcoming. However, because the COA was seen as an elitist body concerned primarily with high-level international sport, persons who were more interested in mass sports programs did not want to relinquish their voice in sport to a COA-dominated umbrella organization.

At the same time, the COA was able to play a supportive role in federal government efforts to improve performance levels, as the following illustrates. Although millions of dollars were spent to make a respectable showing, the post-Olympic symposium held in 1976 noted that the push for medals/performance in Montreal did not reach the root of the problem: "mediocrity was too comfortable for too many people in Canadian amateur athletics" (Farber, 1984). The COA concurred and applied increasingly strict standards for athletes to qualify for Olympic and Pan-American competitions; in this way, it assisted the federal government pressuring sports associations to concentrate on better athlete performance levels. The COA thus served to buffer the federal government from criticism by the sports associations. Frustrations about the government's refusal to take promising young developing athletes to the Olympic Games were directed at the COA instead of at Sport Canada.

The voluntary sports associations also made sporadic attempts through a succession of national umbrella organizations to speak for amateur sport in Canada. The Canadian Sports Advisory Council had hoped to play the primary advisory role in recommending sport policy to the federal government, but, as mentioned previously, the NAC took over this function. Indeed, the CSAC was asked, and agreed, to change its name to the Canadian Amateur Sports Federation in 1962 to avoid confusion with the NAC.

The NAC lost its sport policy-making responsibility in 1968 when John Munro and Lou Lefaive, director of Sport Canada, put down the "palace revolt" led by the NAC's chairman, William L'Heureux. With this loss, the time was ripe for the Canadian Amateur Sports Federation to fill the gap. The Federation undertook a review of its role in 1970 and subsequently changed its name to the Sports Federation of Canada (SFC). The SFC also moved from Toronto to the National Sport and Recreation Centre in Ottawa and appointed its first full-time executive director in 1971. By 1973, eighty-one sports and recreation organizations were members of the SFC, but it never realized its objective to become "the link between sport in Canada and the federal government" (Fawcett, 1977:34). The national sports associations were beginning to realize that they had jeopardized their own autonomy vis-à-vis the federal government by accepting monies, administrative services, and technical support. Consequently, they were reluctant to relinquish even more autonomy to a single umbrella organization such as the SFC. The more powerful national sports organizations preferred to lobby on an individual basis with the federal government because they believed that this was a more effective and rewarding approach.

In 1979, the COA presented a proposal to Prime Minister Joe Clark to establish an "amateur sport trust," which would provide funds to amalgamate, under the aegis of the COA, the two existing national multi-sport organizations in Canada: the COA and the SFC. The Conservative government intended to give up to the provinces the right to hold lotteries; the COA instead proposed that the government keep Lotto Canada and use the funds accruing from it for the "sport trust." This new umbrella organization was to promote and develop Canadian amateur sport at the national and international levels, and with the assistance of national sports associations, greatly increase private sector support of sport. The proposal was endorsed by the Clark government in a speech given by the Prime Minister at a state reception for athletes, coaches, and officials in October 1979 (Amateur Sport Trust Proposal of the Canadian Olympic Association, December 27, 1979). Subsequently, however, the Conservative government handed the rights for the sports lottery over to the provinces, thus putting an end to this initiative. There were other attempts at unification, but nothing materialized and the national sports associations were left to face the 1980s with no unified voice, ill-equipped to resist further invasions of their autonomy by the federal government.

Tightening the Grip (1980s)

At the same time as the arm's-length agencies were contributing to a greater control of sport by the federal government, other events in the mid-1970s were pushing the government in this direction as well. Efforts to improve the performance levels of Canadian athletes were bearing fruit. The 1976 Montreal Olympics saw a substantial improvement in the unofficial points standings compared to the Munich Games four years earlier, and the extensive television coverage of the 1976 Games was generating greater interest in international sport. Prime Minister Trudeau's vision of sport as a unifying factor was becoming a reality. These developments all contributed to the appointment of Iona Campagnolo as the first Minister of State for Sport in 1976. The increased visibility of sport also created interest in the House of Commons, where calls were made for a policy paper on sport. Thus were the seeds of the 1977 Green Paper on sport sown. This was to lead to new sport policies which would place the federal government at the centre of Canada's elite sports programs.

The Green Paper, tabled in the House of Commons in October 1977, was historic because, for the first time, the government had prepared a position paper on sport which was to be debated and discussed in public. Members of the sports community responded enthusiastically when presented with this unique opportunity to provide input to federal government sport policy.

Almost every brief submitted in response to the Green Paper criticized the government for its single-minded promotion of excellence at the expense of mass recreation. International athletes and sports activists Bruce Kidd and Abby Hoffman argued that separating sport from recreation presented the Canadian public with an unfair choice. Most sports associations indicated that they wanted more funding with less accountability to the government. At the same time, they wanted to be free of government and arm's-length agency control. However, no proposals were forthcoming as to how these apparently conflicting goals could be reached, largely because the organizations' lack of unity prevented them from developing a strong, common voice which could be used to express their demands.

The frustrations expressed during the public hearings appeared in a *Globe and Mail* headline on January 15, 1978. "Give It Another Try, Athletes Tell Ottawa" summed up the dissatisfaction with the Green Paper's contents and general thrust. Iona Campagnolo concluded the discussions at the final hearing in Ottawa by saying that the "exercise had been valuable" but commented on the criticism of the government proposals by saying that "the pros and cons are in the eye of the beholder" (McCabe, *Globe and Mail*, January 16, 1978).

The subsequent White Paper was written by a few key senior public servants, with little apparent regard for the concerns expressed in reactions to the Green Paper (T. Bedecki, personal communication, March 1984). The national sports associations and other sports bodies across the country had lost a chance to significantly influence future government sport policy, at least in part due to their inability to form a united front.

The impact of the 1979 White Paper on sport was dampened considerably by a number of events. First, the sports organizations were never fully convinced that the process had not been somewhat of a sham. The short time allowed for responses to the Green Paper, the long delay in the issuing of the White Paper, and the perception that recommendations had been largely ignored created much scepticism. Second, the White Paper was issued after Parliament had been dissolved and shortly before the Liberal government fell in 1979. The uncertainty and political instability of the next eighteen months hindered any Fitness and Amateur Sport initiatives to implement the proposals in the White Paper. The Liberal government returned to office in 1980, but Iona Campagnolo was no longer a member of the government. The new Minister, Gerald Regan, needed time to be briefed on the issues surrounding sport and it was not until June 1981 that he produced a second White Paper, *A Challenge to the Nation: Fitness and Amateur Sport in the 80's*, which was more in tune with the events of the early 1980s.

The 1979 White Paper had addressed the issue of the autonomy of sports organizations and recommended that a Sport Council be established, as an arm's-length agency, to determine national sport policy. It was to be comprised of representatives of the national sports associations, umbrella organizations, and volunteer organizations. Fitness and recreation activities would remain in Health and Welfare Canada, while those elements of Sport Canada in the Fitness and Amateur Sport Branch were to be transferred to the Sport Council. Thus, the primary responsibilities of the Sport Council were to be in the areas of national and international sport, and the pursuit of excellence at these levels of competition. The 1981 Regan statement, however, made no mention of this proposal. This left the matter of elite sport policy largely in the hands of the Minister and the Sport Canada bureaucracy. Thus, the government was free to pursue its own priorities for "elite" or what came to be known as "high-performance" sport. The rhetoric in the White Paper about shared government and private sector responsibilities for elite sport and the desirability of a quasi-independent Sport Council was again ignored.

The specific recommendations in the Regan White Paper made it clear that high-performance sport was foremost in the minds of the federal government officials. National training centres were to be established, assistance to athletes based on performance was to be increased, and a new hosting policy for major sports events was to be implemented. Priority funding was to be allocated to sports demonstrating a commitment to, and a consistent record of, excellence. National sports technical services were to be augmented to assist in the further development of high-performance athletes (Canada, *FAS Communiqué*, June 23, 1981). The 1981 paper was careful to point out that:

> ... the federal government does not manage amateur
> sport programs. ... However, because of the growing
> complexity of administration, the federal government
> feels it necessary to work with the national associations
> in the development of adequate management, account-
> ing, and monitoring processes without interfering with
> the autonomy of the national associations. (Regan,
> 1981:7–8)

In response to requests from the national sports associations, the Minister gave the assurance that, as associations demonstrated their competence in administrative and financial matters, the federal government would be prepared to offer a block funding system. This would permit greater flexibility both on a short-term basis and for long-term planning. The national sports associations, however, would be required to submit a complete financial audit on an annual basis.

Despite increasing federal government control, the sports associations still remained central to the promotion of high-performance sport. About one-third of the Fitness and Amateur Sport expenditures of almost $60 million in 1982–83 was in the form of contributions to national sports organizations. The Canadian Ski Association received the largest sum, about $1.7 million. The Canadian Intercollegiate Athletic Union and the Canadian Track and Field Association each received approximately $1 million (FAS *Annual Report*, 1982–83). In addition, the national sports associations were also supported by contributions of $2.3 million and $4.5 million to the Coaching Association of Canada and the

National Sport and Recreation Centre respectively. Despite these generous contributions the sports associations continued to lobby for unconditional grants, insisting that they knew how these monies should be spent in their particular sport. However, Abby Hoffman, the new director of Sport Canada, spent much time and effort persuading these bodies to develop clear and concise plans for improving the performance of elite athletes. Pressure was exerted on the sports associations to set specific performance goals tied to corresponding funding requirements to attain these goals.

Given the increased importance of sport and the growing government involvement in the 1970s, it was inevitable that sport would be used as a political instrument, further impinging on the autonomy of voluntary associations. In 1976, despite the permission granted Taiwan to participate by the International Olympic Committee, Prime Minister Trudeau denied visas to the Taiwan Olympic team for refusing to back down on its intention to display its flag and play its national anthem. When the federal government imposed an economic and cultural boycott on the USSR because of its military intervention in Afghanistan, the Canadian Olympic Association followed suit, despite an earlier vote by its executive committee overwhelmingly in favour of going to Moscow for the 1980 Games. The federal government also insisted that athletes and sports events organizers support its boycott of South Africa and its apartheid policy. All these examples illustrate the government's usurpation of an area of interest which had previously been the domain of the voluntary sports associations.

Another political feature of the early 1980s was the inclination of Ministers of State for Fitness and Amateur Sport to seize on controversial issues and make popular pronouncements on sport policy before consulting with appropriate public servants and national sports associations. When drug scandals involving Canadian athletes broke out at the Pan-American Games in Venezuela in August of 1983, and shortly after, when Canadian weight lifters returning from meets in eastern Europe were apprehended with steroids in their possession, Céline Hervieux-Payette stated that sports associations must either take immediate steps to stop athletes from using performance-enhancing drugs or lose government funding. Simultaneously, Sport Canada developed a plan to ensure that sport-governing bodies were taking adequate measures to discourage athletes from using steroids and other performance-enhancing drugs. The result was *Drug Use and Doping Control in Sport: A Sport Canada Policy*, issued in 1984, with specific directives to follow.

Jacques Olivier, who followed Hervieux-Payette as Minister of State for Fitness and Amateur Sport, pounced on the bilingual issue as his platform for gaining publicity. At the 1984 Sarajevo Winter Olympics, Olivier stated that amateur sport had "stonewalled" bilingualism (*Globe and Mail*, February 9, 1984). Canadian sports associations and, indeed, Sport Canada itself had fallen well behind other national organizations in the development of bilingual services, particularly the provision of French-speaking coaches and translation services at meetings and conferences. The Minister showed no compunction in threatening to withhold federal government funds. He ordered Sport Canada officials to review all its contracts to ensure that the principle of bilingualism was being upheld. In April of 1984, Olivier instructed that only one-quarter of the $46 million be sent to the sports associations. The rest would be withheld until the Minister was satisfied that bilingual services were being provided. Twenty-two national sports associations were singled out for special attention (*Globe and Mail*, April 19, 1984).

Olivier also criticized the Canadian Olympic Association and especially the 1988 Calgary Olympic Games organizers for their lack of co-operation in bilingualism efforts, particularly in view of the $200 million contribution the federal government had committed to the Games. Reflecting on his role as Sport Minister, and alluding to the tenuous nature of the position, Olivier remarked that:

> As minister I do not have the right to intervene directly in the working of federations and the Canadian Olympic Association, but, before signing an agreement with these organizations for the granting of millions of dollars, I can impose certain conditions. . . .
> I may not be there (as minister) very long, but the new agreements I am about to sign will be lasting. . . .
> (*Globe and Mail*, February 9, 1984)

Many of the matters raised by the respective Ministers were valid concerns. But they also indicated that, by the early 1980s, the federal government was so confident in its primary role in the development of high-performance athletes that it could publicly threaten the voluntary associations, ostensibly responsible for sport, with removal of governmental funding. The complete lack of public protests or outcries over this stance suggests that the struggle for autonomy in sport had been decided in favour of the government.

Consequences

What, then, are the consequences for national sports associations of this intervention of the federal government in high-performance sport? Certainly, the dramatic growth of the sports bureaucracy has changed the way in which sport is conducted in Canada. Not even the most zealous sport enthusiast would have anticipated the size and scope of the bureaucracy. The Fitness and Amateur Sport Branch staff quadrupled in size from 30 in 1970 to 121 in 1984 (Canada, DNHW, 1971–72, 1984–85). In the same time period, the professional, technical, and clerical staff that supports the national sports associations housed in Ottawa grew from 65 to 532 (H. Glynn, personal communication, April 4, 1984).

Increased federal government involvement in promoting high-performance sport and the success of the Canada Games stimulated a parallel bureaucratic growth in most provinces, which previously had concentrated primarily on mass recreation and fitness programs. For example, the Ontario Sports Centre, established in 1970, had a full-time staff of 90 by 1984. About 130 full-time administrative and technical personnel were also attached directly to provincial sports associations (A. Furlani, personal communication, May 9, 1984).

This formidable sports bureaucracy, along with the Coaching Association of Canada and the provincial coaching development delivery systems, has provided an administrative and technical competency for amateur sport unthought of in the 1960s. This support system is the envy of many western nations and is a major factor behind Canada's growing stature on the international sport scene. But this sports bureaucracy is not without its problems. As mentioned earlier, the new sports bureaucrats often find that they serve two masters — the sports organization for which they work and the governmental agency which supports them. When this conflict has arisen, it has usually been resolved by siding with the government position. The sports organizations' acquiescence has allowed the federal government a freer hand in pursuing its goal of high-performance sport and has also contributed to the disappearance of an independent voice for sport.

The bureaucracy also poses problems for promoting participatory sports, as opposed to the favoured elite sports. Many bureaucrats initially were recruited from the ranks of former athletes who had some business experience. The propensity of these individuals has been to sell sport as other commodities are sold in the marketplace. Perhaps the most offensive example of this was the brief prepared by the Council of Executive Directors at the National Sport and Recreation Centre in Ottawa (Council of Executive Directors, National Sport and Recreation Centre, "Corporate Sponsors and Amateur Sport: An Unbeatable Team," 1983). The document defended the practice of associating high-performance sport with the sale of tobacco and alcohol. Moreover, the brief was prepared in the face of growing concern by the Department of Health and Welfare about such promotions. In this instance, one government position (Sport Canada's) was in opposition to that held by another government agency with which the sports community was in agreement.

Another problem with the sports bureaucracy is the power of the executive and technical directors of national sports associations. Occupying a central position in communications between Sport Canada and their respective associations, these bureaucrats also bring to their jobs specialized managerial and technical competencies. As a result, they are in a position to exercise much influence in struggles over association policy and direction. Their advantage is further enhanced because they hold full-time positions with clerical and research support, whereas voluntary national executive members operate with fewer resources, including time, with which to put forward their positions. Finally, the education, sports, and career backgrounds of the professional staff make them most receptive to the rational approach to high-performance sport presently championed by Sport Canada. The socio-economic, educational, and sports backgrounds of the Sport Canada bureaucrats and those of the national sports associations are very similar. It is not surprising, therefore, that the new sports bureaucracy has not, for the most part, championed the participatory sport-for-all philosophy.

Nor has the bureaucracy addressed the question of gender or class inequality to any great extent. Sporadic efforts were made in the 1970s by Sport and Fitness Canada to increase female sport and physical activity participation rates. These efforts were intensified in the 1980s. Although commendable, they have made only a modest dent in gender imbalance in high-performance sport participation roles. The composition of Canada's 1984 Olympic team (22 per cent female), of athletes competing in Ontario universities (one-third female), of secondary school athletes in Ontario (40 per cent female) (Sopinka, 1984), and of athletes competing for national Canadian university championships (30 per cent female) (Vickers, 1984) all attest to the substantial gap between male and female elite sport participation rates in Canada.

This gender imbalance is seen to be even more problematic when the composition of the executives of sports organizations is examined. A number of studies (Bratton, 1971; Gruneau and Hollands, 1979; Slack, 1981; Theberge, 1980) have shown that females are under-represented on the executives of national and provincial sports associations, even when the percentage of female participants is taken into account. This bias is also demonstrated in the composition of executive and technical directors at the National Sport and Recreation Centre; 83 per cent of all positions were held by males in the early 1980s (Fitness and Amateur Sport, 1982). The female administrative apprenticeship program sponsored by Fitness and Amateur Sport has since resulted in a partial reduction of this imbalance. Executive and administrative ranks dominated by males are not likely to redress gender inequality in any vigorous or effective manner.

In addition to gender inequality, class imbalances exist in the composition of the executives of sports associations (Bratton, 1971; Gruneau and Hollands, 1979; Slack, 1981). The extent to which an administration dominated by persons from the upper socio-economic class is interested in redressing socio-economic inequalities in participation rates is problematic. In contrast to its response to gender discrimination, however, the federal government has shown little interest in providing more access to competitive sport for persons from lower socio-economic backgrounds.

Indeed, the voluntary executive members of national sports associations have also contributed to the federal government's penchant for high-performance sport. These executive members take advantage of outstanding international performances to promote a sense of pride within the association and to elevate the status of the voluntary executive members and the paid coaches and bureaucrats. The elitist inclination of national voluntary executives mitigates any concern for mass sports programs. It is clear that any democratization of the associations will not come from the top. Such a movement probably will come from the grass roots where there is a growing concern about the federal government presence and the pursuit of high-performance sport.

In summary, the federal government has firmly established its presence in sport. Through its control of funds to national sports associations and its indirect control of the national arm's-length agencies (the Coaching Association of Canada and the National Sport and Recreation Centre), and as the employer of the bureaucrats who administer these agencies and the national sports associations in Ottawa, the federal government dominates sport policy-making in Canada. It focuses these policies towards the further development of its corps of "state" athletes at the expense of expanding participatory sport opportunities. As well, these policies are carried out to the detriment of redressing inequalities in participation according to gender, socio-economic status, physical and other handicaps, and additional conditions considered to be disadvantages by some sectors of society.

A Proposal for Change

Various solutions have been advanced to redress the present imbalance in sport policy-making in Canada. Some people advocate sport becoming financially independent of government and depending instead on the private sector for support. This is the direction that the Conservative government Sport Minister, Otto Jelinek, is taking. This proposal ignores the fact that one master would be simply replacing another. Instead of serving the interests of government, sport would be engulfed by efforts to sell goods and services, and the commodification of sport, which has already dominated professional and much of amateur sport, would be complete.

A second solution suggests that all could be put right if the national sports associations regained their independence from government, received federal funds, and were allowed to decide how best to allocate these funds to develop their respective sports. The shortcoming of this line of argument lies in the composition of the volunteer executive members of most national sports associations: they represent vested class, gender, and social interests which are often at odds with an interest in sports programs for all Canadians. As well, the sports community has shown itself to be divided and ineffective at arriving at any consensus on a unified sport policy for Canada.

A third approach argues for some reasonable balance of power in sport policy-making. Government has a legitimate and essential role to play in sport. The responsibility to provide opportunities to develop potential talent and to maintain a strong Canadian sport identity is a justifiable government objective, as are similar objectives in other cultural spheres. However, sport needs to be protected from transitory political whims and narrow policy objectives. One step towards this goal is the establishment of a strong, independent, widely representative national Sport Council. This concept, presented by the Task Force in 1969 and again in the 1979 White Paper on sport, was a naive expectation of the sports community when the Fitness and Amateur Sport Act (Bill C-131) came into being in 1961.

Certainly, few would argue that a National Sport Council would resolve all of the issues that have been raised. But such a body would ensure wide geographic representation and a variety of views on what direction sport policy should take. This kind of representation on the original National Advisory Council in the 1960s did mean that there was some balance between the advocates of high-performance sport and those who championed participatory sports and fitness programs. Advocates of the creation of such a body are also careful to suggest that the government should have some authority to make appointments to the Council. One important reason for this stance is the federal government's better record, in comparison to the sports community, of appointing women to its various commissions and agencies and of pressing for gender equality.

A second major step towards a more equitable sharing of national sport policy-making would be to incorporate Sport Canada as the executive and administrative arm of such a Council. It could be funded in the same manner as the Canada Council, by parliamentary appropriations (see Franks and Macintosh, 1984, for more details of government funding for culture in Canada). It is significant that such measures were undertaken in Australia in 1985 with the establishment of the Sport Commission. This Commission has its own executive and professional arm and holds the power to distribute government funds, as it sees fit, to national sports and fitness associations and umbrella federations. It has also been given authority to raise monies from the private sector to dispense in the development and promotion of sport.

The establishment of a quasi-independent Sport Council in Canada, with its own executive and administrative arm, would at least ensure that sport policy was representative of different views and was formulated without the threat of the withdrawal of government funding when policy outcomes were not in accordance with current government objectives.

Suggested Readings

The reader is referred to Donald Macintosh et al. (1987), *Sport and Politics in Canada*, Montreal and Kingston, McGill-Queen's University Press, and to Bruce Kidd's article (1981), "The Canadian State and Sport: The Dilemma of Intervention," in *Annual Conference Proceedings of the National Association for Physical Education in Higher Education*, Champlain, Human Kinetics.

Chapter Seven
The Political Economy of Professional Sport

Rob Beamish

The Employer in Professional Sport

The very term "professional sport" implies an employee/employer relationship. In the world of sport, however, such a relationship was not always the case. It was only between 1850 and 1910, when Canada and the United States underwent rapid industrialization and urbanization, that the structural conditions favoured the development of professional sport. With larger groups of people congregated in the cities, there was neither the space nor the opportunity to enjoy traditional types of leisure. There was, however, a potential market for new forms of entertainment, and numerous entrepreneurs staged sports spectacles for profit. These undertakings, along with the growth of the telegraph, the newspaper, and improved inter- and intra-city transport, helped create the conditions leading to the formation of the first semi-professional sports teams. In the case of baseball, scheduled games replaced challenge matches as early as 1871. From these pre-planned contests, it was not long before the first semi-professional league was formed (franchises cost $10.00).

Corporations and Cartels

The very fact that an individual could purchase a franchise underscores the perception of sport as a commodity which could be bought or sold. Once such a notion was established, a fundamental change occurred in the raison d'être of sports teams: providing opportunities for player participation diminished as the teams became more of a profit-making venture for owners.

The most efficient way to ensure profitability is by incorporation, i.e., the establishment of a business corporation. The critical feature of incorporation was that an owner's assets were protected if his team (and historically there have been very few female owners) did not do well financially. The limited legal liability of the corporation permitted debts to be charged against the corporate entity — the team — rather than the owner's personal assets. Second, the existence of the corporation allowed the owner to sell shares to others who wished to invest in the new entertainment industry; although no flood of investment occurred in the early part of the century, it has since become a significant and lucrative aspect of modern professional sport. Further, the corporate entity became an entity that one owner could sell to another.

Throughout the early period of sport development, owners competed for the best talent. Owners bid against each other for players and this hurt all owners, since player costs rose but revenue did not necessarily increase. Teams folded with great frequency. Consequently, owners in a given league soon began to make agreements among themselves to stop the practice of bidding for the same players. The result was a cartel structure in professional sport.

In simple terms, a cartel is an arrangement, through a series of agreements, among firms such that economic competition between them is eliminated. This results in greater economic stability and increased profitability: the cartel members agree on how much they will pay for the various materials and services needed to produce their products, as well as on a universal selling price for the product once completed. Individual profit is gained through joint profit maximization.

The introduction of cartels into sport is actually a natural extension of league structure because sport, unlike many other realms of the corporate world, requires at least two teams to produce a saleable product. Thus, even in the formation of a league itself, there is some agreement among owners about the "ground rules." The extension of these agreements beyond the structure of the league to economic matters is almost a matter of course.

Monopolies in Sport
In the case of sport, the major economic relationships established by the cartel structure are a monopoly position in what economists term the "product market" (or the output side) and a monopsony position on the "supply (or input) side." A monopoly is a one-seller market while a monopsony is a one-buyer market.

To illustrate, a National Hockey League (NHL) franchise guarantees the owner exclusive selling rights throughout a hundred-mile radius of the franchise's location. If another NHL team wishes to locate a franchise within that territory, it must pay an indemnification fee. (The New York Islanders, for example, paid the New York Rangers $4 million to locate on Long Island because that was in the guaranteed market "owned" by the Rangers.) In addition, teams have a monopoly over revenue generated through the sale of radio and television rights for their home games.

The owners enjoy a monopoly because there is only one local seller for the product of NHL hockey and only one seller for the product at the regional and national levels (the league itself represents the owners in television contract negotiations). Several advantages are reaped by the owners as a result of their monopoly position. They have the power to determine membership in this exclusive league. Competition for facilities such as stadiums, parking, and food concessions is also reduced. Owners have sole access to live and televised spectator markets and they can work out various revenue-sharing schemes to maintain the stability of the league. The team owners' monopoly position enables them to influence the media concerning how sport is covered and at the same time the owners can decide, as a group, how they will market their product — is it a spectacle of speed, skill, or violence, for example? Finally, the monopoly position enjoyed by the owners allows them to establish the length of the season, the number of exhibition games, the timing and length of training camps, and the structure of post-season play.

Three groups are affected by the existence of a monopoly. First, it affects the spectators attending live performances; the lack of competition keeps ticket prices high. Second, television networks pay more for television rights because the owners' monopoly means that there are not three or four leagues from which to choose. Finally, the players are obviously affected because the monopoly revenues secured by the owners increase the economic and political power of the latter in all negotiations.

This discussion of monopolies raises the question of why their existence in sport is permitted. Monopolies are legal in professional sport because of the precedent set by the American Supreme Court in 1922. In an anti-trust suit filed by the Baltimore franchise of the now-defunct Federal Baseball League, Justice Oliver Holmes, in a landmark decision, argued that the monopoly enjoyed by the National League was not a breach of the federal anti-trust laws because the business of giving exhibitions of baseball was under state jurisdiction.

On the basis of baseball's particular status, other sports bodies (most notably the National Football League [NFL]) have also applied for exemption from the anti-trust laws, but they have never been granted such exemption officially. Nevertheless, they enjoy such exemption unofficially on the basis of the baseball precedent. Thus, professional sports owners enjoy a situation unique in the Canadian and American economies — a legal monopoly — and it clearly aids the owners' goal of generating income.

Revenue Accruing to Team Owners

The owners' monopoly provides them with six ways of making money which, in turn, increase their position of power.

Ticket Sales
The monopoly position allows owners to set ticket prices as high as they believe the market will bear. Although there is some competition for spectators' money from other forms of entertainment, this does not appear to be a concern for owners: they have a monopoly over a sport to which a core audience is loyal. Even the formation of a rival league has little impact on the owners' monopoly, because the competition rarely tries to compete "head to head" with the established league.

Television Rights
The sale of television rights affords the greatest financial advantages to the professional sports monopoly. This is clearly demonstrated by the example of the NFL. In 1970, the owners sold the television broadcast rights for $49.1 million. By 1982, the owners were able to sell the combined rights to NFL football telecasts to all three major American networks for $400 million per year, for the following five years. Individually, CBS will pay $800 million, NBC $700 million, and ABC $500 million to show NFL football on their networks.

The American and National baseball leagues have also negotiated substantial television contracts, but unlike football, they receive an additional source of revenue. In baseball, each team augments its share of the national rights with the sale of local radio and television rights. In 1982, for example, the Montreal Expos received $1.8 million from the national television contract, and $6.5 million from local television and radio contracts, while the

Toronto Blue Jays added $4.5 million to their revenues from local coverage.

NHL hockey is not as profitable as either baseball or NFL football, but given the size of the Canadian and regional American markets the NHL does well with the sale of television rights. The long-standing Trans-Border Agreement guaranteed that the majority of revenue generated from the Canadian national television rights would accrue to the Toronto Maple Leafs and Montreal Canadiens. In fact, some argue that a Vancouver franchise was overlooked in the first NHL expansion because the Leaf and Canadien owners did not want to divide the national television revenue with another team.

In 1984, however, the American-based NHL teams and the Quebec Nordiques (owned by Carling O'Keefe) attempted to establish television coverage of their games being played in American cities. The remaining six Canadian-based NHL teams filed a $22 million damage suit against the other clubs for violating the Trans-Border Agreement. An out-of-court settlement prevented the suit from coming to court, but the suit indicates the importance of television revenue for the owners of professional sport — members within a strong cartel are willing to take each other to court over this form of revenue.

League Expansion and Mergers

Owners can also generate revenue through the expansion of the league, by the sale of individual franchises, or by a merger with a rival league. Individual franchises are very expensive propositions. In 1967, the NHL sold franchises to Philadelphia, Pittsburgh, Minnesota, St. Louis, Los Angeles, and Oakland for $3 million each. Within three years, Vancouver and Buffalo paid twice that amount to enter the league. In 1977, Labatt's Breweries, Howard Webster, and the Canadian Imperial Bank of Commerce paid $7 million for the Toronto Blue Jay franchise in the American Baseball League.

Expansion through mergers touches on several issues related to the power and wealth of the owners, so it is useful to consider this revenue-generating process in some detail.

In 1972, the World Hockey Association (WHA) was formed as a rival to the NHL. The WHA gained credibility by signing well-known NHL players and by locating franchises in Canadian cities long overlooked by the NHL. Most important, the WHA undermined the monopsony position (the one-buyer market) which the NHL had enjoyed with regard to its players.

WHA owners paid attractive salaries for established professional players and for promising juniors. Not only did the WHA pay well for the graduating juniors, it also signed eighteen-year-old players not yet eligible for the NHL draft. Thus, even though the WHA had no impact on the NHL's revenues, by raising player costs and jeopardizing some of the NHL's inter-league agreements with the junior leagues in Canada, the WHA was recognized as a genuine threat to the established league.

By 1979, the NHL owners realized that the WHA would survive as a rival league and that the Canadian franchises, in particular, were strong. NHL owners had lost the monopsony over hockey players which they had enjoyed, and the existence of the WHA was escalating NHL player salaries. Further, the WHA had filed an anti-trust suit against the NHL; a judgement against the NHL would seriously undermine the value of the franchises in the league. Finally, the Canadian Amateur Hockey Association (CAHA) was using the presence of the WHA to increase the fee that NHL teams paid to junior teams when drafting players. In short, the continued existence of the WHA represented increased costs for the NHL and a potential dramatic deflation of franchise values if the WHA won its anti-trust case.

In 1979, the NHL voted 14 to 3 to "expand" into the WHA. The use of the term "expansion" was deliberate. If the NHL and WHA owners had called the deal a merger, they would have faced the possibility of being challenged with anti-trust legislation on the charge that two leagues of comparable level had merged to form a monopoly. The term "expansion" eliminated that possibility.

The merger/expansion of the two leagues had several implications. The NHL received $24 million which the WHA paid to join the National Hockey League. At the same time, monopsony was established on the supply side with the resumption of a one-buyer market for players. Player costs were thus cut significantly and an ever-escalating price war for talented players was prevented. The NHL owners were not the only winners: the WHA owners gained admission to the established league and access to the privileged positions of monopoly and monopsony.

Tax Shelters
A sports franchise involves a considerable outlay of money. However, because the tax system in Canada and the United States allows owners to write off, over a number of years, a large

part of their franchise fee, they receive tremendous economic benefits. Using professional teams as tax havens is another way owners
generate revenue.

This is best illustrated with a hypothetical example. Imagine that you have bought an NFL franchise for the price of $50
million. This fee can be divided into two components: a franchise
component and a player component. Up to 50 per cent of the franchise price can be assigned to the latter component as a depre-
ciable resource which could be written off in the following way.
(Professional sport is the only business in which employees can
be depreciated.) If $25 million is assigned to player contracts and
depreciated over a five-year period, annual business expenses of
$5 million can be claimed as a deduction. Thus, the first $5 million of revenue will not be taxed. If another $3 million in operat-
ing expenses (player salaries, stadium rental, equipment, etc.) is
incurred, annual expenses would total $8 million ($5 million from
player depreciation plus $3 million from operating expenses). If
an income of $2 million in gate receipts and another $5.5 in television revenues is received, there is a net loss of $0.5 million. In
other words, despite the fact that only $3 million was spent during
the year and $7.5 million in revenues was accumulated, no taxes
are paid on the $4.5 million surplus. Moreover, there is a $0.5 million loss that could be used to shelter income from other parts of
your investment portfolio. This process can be repeated for five
years until all the players have been depreciated.

Increase in Franchise Value

Professional sports franchises are a relatively scarce commodity. As a result, their value increases very rapidly, especially
because of the financial benefits associated with team ownership.
Consider the following: In 1933 the Philadelphia Eagles NFL franchise was worth $2500 and sold in 1949 for $250 000. In 1963 the
franchise sold for $5.5 million and again in 1969 for $16.2 million.
In March 1985, Leonard Toss negotiated the sale of the Eagles to
Miami auto dealer Norman Braman for $65 million. In the same
month, John Mecom, Jr., the majority owner of the New Orleans
Saints, negotiated the sale of that team to a group of investors
headed by Tom Benson. The $64 million price tag represented an
eight-fold increase over Mecom's $8 million purchase price in 1967.
Finally, Clint Murchison bought the Dallas Cowboys for $0.5 mil-
lion in 1960 and sold the franchise in 1984 for $80 million — a
rate of return that is higher than 600 per cent for every year over
the twenty-four year period.

Revenue Through the Sale of Stocks

Revenue can be accumulated through dividends paid by teams to shareholders each fiscal year. Harold Ballard, for example, owns 70.5 per cent of the stock in Maple Leaf Gardens (MLG) Limited — about 600 000 shares. In 1981, the corporation paid a dividend of $3.85 per share resulting in $2.3 million of personal revenue for Ballard. Additional revenue can be generated when there is an increase in the value of shares in a corporation. For example, between 1983 and 1984, the value of a share in MLG Limited jumped from $14.00 to $41.00 per share. For a shareholder like Harold Ballard this represents an increase in potential wealth of $16.2 million!

Who Owns Professional Teams?

Given the value of franchises, and the amount of revenues and expenses involved with modern professional sport, only those with large sums of investment capital are able to own professional sports franchises.

In the 1985 Forbes list of the four hundred richest Americans, thirty-two had ties to professional sport. For example, Edward J. DeBartolo owns the Pittsburgh Penguins, the indoor soccer team Spirit, and the Pittsburgh Civic Arena; his son is president of the San Francisco 49ers. Ed Gaylord, who has interests in broadcasting, publishing, and real estate, owns the Texas Rangers baseball team. Lamar Hunt, who has interests in oil and professional tennis, controls the NFL's Kansas City Chiefs, while Harvey Bright, who has interests in oil, trucking, and real estate, owns the Dallas Cowboys.

But not only individuals invest in professional sport; corporations also seem interested in owning sports teams. In the case of baseball, football, and hockey, there is a strong tendency for corporations involved with cigarettes, alcohol, and the media to have interests in team sports. To cite some Canadian examples: in 1985, Molson's had ownership in the Montreal Canadiens, while Labatt's owned almost half of the Blue Jays, and the Bronfman Corporation, owners of Seagram's distilleries, was linked to the Montreal Expos. Moffat Communications has shares in the Winnipeg Jets hockey team, while Rothmans of Canada, as the majority owner of Carling O'Keefe Limited, also controls the O'Keefe sporting interest in the Quebec Nordiques.

These ownership patterns have implications for the athletes. In labour relations terms, because the owners have vast capital resources, their ability to "take a strike" far outweighs that of the players. Moreover, these teams are only small parts of much larger corporate empires. Labatt's, for example, has $1.2 billion in assets and more than $2.5 billion in annual sales; it is therefore little wonder that, in a small section of the annual report entitled "partly-owned businesses," Labatt's notes its "45% partnership interest in the Toronto Blue Jays, an American League baseball club." In other words, what seem like large sums of money to the average person are merely operating expenses to these corporations, and sport is only one part of an enormous corporate venture.

The final consequence of these ownership patterns is rarely considered. If and when corporations see that other vehicles of investment are more advantageous, and as soon as television networks or advertisers decide that another form of entertainment better serves their financial needs, there is little to prevent them from withdrawing financial support from professional sport. That removal of support could result in the complete collapse of a very elaborate employment structure.

Monopsony in Professional Sport

One of the major consequences faced by a player with respect to the cartel structure of sport is that the owners agree to divide up the players among themselves before a player even has the chance to try out for a team. Historically, professional teams have divided players either by the farm system or the universal draft. Because both systems have been used by the NHL, it is appropriate to cite hockey as an example. Prior to 1967, the National Hockey League had a farm system and a reserve clause in its contracts with players. Under this system, players became members of a professional hockey organization by signing an "A," "B," or "C" card at almost any point in their adolescent hockey career. From that point on, a team enjoyed exclusive rights to all players signed to its cards unless the team chose to release the player from his contractual obligations. The farm system was basically a player development system, although it also served as a means of keeping quality players away from rival teams and as a means of discipline for the players.

With expansion in 1967, the NHL owners eliminated the farm system and implemented a universal draft. In an annual draft of non-professional players, each team selects players from the Canadian and American universities, teams in Europe, and the junior players who have turned eighteen years of age. Teams draft in the reverse order of their final standing the year before the draft. Drafting a player gives the team the exclusive rights to his services, and he cannot try out for another NHL team even though his chances with another club might be far better.

The league's rationale for the draft is that, to some extent, it ensures the equalization of teams, which is in the best interests of the fans. League equality, however, is not just a magnanimous gesture on the part of the owners — it stems directly from economic considerations. The more competitive the league structure, the better the spectator attraction. Further, the greater the uncertainty of the outcome of the game, the more likely people will attend or tune in on television. This means increased revenues for the owners. At the same time, the draft works even better than the old farm system in protecting the owners from one another since it prevents one owner from keeping quality players in minor league affiliates. Specific roster limits for protected players prohibit the stockpiling of talented players which occurred in the farm system. However, like the farm system, the draft maintains the owners' position of monopsony, since a drafted player can only sign with the team that holds his playing rights through the draft. Thus, the player is faced with only one NHL buyer for his services as a hockey player.

On the basis of the above, it is apparent that professional players are in a less advantageous bargaining position than employees in other sectors of the economy. Most notably, non-athlete employees can normally move freely from one employer to another without having to worry about reserve or option clauses in their contracts; this allows them to bargain one employer against another. This is not to suggest that NHL players have no bargaining powers, but the amount of power possessed by a player is dependent on his value to the team. Opportunities for professional athletes are also limited if they wish to play in North America.

Owners want winning teams and this means securing the best talent available. Thus, the highly skilled player has some bargaining power when signing a contract. Also, there have always been alternatives for athletes (though too much can be made of these alternatives). In the case of hockey, from the 1930s to the 1960s, players could play semi-professional and senior hockey and maintain a job outside the sport instead of going to the NHL or a minor league affiliate. Today, players have the option of playing in Europe or Britain. Players could also work elsewhere in the labour force and forego a professional career. All of these alternatives, however, have specific costs for the player and none are as economically profitable as playing in the NHL.

Finally, there is one sense in which signing a player to a high salary is economically sound. Although the owner pays a large salary to the player, the return in terms of media exposure can far outweigh the cost. Consider, for example, the signing of Herschel Walker with the New Jersey Generals football team. He signed a three-year contract worth $4.5 million and, in the first week after signing, the Generals sold 12 000 season tickets, generating more than $1.2 million. Thus, the salary becomes a business expense and is therefore tax deductible, as well as a source of revenue-generating publicity which helps inform consumers about the quality of the product.

The Reserve System and the Option Clause

The reserve system began in baseball when the owners first collaborated to form a cartel. The National League owners agreed informally, in 1879, to allow each team to "reserve" the rights of veteran players for particular teams and that no owner would "tamper" with the players reserved for another team. In 1887, the informal agreement was written into the contracts of all professional baseball players. As a result, when a player played out the length of his particular contract, the team still had the right to reserve his services in perpetuity. Despite successful challenges in the courts subsequent to this 1887 agreement, owners now are exempt from the anti-trust laws and are free to reinstate the reserve clause.

In the case of the NHL, although it never enjoyed formal exemption from the anti-trust laws of the United States or the anti-combines laws of Canada, it employed a reserve clause which was never challenged by any player in the courts.

The NFL never had a reserve clause, although it did have a two-year option clause. Under this clause, according to the standard NFL player's contract, the team had the option of renewing a player's services for the two years following the expiry of a contract. With two one-year contracts and then two option years, an owner could control the entire playing career of most players.

In 1957, the American courts ruled that the NFL's reserve system was an illegal restraint of trade. No player tried to attain free agency status, however, until 1963 when, following R. C.

Owens' move from the San Francisco 49ers to the Baltimore Colts, the owners responded with the "Rozelle Rule."

This rule gave the NFL commissioner Pete Rozelle the power to determine what compensation a club signing a free agent must give to the club losing the free agent. The first two times that free agents were signed, Rozelle imposed strong compensation deals on the clubs signing the agents and thus, in effect, eliminated the mobility of NFL players even when they did play out their options. When compensation is so high, there is no incentive for clubs to sign free agents.

Free Agency and Labour Negotiations

Increasingly lucrative television contracts for professional leagues, in conjunction with the players' awareness that they had no freedom to sell their labour capacity to the highest bidder (free agency status), created a good deal of interest in the formation of player unions. In 1967, the National Hockey League Players Association (NHLPA) was formed and three years later, the NFL followed with the National Football League Players Association (NFLPA).

Supported by their union, players have challenged in the courts the restricted movements imposed by the owners. One of the clear messages given by the courts to professional sports owners is that, while they are willing to grant monopolies in the product market, they are not willing to allow team owners to have restrictive trade practices on the supply side, *unless* the players agree to restricted movement in the collective bargaining process. This is an extremely important caveat.

It assumes that the collective agreements formed between the players and the owners are negotiated in good faith. It also implies that the unions now hold the full responsibility for securing, and maintaining, free agency status for players. The courts will not enforce anti-trust laws as long as compensation agreements are negotiated into collective agreements. This means that the right enjoyed by almost every citizen in the country to move freely from employer to employer is lost to professional athletes if their union is not strong enough to press for full agency. As a result, rather than representing the total breakdown of the owners' power, the unions represent powerful levers that the owners can manipulate to continue the monopsony position they would otherwise lose in the courts.

The fate of free agency appears to lie solely with the unions' power and their determination to negotiate aggressively on the free agency question. The will of a union in this issue hinges on the membership's willingness to employ its ultimate weapon — the strike. The strike is the final form of leverage that workers can use against their employers but this leverage is not nearly as powerful as many people think. A strike requires the majority support of the membership throughout its entire duration. Many workers enter into a strike with great enthusiasm, but as it drags on, the original solidarity becomes progressively more difficult to maintain. Regular wages are suspended and strike pay never approaches these levels. In the case of professional athletes, this is a tremendous cost in both absolute and relative terms. In the 57-day NFL strike of 1982, each player lost tens to hundreds of thousands of dollars, while the league owners saved $63 million in wages. In relative terms, the players' loss was even greater; while on strike for just two months, they lost more than ten per cent of their career earnings. Given this reality, the strike is a lever that sports unions use with tremendous caution. Moreover, unlike workers in some other spheres of the economy, professionals often encounter strong public opposition to their strike action.

While many people acknowledge that strikes are justified in the so-called business sector of the economy, many feel they do not belong in the world of sport. This sentiment is based on the belief that sport is somehow different from the world of business and that business interests artificially intrude into sport and do not rightly belong there. The sentiment is, of course, wrong. Professional sport is, first and foremost, a question of production, sale, and distribution of revenues.

The Pressure For and Against Unionization

Professional athletes are like any other employees. They sell their labour capacity to an employer and surrender a certain amount of their personal autonomy (both at and away from the work site), and undergo some physical impairment (far more so than most other workers), in return for a wage. The employer attempts to increase the productivity and profitability of the franchise in a number of ways already noted. As an individual, the athlete has virtually no power to oppose a team owner, especially in view of the nature of team sports selection. Thus athletes, like other employees in various sectors of the economy, organize collectively to oppose or negotiate with the owner. In sport, however, the tendency to unionize is met with significant resistance.

Unlike other occupations, professional sport represents a very short career span. Given that the majority of players are in the major leagues for less than five years and that the competition for jobs is so intense, many players do not see numerous advantages in joining a union or being involved with the union movement while they are playing. This is coupled with a characteristic common to many professional athletes that mitigates their enthusiasm for unions: most professional athletes are conservative by nature and the idea of belonging to a union goes against their personal political ideology. Moreover, professional sport is essentially an individualistic enterprise. With so much emphasis on the individual's performance and the individualistic nature of the reward structure, there are few incentives to think collectively except as a team against all other teams in the league. Finally, not all players are at the same stage in their careers, and career phase also determines how much energy or commitment a player is willing to devote to union activity. Rookie players are not likely to want to be involved in any activity that might jeopardize their chances of making the team. Similarly, those at the end of their careers may be seeking a position in management or coaching and are unlikely to promote the union or its objectives. Those in the middle of their careers, if they are not too busy trying to meet performance bonuses in their contracts, are the most likely to support the union and its objectives, but this represents only a small minority of players.

As a result, player unions must first overcome definite obstacles in their efforts to unionize (despite their legal right to do so), and then to act effectively. The nature of the sport also affects the ability of unions to provide benefits for their members. In sports like baseball and hockey, there is greater opportunity for individual performers to excel and be rewarded financially. In these situations, unions have greater difficulty. In the case of football, even though there are a number of individual superstars, the majority of the league is comprised of linemen who fare very poorly financially but who last much longer in their careers. As a result, the leadership of the NFLPA is made up of many more linemen than players from other positions. Thus, the union's objectives reflect the interests of those players with very little individual bargaining strength.

Sport as Alienated Labour

As the previous discussion has shown, there is a marked divergence of interests between owners and workers. Owners want to maximize profits and thus are compelled, by the dictates of the market, to minimize costs and reduce, or at least hold in line, employees' wages. It is not surprising that most cost-saving measures involve stricter control of the production process and the use of labour-saving technology wherever possible.

Workers, on the other hand, seek better working conditions, shorter hours of work, increased wages, and greater autonomy and responsibility in the production process. As a result, the relationship between owners and workers involves each group seeking to consolidate its own power and advantage over the other.

In the case of professional sport, despite increased use of legal action and the development of players' unions, the professional athlete remains relatively powerless in relation to the owners. This powerlessness has led a number of scholars to look at the activity of professional athletes as alienated labour.

The alienation theme has two dimensions. The first deals with the creative dimension of labour. When a worker sells his or her labour capacity to an employer, work no longer represents an opportunity to use the production process as one of creative self-actualization. Work is subordinated to the instrumental demands of profit.

Although sport is potentially one of the most creative and expressive avenues of human self-development, the activity is subordinated to a set of highly regimented, restrictive practices in order to enhance team performance and make the game into an attractive spectacle. All phases of the game are controlled by owners, management, and coaches. Whether a player can even participate is a decision made by others. There is a good deal of literature, both analytical and in the form of personal accounts by athletes, which documents that sport, as a realm of creative activity, is a highly alienated environment.

The second dimension of alienation is more theoretical and deals with how players actually create the structure that opposes them. Throughout this chapter, employers are referred to as owners, but this is somewhat misleading. As the NFLPA pointed out to its membership in 1981, the owners of sports franchises actually own very little. They possess membership in an exclusive club through ownership of franchise rights, but they rarely own much more. While they own some equipment, they rarely own the stadiums in which their teams play or practice. In effect, the owners of the professional sports franchises are only promoters. They promote the league, set up performance dates, and sell tickets. Owners can just as easily promote rock concerts, circuses, or ice shows as they can sports events. In other words, the players are the show; they are the real producers, and the owners, with minimal risks, profit from the efforts of the players who risk their careers on every single play of the game.

In terms of objective alienation, the players not only produce a product that they do not own, they also produce a product which returns high rates of profit, thus further reinforcing the owners' position of power and domination. The players are creating an objective set of structures that stand outside themselves and, in effect, oppose and ultimately control them as athletes. This opposition between the players and the object of their creation — the owners and their profits — lies at the heart of the dynamic of the political economy.

Conclusion

In industrial capitalist societies like Canada and the United States, the majority of people have scarce resources; few citizens could live for very long if they did not work for some employer in the public or private sector. Wage workers have to try and sell the one commodity they all own that has economic value on the marketplace — the ability to do work (labour capacity). When people agree to work, they give a certain amount of effort to the employer. They also surrender some autonomy to the organization and dictates of the workplace. Finally, they may suffer some degree of impairment (even if it is only in the form of fatigue, though it can be much more serious than this). In return, workers receive a wage, some satisfaction from the work (or from being at work, at least), and gain some status and/or prospects for a career.

The employer, for his or her part, has specific resources which he or she is willing to invest in commodity production for the primary purpose of producing a profit. While the production and sale of products in the market requires many prerequisites — for example, raw material, capital equipment, a work site — it is fundamentally dependent upon the labour capacity of the work force.

Despite the ubiquitous nature of the wage/labour relationship, until very recently little attention was paid to the work of professional athletes. Through an examination of the economic and other aspects of sport, this chapter has illustrated the close parallel existing between professional sport "work" and work in other sectors of the capitalist economy.

Suggested Readings

For a more detailed discussion of the theoretical framework associated with the political economy of sport, see Rob Beamish (1981), "The Materialist Approach to Sport Study: An Alternative Prescription to the Discipline's Methodological Malaise," in *Quest*, XXXI, 1, or Rob Beamish (1982), "Sport and the Logic of Capitalism," in Hart Cantelon and Richard S. Gruneau (Eds.) (1982), *Sport, Culture and the Modern State*, Toronto, University of Toronto Press. J. Barnes (1983), *Sports and the Law in Canada*, Toronto, Butterworths, and A. Johnson and J. Frey (Eds.) (1985), *Government and Sport: The Public Policy Issues*, Totowa, New Jersey, Rowman and Allenheld, contain more detailed discussions on specific topics in the political economy of sport.

Chapter Eight
University Training of Physical Educators

Pierre J. Demers

There is a big difference between what physical educators offer
and what the various segments of the population want in the way
of sport and recreation. This supply/demand gap is not due to the
poor quality of the services offered by physical educators, but to
the inadequate understanding of what the public wants. In this
modern age of "special populations" (the sometimes artificial cross-
sections which reflect the fragmentation of the ways of life engen-
dered by capitalist industrial society), there is every indication that
the university training of physical educators does not prepare them
to meet the needs of these special populations (the handicapped,
the elderly, pregnant women, and so on). Because of the tightness
of the job market, physical educators are often forced to work in
areas where they have little knowledge of the needs of those they
serve. Poorly designed university training programs are partly to
blame for this situation.

There are innumerable publications dealing with the problems of training physical educators. For example, Boileau (1982)
lays much of the blame for the criticism levelled at physical education on what he calls "sportism." The emphasis placed on sports
education in physical education courses at the expense of other
physical skills would get considerably less support from parents
and students if they appreciated all the implications of physical
competition. Chauvier (1979), Demers (1979, 1982, 1984), Deschênes (1984), Ross (1978), Paplauskas-Ramunas (1968), Sheedy
(1976), and Zeigler (1983) have all cast doubt on the conceptual
bases underlying the dominant concept of physical education.
Among the problems they have mentioned are overspecialization,

obsession with technique, lack of a humanizing approach, and ignorance of the impact of certain presumptions about the nature of physical activity (such as focusing exclusively on the physiological implications of physical exercise). Other writers have studied the various occupations involved in physical education, some proposing the introduction of professional status as a solution to the problems of market control (Larouche, 1984) and others the opposite course, "deprofessionalization," to better meet the emerging needs of contemporary society (Harvey, 1982). The aim of this chapter is to describe the present situation in physical education and to propose suggestions for possible reforms.

Two cornerstones of the modern view of physical education seem responsible for its poor design: the exclusively biophysical conception of the nature of physical activity, and strategies of intervention that relate to the professional interests of physical educators rather than those whom they wish to serve. In addition, there are few differences in the training programs offered by the various universities. There appears to be one dominant view of physical education, a primarily biophysical view, prevailing at most universities.

The Historical Sources of the Dominant Contemporary Model

The Great Social Dynamic Forces

The model that currently prevails in the training of physical educators, kinanthropologists, or specialists in human movement, depending on the terminology one chooses, did not arise by accident. Nor was it the result of some Copernican revolution in physical education which brought it from the dark ages into the age of enlightenment. It is a product of the history of physical education as an occupation that has recently sprung from the social division of labour created by industrial society. Some sports and physical education historians, particularly those who assume the transhistorical character of sport, would interject that sport has always existed and that the gymnasiarch of the ancient Greeks is the archetype of the modern physical educator. We do not deny that many different physical education occupations have emerged throughout history, but maintain that advanced capitalist societies are historically distinct social formations, which give rise in particular to a specific division of labour, within which contemporary physical education has developed.

Numerous factors have influenced the development of physical education, including religious concepts, as discussed in the chapter on the Quebec clergy. Many publications highlight the role played by individuals in the history of physical education, although there is a tendency in these publications to overstate the influence that isolated individuals can have on an institution. There are countless other factors. However, since we are concerned here with contemporary physical education, let us focus our attention on a few general circumstances that form the framework within which the dominant contemporary model is built. Two variables seem fundamental to this process. The first, already mentioned above, is the configuration of the social division of labour. More specifically, professionalism seems to have had considerable attraction for physical educators. The second variable is the growth of knowledge within industrial society. The effects of these two factors are closely interrelated; therefore we will deal with them together. Finally, the inherent tendency for advanced capitalist societies to "commodify" every social product, that is, to make it an object of consumption, has not spared physical education.

Aside from the institutional sources at the very foundations of advanced capitalist societies on which rests the inherent logic behind the social and technical division of labour, the continuous process of occupational specialization is probably the factor that has most directly influenced contemporary physical education. It is the chief cause of the emergence of physical education as a distinct occupation within the social division of labour. Initially appearing in the schools, physical education later expanded to encompass a larger reality, from coaching elite athletes to working with "special groups" and helping business people keep fit.

Specialization has done more than make possible the emergence of physical education as a distinct occupation. Its growth has resulted in fragmentation of the field, particularly in the universities. Not only are the areas of application becoming increasingly specialized, but knowledge has become so fragmented in the universities that, considering the eclecticism that exists in training programs, those who have sought to create a single science or discipline (Zeigler, 1983; Ross, 1981) have been reduced to attempting to build bridges between many solitudes. In this respect, the differences in position between those favouring the humanities and those favouring the biological sciences seem almost irreconcilable.

This fragmentation of knowledge is linked not only to the increasing social division of labour, but also to the growth of scientific knowledge, which itself produces a division of scientific labour, the continual partitioning and specialization of knowledge. Even more important with respect to knowledge in advanced capitalist societies is the imposed dominant scientific model. The dominant contemporary representation of science is based on the model of the natural sciences, and in the case of physical education, specifically that of the biological sciences. Since physical education acts primarily upon the body, has long been defined in opposition to or as complementary to intellectual education and, in the effort to break sports records, is often seen as a process of enhancing physical performance, there is a strong tendency to regard physical education as a biological science, a science of the efficiency and rationality of physical movement and functions. In this sense, sports sciences would be, to paraphrase Habermas, an extension of rationality to attain one end, performance, which is characteristic of modern societies: " . . . technical evolution lends itself well to a model of interpretation according to which the human species has projected, one after another, the elements upon which rational activity with respect to an end is based and whose roots are in the human organism in the form of technical means" (quoted by Harvey, 1983:74).

In conforming to the dominant model, knowledge in physical education has confronted certain epistemological problems; the model has also had practical repercussions, as we shall see later. Before proceeding with a discussion of these problems, however, we should stress here that the foregoing is not a call for the rejection of science. But it is important to keep in mind that the dominant scientific model is not free of problems; science does not provide completely neutral knowledge. Every scientific activity has social repercussions, some of which are not intended by the scientists themselves. Thus the social conditions of the production of scientific knowledge are of considerable importance, for they often determine the type of knowledge that is favoured and the direction to be taken in seeking solutions. As Giard, like others before him, points out, the problem is not one of knowing whether or not to condemn science as it currently appears; it is rather that

> Anything is possible, but is it desirable? . . . We are in a time of taking responsibility, rejecting options, and making choices, in order to avoid excessive risks, to ensure a future that is neither hideous nor perpetually

> dangerous, without sacrificing in doing so the indispen-
> sable progression of discoveries and technology. Be-
> tween science fiction and a return to the Middle Ages,
> between rampant futurism and a regressive opposition
> to science, there must be a balance, a wise solution. . . .
> (Giard, 1977:44)

If this quotation seems extreme in relation to current applications of the "science of human movement" (although those applications that involve the doping of athletes approach the most
apocalyptic scenarios), it is nonetheless instructive in exposing
the dangers of a blind quest for knowledge. This problem is all
the more important since, in societies where everything scientific
has considerable prestige, the dominant model of science becomes
attractive to those who seek power, because science can impart
great legitimacy to their precepts.

Indeed, it is by declaring themselves possessors of an
exclusive science and technology and by using science as the foundation for their credibility that professional groups have attempted
to build their monopolies. Professionalism can be defined as the
pursuit of certain prerogatives granted under the law, notably the
exclusive right to perform certain acts. It is a social organization
of labour in which the producers of a service have a monopoly,
a monopoly that also makes the users of the service dependent
on the producers (Gyarmati, 1975; Illich, 1977). Professionalism
has been used by a number of occupational groups seeking upward
social mobility. Among those which come readily to mind are
doctors, lawyers, and — closer to the field of physical education
— physiotherapists and ergotherapists. A large percentage of physical educators, often with university professors leading the way,
have set out to acquire professional status. It is understandable
that professionalism, regarded by the middle classes as the symbol
of success, has held such an attraction for physical educators who
come from these classes.

The second factor mentioned above is the "commodification" of physical activity. This process manifests itself in the
production of records, books, and television programs on physical fitness, especially "dancercise." Indeed, to a certain extent,
the practices promoted by physical educators were pioneered by
the commercial programs of Jane Fonda. Professional sport (see
the chapter by Beamish) is also a form of commodified physical
activity. The power of the sports industry and professional sport
has made the commodified forms of physical activity into the
dominant models.

The Institutional Dynamic of Physical Education

The contemporary model of physical education is not only the product of the historical factors discussed above. It is also the result of the historical dynamic of physical education, of specific economic circumstances shaping its development, not least of which are the actions of those who have worked in the field, and of the struggles between various factions to impose a particular model on the discipline.

The many writers who have recounted the history of physical education in Canada remind us that physical education as a distinct occupation is the result of several competing tendencies. For example, in his study of the history of physical education in Quebec, Donald Guay (1981) mentions a number of conflicting historical currents, including militarism, sanitarianism, humanism, and scientism. On the basis of his classification, Guay argues that the dominant model of contemporary physical education is scientism or, as described above, the biophysical approach. Guay says the following of the proponents of this approach in Quebec: "Subscribing to the Western current of thought according to which physical education is based chiefly on *available scientific evidence*, they aggressively propose a scientific physical education based on *the science of man in motion*, which is capable of supplying *physical education with all data about the phenomenon of human movement and its effects on the many dimensions of the personality*" (1981:57). Guay adds that this approach soon narrowed to the physical dimension of the individual.

This particular model gained credence as a result of circumstances that presided over the development of modern physical education. First, the progressive introduction of training programs for physical educators into the universities gave rise, especially in the mid-1960s, to a tendency to "scientize" the occupation. Before this, virtually all physical educators had been trained in teachers' colleges, and they were primarily regarded as school teachers. This continues to be the major occupation of physical educators. For those not interested in teaching, sports federations and municipal recreation services also provided good prospects for employment. Thus the training of physical educators had for a long time produced primarily teachers, sports organizers, and specialists in sports activities.

During the 1960s, however, an increasing proportion of university professors were looking for more scientific programs in physical education. There are a number of possible reasons for this search. First, physical education professors who had been working only a short time in the universities were trying to make inroads into the more established university community. In fact, they were strongly encouraged to do so by university administrations, which constantly stressed the importance of generating scientific knowledge in the university system. They were seeking academic and professional status not only within their own universities, but also from the state and the government agencies that provided research funds. Secondly, they wanted to improve the image of physical education within society. The prestige of science within contemporary society made the scientific model even more attractive. Consequently, the new physical educators, especially those who saw themselves as academic researchers, steadily joined the army of experts who had appeared in other areas of society.

The American influence seems to have been a determining factor in Canada, notably for the model that became the cornerstone for the science of human movement. This influence was exerted in particular through university professors who had received their post-secondary education in the United States and who imported the models currently in use there. The geographical and cultural proximity of the United States also enhanced the acceptance of American models. The most significant aspect of the American concept of physical education was its emphasis on one particular type of approach, that of medicine. Kenyon (1967) notes that the emphasis placed on the physiology of human physical activity was largely due to the tradition that the physical education movement inherited from American medicine. The principal founders of the American approach were all medical doctors, and Kenyon concludes that physical education adopted a rather narrow orientation based on the model used in specialized medicine. This "biological" influence had a strong effect in Canada, increasingly supplanting other approaches. There were other reasons for this besides the educational background of Canadian physical education professors. First, Canadian physical education, like other aspects of Canadian society, was to some extent the victim of American cultural imperialism. Furthermore, American ideas were even more successful in penetrating physical education circles in Canada since Canadian professors, who were being encouraged by their universities to complete their doctoral studies, elected to attend, in large numbers, institutions in the United States. As already mentioned, research in these universities centred increasingly on the biological aspects of physical activity.

Indeed, the emergence of kinanthropology or sports science was entirely consistent with the logic of specialization espoused by the adherents of the biophysical approach, and a new division of scientific labour was created, this time within physical education itself. These adherents in effect tried to distance themselves from traditional physical education, which was more concerned with the formative aspects of physical activity in relation both to personality and body, by pursuing the scientific study of human movement, which would leave no part of the organism hidden from instrumental rationality.

This approach therefore led to a new form of technical intervention in connection with the body (Sheedy, 1982). The development of movement technique often became more important than the development of the individual. Although draped in scientific neutrality, this approach was nevertheless based on certain ideological assumptions about the nature of physical activity. According to Harvey, the approach rests

> . . . on two ideological assumptions, one implicit, the other explicit. Explicitly, there is a belief in the existence of a universal science, a model borrowed from the natural sciences, which sports science need only accept to become an instant member of the select club of the sciences. This science would also make it possible to discern once and for all what is "natural" in physical activity.
>
> Implicitly, it is postulated that human performance is endlessly perfectible. Thus research is directed primarily towards the improvement of performance, which leads to a mechanistic view of the body. (1983:69)

Sports science would therefore be devoted primarily to research on physical performance; it would have a bias in favour of breaking records or achieving the best technical execution.

Beamish (1982b) has discussed the political aspects of the study of sport based on the natural sciences model. He argues that research carried out within the scientific framework is subject to certain political biases regarding sport, even though the researchers claim to be non-political. The first bias identified by Beamish comes from the unconditional acceptance of the dominant assumptions about sport by sports scientists. Like Harvey (1983), Beamish notes what Habermas and other members of the Frankfurt School had earlier demonstrated, that is, research directed towards technical rationality, far from being a liberating factor, creates new forms of domination. This is particularly true for modern sport, which is devoted to the never-ending quest for a new linear record.

This is reflected, for example, in the athlete's total dependence on the best method of "performing." According to this way of thinking, which is dominant in modern societies, " . . . sport is not associated at all with re-creation, freedom of movement, freedom of expression, or intrinsic qualitative enjoyment. Rather, sport is progressively conceptualized in work-like terms, constrained by rational planning and calculation and its performance oriented with the measurement of success supplied by some external quantitative means" (Beamish, 1982b:11). Sports science only reinforces this tendency. Rather than emancipating, it establishes new forms of domination over the body. Beamish also argues that the institutional support for sports science and competitive sport by the state, businesses, and even professional associations of physical educators raises the problem of the allocation of resources. In effect, since this representation of knowledge is generally accepted as the only legitimate one, the research resources are almost all aimed directly or indirectly at breaking sport records or at finding rational means of improving the performance of the human body as a machine.

    As a result, the adherents of sports science have shirked the critical functions inherent in university research, as has been shown elsewhere (Demers, 1984). Only a critical outlook effectively makes the progress of knowledge possible. Not only have the adherents of sports science seldom looked critically at the dominant representations and institutions of sport and physical education, but much of their work has reinforced the dominant models and the forms of power that they convey. This tendency is clearly visible in the production of scientific articles. "Of the 131 articles published in the *Canadian Journal of Sport Science* from 1979 to 1981, 73% dealt with material that would directly enhance linear sport. . . . An additional 13% of the articles presented material that would indirectly contribute to athletic performance" (Beamish, 1982b:10).

Physical Education and Public Needs

Thus, university training in physical education is now largely dominated by sports science. A high percentage of graduates receive predominantly biological training and are taught to have a mechanistic view of the body in their work. Moreover, with medicine as the ideal benchmark against which to measure themselves and whose legal prerogatives they enjoy, some groups of physical educators, notably the adherents of sports science, are leaning heavily towards professionalization.

With the overemphasis on organized sports activities, other forms of physical activity are forgotten. As a result, many people, particularly young people, lose interest because of the inadequacy of what is available. Can the scientific analysis of technical movements lead to anything other than technical training? This training encourages an approach of the same type, that is, a preoccupation with teaching the technical aspects of sports activities, whereas many of the groups with whom this approach is used are not interested solely in organized sports. Future decisions must be based on a definition of physical education that better reflects the needs of the target population rather than the specialized technical skills of the individuals responsible for serving them.

Furthermore, physical educators seem to have a tendency to pass moralizing judgements on the public — the kind of judgements that are inspired by a paternalism that characterizes the way professional groups perceive the people they serve. There is an assumption that the public has nothing but flaws and bad habits that must be corrected. This perception is probably due to the fact that the scientific, technical orientation of physical educators leads them to apply technical criteria to popular practices and motivations, whereas for the vast majority these technical concerns are, understandably, of little importance.

Physical conditioning as it is organized by physical educators in universities and sometimes used by the state as a means of intervention (see the chapter by Harvey and Proulx) may be a perfect example of this tendency. The term "conditioning" itself suggests a certain orientation in the approach of physical educators. In fact, this is what prompted some writers to wonder whether physical educators are agents of dependence rather than agents of emancipation (Harvey, 1982). Does not "to condition" mean, among other things, to make someone behave in a certain way?

Given the social variations in sports preferences and choices of physical activities in general (see the chapters by Boulanger and Laberge and Sankoff), we can say that the most common activities involve not only sports, but also physical recreation, relaxation, fun, and self-expression. As Levasseur notes, "the most popular activities are the relatively simple ones, which require little organization, can be engaged in by one person or a group, take place in many different settings, have no particular rules or regulations, require no competitive bond between participants, and require a minimum of equipment" (1982:21).

In a society in which we are constantly subjected to stress and conditioning of various kinds, we have the right to ask ourselves why similar methods are used in physical education. Why concentrate on physical conditioning and the pursuit of maximum physical performance when the physical education that people need is found in relaxation, recreation, and diversion, which help them break free of their daily routines? Obesity, excessive stress, and burn-out are all symptoms of problems created by the conditions in which we live. Hence, should we not develop opportunities for living at a different pace and for creating a new balance in social expectations? Should we not advocate approaches in which physical activity is used as a tool of liberation rather than an additional source of stress and alienation?

All the evidence suggests that we are faced with two solitudes. On the one hand, physical educators have developed a wide array of techniques for working on the body, which are based on technical and functional criteria. On the other hand, popular practices and needs seem to have a completely different orientation. If this analysis is correct, it can serve to explain Boileau's (1982) finding, that physical educators are low in public esteem. In his study, which is aimed at determining the variations in social status of physical educators, he comes to the conclusion that the general public is becoming increasingly dissatisfied with the concerns of physical educators (particularly those in the schools), and specifically the pivotal role they often attribute to competitive sports activities.

Could this be called a crisis? At the very least, it may be assumed that university training is not properly attuned to public expectations. The universities appear to have taken little interest in these expectations, preoccupied as they have been with the pursuit of positivist knowledge of how to work efficiently on the body.

Towards Health Education

The foregoing gives us ample reason to seek a new model. It seems possible to suggest a few paths towards this goal, although in so doing we are moving from analysis to theory. In any case, it is time to put some serious intellectual effort into establishing a new conceptual framework for physical education. A modest start is presented in the pages that follow.

A series of important variables must be taken into consideration. First of all, an in-depth examination of the role assigned to physical education in society is essential. In addition, public expectations regarding physical activity must be taken into account. These expectations stem both from the specific tastes of the various social groups served by physical educators and from the constraints imposed by different environments. Training should be geared to these expectations, rather than exclusively to the interests of physical educators. Furthermore, as several of the authors cited have proposed, it seems necessary to seek, in the conceptualization of physical education, a better balance between the biological, psychological, and social dimensions. It is also important to find approaches that do not impose new forms of control on the body. A physical education geared to helping individuals take charge of their own bodies seems to hold the most promise. The fundamental objectives of physical education should be the promotion of health, the prevention of disease, the recovery of control of the body, and personal and collective self-management of physical health. More immediate goals could be incorporated into the framework of these ultimate objectives, including training in sports but especially the total development of the person. In accordance with this approach, then, physical education would be, first and foremost, health education.

Such an approach will not be easy to introduce. For one thing, institutional inertia and the strength of the dominant ideology, which works for the preservation of existing structures, must be expected. In addition, it must be kept in mind that there are many different groups involved in the health sector. Some of them work to cure disease, others to prevent it, which is precisely what physical educators and health educators could be doing.

Finally, any new approach in physical education will have to come to terms with the dominant models of the individual's relationship to his or her body, those of competitive physical activities and those of daily care (such as physical conditioning) sanctioned by the consumer society. As previously pointed out, the "commodified" forms of physical activity portrayed by the media have a substantial influence on the idealized image of the body.

It is in physical educators' interest to develop specific teaching methods that will enable those groups and individuals whom they serve to take charge of themselves. Health education must make people aware of aspects of prevention that can be self-managed. Physical educators would thus become an additional resource of information about health, while pursuing their concerns with the development of physical practices related to sport.

All this presupposes a major overhaul of physical education training, the striking of a new balance among different approaches by the various disciplines, as well as the reorientation of research so that it would no longer focus exclusively on improving physical performance, but would also be aimed at freeing the body from the external pressures that assail it. Thus, rather than being merely scholastic and "biological" physical education would be *an integrated social approach to the overall development of the individual and of the community.* Instead of concentrating on means (such as improvement of skills in sports and physical conditioning) and biophysical results, which are quantifiable and therefore easily measurable, it would branch out to include broader objectives such as education, health, and ecology. Then, physical education could be defined as the whole educational process that teaches each individual to take charge of all matters connected with his or her body and health.

Obviously, the pursuit of such objectives would require a different training for physical educators from that currently offered in the universities. In particular, this training would be gradually separated from technical training in sports activities, at least for those not interested in a coaching career in competitive sports. This is not to condemn sports as such, but rather the dependence on the competitive sports model, from which its objectives are borrowed. Also of great importance in the new approach to physical education training would be the effects that the environment has on the choice of activity and the social constraints which restrict participation. Finally, the new approach would offer a range of activities in addition to organized sports, thus enabling physical educators to meet the expectations of groups — whether they are "special groups" or not — who have never been interested in organized sports and are attempting, in their own way, to take charge of their bodies. In this connection, it is worth considering what is sometimes called anti-gymnastics, which, in contrast to the kinetic, functional approach that currently prevails in physical education, are aimed at rediscovering the self through attention to bodily sensations. But it must also be kept in mind that, taken to the extreme, the latter approach can lead to an exclusively "psychologizing" view of the relationship to the body, currently fashionable with the upwardly mobile middle classes.

Thus, in distancing themselves from the dominant and dominating role of expert in the rational and technocratic management of the body, physical educators would become genuine agents of cultural emancipation. There would be no reason to wonder whether physical education should be patterned after the leading professions. Professionalism would no longer be compatible with the new directions taken by physical education. It would no longer be a case of training professionals to perform rational, instrumental work on the body, but rather of training a new breed of social organizers concerned with the cultural emancipation of the body.

The foregoing are, of course, very rudimentary reflections, but they at least have the merit of shifting the study of the difficulties in physical education, especially in the university training of physical educators, to much broader considerations than "sportism" and the "technification" of physical activities. Is it not true that physical educators have always defined themselves as those who are responsible for the education of the body? Is it not time to introduce an approach to physical education that is compatible with this objective?

Suggested Readings

Paplauskas-Ramunas' book (1968), *Development of the Whole Man through Physical Education: An Interdisciplinary Comparative Exploration and Appraisal*, Ottawa, University of Ottawa Press, discusses useful parameters for the development of a new type of university training in physical education. On the history of physical education in Quebec, see Donald Guay (1981), *L'histoire de l'éducation physique au Québec: conceptions et événements (1830–1980)*, Chicoutimi, Gaétan Morin. For a collection of papers on the future of physical education in Quebec, see *L'éducation physique, où va la profession?*, Montréal, Les dossiers Beaux-Jeux, 7, Bellarmin-Desport, 1982.

Despite the fact that native Canadians taught the game of lacrosse to the early colonial inhabitants, the discrimination contained in the early definitions of amateurism prohibited them from participating in organized amateur matches later on. Public Archives Canada/C-9781

Intermediate league champions, "National" lacrosse club, 1897–1898.
Laprés & Lavergne/Public Archives Canada/PA-51557

The first organized hockey games involved university students playing under the McGill rules. Today hockey is one of the most democratized sports in Canada, with participation across the whole spectrum of social class. Associated Screen News Ltd./Public Archives Canada/PA-149163

"Play on the Street." It is often argued that play is liberating but, for many children in inner-city neighbourhoods, their choice of play activities is constrained by inadequate facilities. Public Archives Canada/PA-108313

The class structure of Canadian society is often dramatized through sport. Whereas private school educators promoted team games as a way of developing amateur gentlemen, the public education system (including native residential schools) emphasized mass calisthenics as a means of developing social control and discipline. Jack Long/Public Archives Canada/PA-160943

Weightlifting at the Seaman's Club, 1945. Jack Long/Public Archives Canada/PA-160941

Nurses exercising in gymnasium of the Residence for Nurses of the Hospital for Sick Children, Toronto, 1907. Public Archives Canada/C-90777

Although it is still most common to see women engaged in the so-called "feminine" activities, traditional male activities like bodybuilding are gaining legitimacy as female activities as well. Model, Kim Hughes/Photographer, Fortuna Privis

Organized labour in Quebec argues that programs in the workplace are more geared to worker productivity than they are to the promotion of health among employees. G. Carrière/Health & Welfare Canada/Public Archives Canada/PA-160976

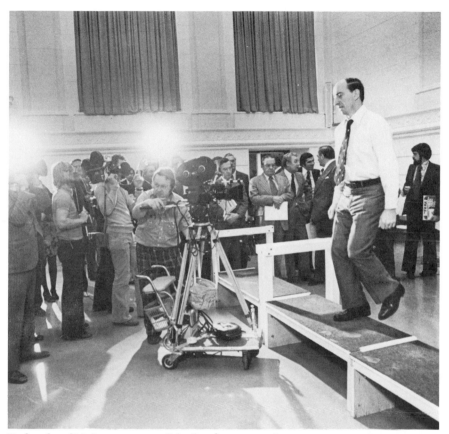

Federal politicians responsible for fitness and amateur sport have gained widespread publicity and exposure because of the increased government presence in sport and fitness. D. Paterson/Health & Welfare Canada/Public Archives Canada/PA-160975

Part Three
The Ideology of Sport

Like any institution, sport carries meaning: it is the vehicle for particular images of the social order. It has its own ideology, one interwoven with the dominant ideology of society. Thus it is the subject of a social discourse: every day different opinions are advanced on what values it should carry, on what does and does not constitute a sports activity; everyone has an interpretation of the meaning of actions by those involved in this sector. If ideology is a "representational system through which a group perceives itself and builds its social environment, distribution, conflict, belonging, common objectives, and values" (Ansart, 1972:213), every ideology is the vehicle for the social project of the agents who disseminate it. At times it legitimizes the established order, and at other times it attempts to delegitimize this order — when it supports replacement models.

The chapters that follow focus primarily on the dominant ideologies of sport, both because replacement or challenging ideologies are not exactly numerous in this area, one often considered highly conservative, and also because there is almost no work on the rare attempts at change.

The analyses assembled here are based on the supposition that the meaning and structure of cultural events are tied to the dominant ideology and the social structure, which is not to say that the former is only a pale reflection of the latter. This structure leads individuals to consider one definition of sport as being a matter of course and not subject to debate, whereas in fact it is only one definition among many.

Ever since television moved into the area of sport, it has proved to be a powerful vehicle for the dominant ideology. It has set off a new boom in the commercialization of sport and has sanctified its event aspect. Finally, it has helped change the meaning of the practice by stamping it with new significance, by "re-presenting" a particular image of the sports "hero"'s performance. Hart Cantelon and Richard Gruneau believe that research on the effects that the sports event has on the public is in the mainstream of research on sport and the media. This particular aspect of the sports event, its structure, is something no one has ever examined at length. This structure nevertheless has a crucial influence on the meaning of spectator sport.

Semiology, that is, the study of the use of signs in social life, is a useful tool in the analysis of ideologies. Derived from structural linguistics, semiology reveals the meaning of communication and its underlying social message. According to Margaret MacNeill, ideologies are not conveyed solely by linguistic signs or words. Semiology in fact distinguishes between linguistic, olfactory, gustatory, kinesic, auditory, and iconic signs. MacNeill studies the social view of the female body conveyed by images (iconic signs) disseminated in the media. Taking as examples a "dancercise" program and a televised female bodybuilding championship, she shows the relationship between the dominant ideology in Canadian society and the signs conveyed by the media concerning the female body.

Women have never been encouraged to participate in physical activity. While women today are physically active, the type of activity which they can engage in is still subject to debate. The media present predominantly aesthetic activities as being most appropriate for women. Moreover, they help create a particular image, that of a woman who wants to be physically attractive to men. MacNeill's study highlights the inequality between the sexes in Canadian sport.

Sports literature is another vehicle for the dissemination of the dominant ideology of sport. Although Robert Hollands makes no reference to works produced in French, this holds true, with a few slight variations, for all of Canada. For one thing, a number of sports biographies distributed in bookstores in French Canada are translations or pale imitations of works that have already appeared in English. For another, similarities between Hollands' observations and those of other writers, notably Gritti in a 1975 study on the journalistic treatment of sport in France, suggest that there is a prevailing sports hero myth in all advanced capitalist societies, a myth consisting of certain constants found in all social groupings. Moreover, it is clear that French Canadians have their own sports heroes, who have traits that are not unlike the images that francophones have of themselves. To our knowledge, there exists only one preliminary study on this subject (Plante, 1975).

In his study, Hollands also uses the analytical framework of political economy. He notes that writers, far from being completely free in their means of expression, are strongly influenced by fundamental, common ideas in choosing literary techniques that will fit in with the publishing industry in the capitalist system. The same kind of dilemma faces sports journalists. When the latter have to write an article, for example, their task is made much easier if they can meet with the coaches and players to get the information they need. They can, however, be refused access by the owners of professional teams, which necessarily reduces their freedom to report. Thus, far from being completely free, sports journalists and sports fiction writers produce work that conforms to a predetermined framework.

There is no unanimity in the ideology of sport regarding its instrumental aspects. The chapter by Pierre Brodeur highlights this question. His chief concern is to bring out the social issues of a practice that has become the panacea of modern times and is promoted by physical educators and kinanthropologists: physical fitness in the workplace.

Now that private enterprise is assuming increased importance, with the worker being pushed into the background, this chapter has much valuable information to impart. First, readers will note once again that even activities that are supposed to be exclusively physical also have a social impact. Second, they will see that physical fitness in the workplace, aside from any physiological benefits it may produce, may also constitute a form of alienation and may cost those for whom it is intended some autonomy and freedom if they fail to guard their own interests.

Brodeur shows that the domination of favoured models is never total. As the state and private enterprise focus on a particular issue, promoting, with specific objectives in mind, the introduction of physical activity in the workplace, the union movement is seeking other forms of organization.

Chapter Nine
The Production of Sport for Television

Hart Cantelon and Richard S. Gruneau

Introduction

It is generally acknowledged that the popularity of sport in North America has been significantly influenced by the medium of television. "Television made it a new game" and "football was made by television" are two of many statements which have emphasized this bond, and the statistics seem to support the supposition. Audience ratings consistently indicate the popularity of televised sport.

Consider just one example relevant to Canadians. At the 1986 World Junior Hockey Championships, the gold medal game between the USSR and Canada attracted 4.5 million Canadian viewers, almost half of whom watched the entire contest. As a consequence, it was the top-rated Canadian show for the week (*Globe and Mail*, January 25, 1986:D2). Similarly, an examination of CBC *Annual Reports* indicates that "Hockey Night in Canada" has had one of the largest viewing audiences of any program on Canadian television. This continues to be true even in the fragmented viewing markets created over the last several years by cable and pay television. For example, in a 1981 paper, audience researcher Barry Kiefl noted that the average quarter-hour audience for "Hockey Night in Canada" (2 755 000 viewers) ranked in the top ten programs in a sample winter viewing week. This rivalled the audiences drawn to successful "prime-time" programs such as "M.A.S.H." and "Dallas."

Such viewer interest has not been confined to hockey. Canadians have also been heavy consumers of the major American team sports and of international sports events such as the Olympics and soccer's World Cup — events where world-wide audiences may exceed a billion viewers. It is important to understand that North American and European networks have done more than simply *respond* to a deep-rooted interest in sport in western societies. Over the last thirty years they have also *cultivated* potential sports audiences, and have worked to expand them.

One consequence of this has been a greater volume of sports programming. From being represented by only a handful of programs in the 1950s, sport has come to be an omnipresent part of television. By the late 1970s, it was estimated that North American networks produced over 1200 hours of sports programming annually, approximately 15 per cent of all scheduled programs (Loy et al., 1978). In Canada, a 1975–76 CBC report noted that the "sports and outdoors" category made up 13.7 per cent of its program content, 76 per cent of this being devoted to Canadian sports. Along the same lines, a *Special Report on Broadcasting* (1977) by the Canadian Radio-television and Telecommunications Commission (CRTC) found that, in 1976, sports made up 5.8 per cent of the distribution of viewing time for English-language television. What makes this latter statistic even more striking is the fact that it did not include the heavy weekend coverage of sport.

The cultivation of larger sports audiences has also had another, less measurable effect. In order to become more "attractive" to viewers, sports programming has been incorporated into the world of sophisticated production techniques, entertainment values, and network competition. With replays, split-screens, slow motion, and "colour" commentators, sports programming today has a much different look than in the early years of television transmission.

Television Sports Research: The Focus on Effects

Researchers concerned with mass communication and cultural studies have generally identified three distinct areas of analysis: the organizational/institutional features of production, the message which is produced for the audience, and the effects of the message on the audience (Corner, 1983).

North American scholars particularly interested in the sport/television relationship have tended to work in the area of message dissemination, that is, the effect of the message on the audience. The majority of this research has been of two types. The first and most prevalent approach has focused on televised sports violence and its effects on audiences (Goldstein and Arms, 1971; Hrycaiko et al., 1978; McMurtry, 1974). A second approach has sought to evaluate the effects which television coverage has had on sport (Birrell and Loy, 1979; Horowitz, 1974). Within the former approach, the research has targeted various audience groups (children, males, females) or different forms of violence (legitimated within the rules of the contest, like boxing, or outside the rules, like fighting in hockey). In the latter research, the emphasis has ranged from the "corruption of sport thesis" (that is, sport has been made to "fit" television and this has changed its nature) to evaluations which stress the positive (e.g., raising player salaries, promoting participation, reaching a wide audience).

Although this television "effect" research has contained some important insights, the focus on the consequences for the audience or the sport has also been limiting in some fundamental ways. In emphasizing "effect," implicit (and often explicit) assumptions that television is a very powerful instrument of manipulation have developed (Gurevitch et al., 1982). Rather than suggesting that television messages are received/interpreted on an individual basis, for instance, researchers portray audiences as homogeneous entities that passively accept the audio-visual package produced by the network. Moreover, the research has tended not to address the fact that the television medium itself is influenced and contoured by the nuances of the industrial capitalist state (that is, like sport, television is a product of the particulars of Canadian political economy). While addressing the effects of violence, for instance, researchers have given little thought to why some sports forms rather than others appear on television, or to the place of violence within Canadian society generally. Short studies which move directly to "effects" and "attitudes" have foregone the important task of understanding how messages are produced.

This is not to say that these studies have not made a contribution to sport and to the mass media. The problem is one of depth and perspective. While most research has been concerned with how television affects sport, it barely skims the surface of the complex ways in which games are constructed and produced for television. Nor does the research deal with the significance of this production for evaluating broader issues in political and cultural life. Research which does look more clearly at television's effect on sports forms has been conducted by Cominsky et al. (1977). The researchers conducted a detailed content analysis of the audio portions of six National Football League (NFL) games shown over a three-week period during the 1976 season.

The findings of this research have been widely noted. Over 25 per cent of the sentence units analysed offered some sort of "dramatic embellishment" of game action. The researchers concluded that commentary heavily influenced the audience reaction to the game and the right verbal cues could turn a one-sided contest into an exciting spectacle.

Much of the "effects research" has contributed important insights into the complex nature of the sport/television relationship. Yet, there is also a sense in which research dealing with this relationship in North America has been limited by its concerns about media effects, related questions of message content, and the apparent "needs" which audiences either bring to, or derive from, particular messages.

Over the last decade, cultural studies in Europe and North America have attempted to respond to these limitations. Rather than emphasizing the analysis of television effects and message content, these researchers have sought to analyse the specific processes of television production and their relationships to the significative properties of televised sports entertainment. A number of British researchers have been leaders in this area (Buscombe, 1975; Whannel, 1981; Peters, 1976; Colley and Davies, 1981), and one concept which occurs throughout much of this research is that television production can be understood as operating through a series of "codes."

Cultural Codes and Cultural Production

The study of codes and how they are related to ways of viewing the world has been the specific domain of semiology. Although it is a complex concept, a code can be loosely defined as a set of structures and rules through which meanings are organized. Language, for example, embodies a number of codes that are used every day. The structures of language include the characters or alphabet, grammar, and sentences. These components of language only become meaningful when they are organized through rules of discourse that allow understanding to occur between individuals.

Television, as a particular form of mass media, has its own specific codes. These codes underlie the technical and narrative conventions (e.g., editing styles, camera locations, sound use) associated with the production of programming. In sports broadcasting, the expression of these codes can often be found in the

preference for a particular type of narrative (for example, the orig-
inating question: "who will win?") and the audio and visual story
that develops from it. The transmission of a sports event would
not make much sense, nor have much meaning, if it were not
framed through a narrative code. What makes these British studies
of televised sport different from those most often conducted in
North America is that, in exposing and analysing the codes of television, the researchers are addressing the question: how are messages produced for the audience? As such, they reveal a great deal
about the culturally dominant assumptions in a society.

Because the analysis of codes and images requires a consideration of the broader forces which have been involved in their
constitution, there has been a tendency in cultural studies research
to emphasize the relationships of the media with other cultural
forms, with ideologies, and with political and economic conditions.
One of the most important concepts to emerge as a result of this
tendency is the notion of "cultural production," that is, the notion
of viewing culture as a dynamic process. This cultural process is
made and struggled over in the context of differing resources in
a society. It also involves the capacity of some groups and classes
to exercise a disproportionate influence over formal and informal
conventions which circumscribe the production and reproduction
of given cultural practices (Barrett, 1979; Hall et al., 1980).

Approaching the Question of Production

There are two related contexts within which sport is produced
for television. The first is the broad political economic context of
production, that is, the economic, social, and political factors
which exert pressure on the organization of both television and
sport. The key research questions to be asked are two: how are
broadcasting and sport organized in capitalist societies, and what
identifiable implications can be drawn from the organization?

Without doubt there is an important set of pressures on
cultural production which arises from the commodity-producing
logic lying at the core of capitalist social processes. Jhally (1984)
has developed this idea into a theory of the evolution of the sports
media complex. He argues that sports organizations sell sports
events to television broadcasters, and the networks then use these
events as a basis for selling audiences to advertisers. It is the
capacity to deliver large audiences with clearly identifiable
demographic characteristics which makes sport so attractive to

the television industry. And it is the competition for these audiences in North America that greatly influences the type and format of the televised sports which are shown.

However, there is a wide variety of compounding factors involved in the production of sport for television. For example, available technologies, working conditions of technical personnel, technological limitations of equipment, and social backgrounds of commentators all create a more immediate context of production which requires analysis. Unfortunately, there is a noticeable absence of studies which have considered this aspect of the production of sport for television in any detail. Most of the work has been British and many of these studies have been influenced by similar investigations into the production of television news. One particular series of studies which has received considerable attention in British media research has been the Glasgow University Media Group's ongoing work *Bad News* (1976), *More Bad News* (1980), and *War and Peace News* (1985).

In its investigations, the Media Group carefully documented the production of British newscasts. As the Group itself asserted:

> Our argument in *Bad News*, Volume 1 of this study, was that routine news practices led to the production of bad news. For example, viewers were given a misleading portrayal of industrial disputes in the UK when measured against the independent reality of events. They were given restricted accounts and somewhat one-sided evaluations of such events. In general we examined the routine practices of television news production as they appeared on the screen. (Glasgow University Media Group, 1980:3)

The parallel between how news is produced for television and the production of televised sport is closer than one might initially imagine. For example, journalists of both television news and sports broadcasts give the impression that what they are presenting is neutral and objective. They are simply showing the audience "how it is." Of course, with its many replays, slow-motion sequences, pre- and post-game analyses, television sport admits to a high level of mediation. Yet, underlying a surface acknowledgement of the importance of production techniques to define and frame events is the suggestion that, as in watching a newscast, one is witnessing a "real event." Other comparisons between sports coverage and news coverage include the fact that the two branches of television programming use similar equipment and technologies, and are geared towards coverage in often difficult outdoor locations. Furthermore, there appears to be a notable similarity in the working environment, job pressures, and professional ideology of production personnel in the two settings.

Bad News is one of the first detailed studies of how the production of news is shaped or contoured which has not regressed into a conspiratorial type of analysis. Instead of pursuing the view that the news is unequivocally biased and manipulative, the Glasgow Group delves into the complex and contradictory ways by which the news is limited in and through its production. Emphasis is placed on the structure of the newsroom itself, the physical environment, the organization of authority, and the day-to-day routines experienced by journalists. In other words, an attempt is made to link *ways of seeing* to a political economy of the newsroom in terms of broader forms of social and cultural organization.

Yet, while *Bad News* provides some important guidelines and reference points for the study of television in general, many of the categories used by the Glasgow Media Group require considerable modification and reformulation for the study of sports broadcasts. Most notably, the Glasgow Group's analysis tends to discuss sport *within* news broadcasts but does not deal with it independently. Furthermore, the Glasgow Group tends to be insufficiently sensitive to historical factors influencing television production and the Group often uses content-analytic techniques that are not readily transferable to the analysis of connotative codes.

Such caveats notwithstanding, close links between studying the production of sport for television and the general objectives pursued in *Bad News* can be seen. Both begin with the premise that television modifies and (re)presents social reality as something that is natural. In this sense, the sports researcher's primary objectives can be stated as follows: (1) to analyse sport on television in order to come to grips with how, and in what ways, games have been transformed through their association with television, and (2) to assess, through an examination of the particular images and codes produced in sports broadcasts, the implications for the broader social and political significance of sport in modern life.

The paucity of research into the production of sport for television is closely linked to the conventional wisdom which suggests that sport is somehow separate or different from the "real" world and consequently that the images and representations produced by televised sport are trivial, natural, or separate from other news items. The Glasgow Group believes that it is important to analyse the ways in which television (re)presents live events. This point has even greater significance in light of a comment made by the Glasgow Media Group (1976:26): "Only sports, political speeches, and other events deemed important enough to warrant the use of the Outside Broadcast Unit which then broadcasts live into a bulletin can be seen as they happen." The Media Group is not implying here that sport is presented in a completely objective way by television. All televised sports events, for example, are filmed from a particular location in the stands, using certain technical conventions, and they are framed and structured by commentary and narrative.

Perhaps even more important is the degree to which the apparent innocence of sport provides a significant site for the construction of myth and ideology (see Hargreaves, 1982b, and Gruneau, 1983). With sport's seemingly "neutral" emphasis on the body, and supposedly equal conditions for competition and possibilities for success based on merit (Baron de Coubertin, the founder of the modern Olympics, used to refer to sport as "the democracy of ability"), the rhetoric of sport contains a powerful tendency to represent particular objects and social relations in ways that mask their socially constructed character. This has the result of "naturalizing" particular meanings and social relations of sports practice. Socially constituted and culturally specific meanings and relations are thus presented as natural and universal. For example, professional hockey which is seen on television is considered to be the definitive form of the game, rather than the pick-up game that occurs on outdoor rinks across Canada.

Such ideological resonances do not reside "within" sport itself so much as within the dominant structures which define and organize sports practice and in dominant practices and structures of representation. Thus, the argument returns to the impact of the television medium in giving preference to these dominant modes. As the most important and influential contemporary communicator of sport, television serves to "naturalize" these myths about sport. It is useful, therefore, to consider several studies to illustrate how, through the production process, the manufacturing of consent and the naturalizing of sports myths occur.

The Production of Sport for Television: Recent Cultural Studies Research

The British Film Institute (BFI) monograph *Football on Television* (1975) forms an important watershed in production research both in the scope of the study — it included chapters on the program guides as well as the television production — and in its seriousness. As the general editor Edward Buscombe noted, prior to the BFI monograph, there were few attempts to critically examine sport in television. In their analysis of the 1974 World Cup, Buscombe and his associates focused their attention on the general assumption that television merely recorded sports events.

Peters' *Television Coverage of Sport* is also a serious attempt "to investigate the various ways in which the media, particularly the visual side of television, present sport" (1976:1). Like the authors of *Football on Television*, Peters concentrated on a high-level sports event, the 1976 Summer and Winter Olympics. In fact, it has been a common practice to concentrate on major sports competition, because these are acknowledged as important television "events." Certainly Colley and Davies (1981) and Whannel (1981) follow this general trend. The former investigate the 1981 Football Association (F.A.) Cup final, while the latter is concerned with the British coverage of the 1980 Moscow Olympic Games.

As a general introduction to their sport case studies, the authors pay particular attention to the assumption that television merely presents a "live" event. In so doing, their reports closely parallel the Glasgow University Media Group's investigation of the news. Just as the latter revealed how the news broadcast was selective, so too the sport studies note the mediation by television. The premise developed by the authors argues that one structure (sport) with its particular form and pattern, when combined with another (television) with a decidedly different form and pattern, will produce a third structure (*sport in television*). The research then sets out to demonstrate how this occurs.

Peters (1976:5) tends to concentrate on the technical limitations which dispel the myth about "live" televised events. He notes the capabilities and distortions which occur with the standard television cameras, their placement, and the use of different lenses ("wide-angle lenses have a tendency to exaggerate distance and to curve straight lines as well as to make parallel lines converge"). Further, the majority of televised sport follows the conventions of classic film in employing the 180-degree rule, which dictates that, if people are placed opposite each other and the camera is showing them from one side, the director may not cut to a shot showing the characters from the opposite side. In addition, the objective of the producer is to use the equipment in such a way that, through a set pattern of camera angles, variety of shots (long, medium, close-up), and the strategic placement of the cameras, the television coverage offers the producer's idea of the experience of the ideal on-site spectator.

Peters (1976) suggests that this creates a kind of verisimilitude (that is, the appearance of truth or reality). In fact, the viewer experiences what no on-site spectator can see — the combination of images produced by camera cuts, variety of shots, and angles of shooting. Nevertheless, these images are edited in such a way that the transition from one camera to another, from one shot type to another, appears "natural." The instances in which the camera is seen to "intrude" are kept to a minimum; and when the camera does intrude (for example, during the 30-second commercial breaks), the viewer "learns" that nothing important is happening at the sports site anyway.

If the research did nothing more than note the technical constraints which exist in television production, it would dispel considerably the myth that the medium is somehow a window on the objective world. But, as Whannel (1981:1) notes, every production consists of much more than actual event coverage. There is pre-planned studio material ("opening and closing title sequences, introductions and links, interviews, results and statistics, preview and postmortem discussions") which frames the actual event and places it in a particular context. This studio material may even include editorial decisions made by other media (newspapers, magazines) as to what is important (Buscombe, 1975:8–15). The importance of this material cannot be underestimated. It serves to transform the visual into a dramatic story to which the audience is invited to "attach" itself (Whannel, 1984). The predominant theme worked out in the production is "who will win?" In posing this initial enigma, the production can then progress towards a resolution. Whannel notes (1981:6):

> So as not to answer the question too soon, a number of strategies are adopted (by the producers and commentators). The most relevant . . . are constant reformulation of the question (based on game events), the promise that there will be an answer, and the provision of a partial answer.

Yet, in working out this resolution, the television producer utilizes highly selective techniques and particular forms of narrative. These all tend to reaffirm for the viewer that what is being presented are natural and universally accepted notions of what constitutes sport.

Whannel (1981, 1984) has attempted to demonstrate how this process of selection serves to organize and to give coherence to the world. This affirmation includes at least four aspects of television production:

> First, hierarchisation, the process of signalling that some things are more important than others. Second, personalisation, the presentation of events from an individualised perspective. Third, narrative, the telling of the events in the form of stories. Fourth, the placing of events in the context of frames of reference. (Whannel, 1981:2)

Examples from televised sport illustrate how each of the aspects serves to contour the sports production so that the viewer receives a highly specific package.

1. *Hierarchy*. Hierarchies in the production occur on two levels: the actual sport which is selected for television, and those priorities which are made within the contest itself. It should come as no surprise that Canadian English-language television coverage of sport concentrates on male, professional, team games (Cantelon and Gruneau, 1984). The wider implication for such priorities is that the viewer "learns" that one gender is more important than the other, or that particular events or games are more crucial than others. In other words, a social value is appended to a particular choice of coverage. An illustration of this is perhaps appropriate here. As already noted, "Hockey Night in Canada" is a long-standing popular television production. Certainly the cultural importance of the sport in Canada warrants its selection as an obvious choice to be televised. But what form of the game do we see on television? We see the highly competitive game played by the most technically skilled and physically capable males. Yet, the forms of hockey most played in Canada would in no way match that seen on television. Hockey played by professionals has been naturalized as "the" form of the game. Any other form (pick-up games in the park, those played by females or youths) may appear on television, but the established hierarchy implies that they are less important.

This hierarchy is evident in the research being discussed here. Peters' (1976) coverage of the 1976 Olympic Games led him to some revealing conclusions. He noted, for example, that the scientific training regimes and pursuit of quantifiable goals which characterize contemporary sport have resulted in longer schedules for even the recreationally oriented participant. Yet one gets the impression that sports are still seasonal (hockey is played in winter, for example) because they are covered in a seasonal fashion by television. Further, along with the selection of sports for television there is the ranking of particular fixtures for coverage. Track and field in the 1976 Olympics received much more coverage than other track meets, even though the latter may have had their share of successful world record efforts. Peters' observations led him to assert:

> Such events (the Olympics) are seen to be the apex of the various sports or the one occasion when those not normally bothered about sport join forces with the fanatics to share in a common cultural experience. (Peters, 1976:6)

The television production, in other words, suggests to the viewer that this is important. It is part of a universal notion of sport and of history. This is powerfully demonstrated by Colley and Davies (1981) in their analysis of the F.A. Cup final. The pre-game build-up included the following report:

> ... in 1928 Blackburn Rovers surprised Wembley by beating the then omnipotent Huddersfield — and women were enfranchised. In 1936 Ted Drake scored the only goal for Arsenal against Sheffield United — and Edward Fox gave up his throne. In 1939 an unfancied Portsmouth side routed a nerve-racked Wolverhampton 4-1; something else happened that year but it does not readily come to mind. (Colley and Davies, 1981:7–8)

Although facetious, it does suggest the powerful hierarchies that are recognized in televised sport selection, and the rightful place in history of the sport which is selected.

But hierarchies are also evident *within* the game. Again Peters (1976) notes that, despite the fact that the first week of the Montreal Games was taken up with gymnastics competition, the commentary emphasized the importance of track and field. Even though the BBC covered over twenty different sports during the Olympics it was obvious, from a close reading of the audio and visual codes, that it was track and field (and particular events within the sport) which was favoured with greater exposure. Like Peters, Whannel discovered a clear-cut intra-sport hierarchy. He noted the obvious dominant coverage awarded to the two British runners, Sebastian Coe and Steve Ovett. Although readily admitting that theirs was a good story —

> After all, Coe and Ovett are two of the most successful British athletes ever, they were currently world record holders in their main events, and almost unprecedently joint holders of the 1500 metres world record. They had virtually never raced each other and were to meet in both the 800 metres and the 1500 metres in the world's premier event, the Olympic Games. (Whannel, 1981:8)

— Whannel notes that the BBC's acceptance of Coe and Ovett as the dominant story was not simply natural. The choice was rooted in cultural assumptions about what makes "good" television for the British audience. Coe and Ovett meet the criteria of quantifiable excellence. They hold world records. The Olympic Games is the showcase competition in which such excellence is to be proven. Both runners are British, male, and, as Peters discovered, compete in the Olympic sport most covered by British television. Finally, the long tradition and success of middle-distance running in Britain favours particular distances as "the blue ribbon events." In short, the specific hierarchy of television coverage is clear.

2. *Personalization*. In North America, just as there is a strong assumption that television "tells it like it is," there is an equally strong suggestion that the focus on the individual is "good" television. Certainly this is the conclusion reached by British authorities when comparing "their" coverage of World Cup soccer to that of the West Germans (Buscombe, 1975:47–53). The "personality-centred" British producers were lauded for "the enormous technical virtuosity" which could not be bettered. Whannel (1981) has described this particular approach as the personalization process. It includes the tendency to focus on the individual, even within a team structure. It entails the finding and subsequent coverage of one or two "heroes." Interestingly, in Canadian English-language television coverage, the superimposed statistics and notes about performers are called "hero notes." The studio material is utilized to predict possible candidates for the hero role while the actual game conditions prove or disprove the prediction.

Such orchestrated studio material requires the services of an expert for commentary and discussion. This personalization has been a major approach of Canadian television since the early 1960s. A 1965 article in *Maclean's* quotes Len Casey, executive producer of CBC sports, as saying that sports programming in Canada "should be revolutionized." Part of this revolution would be the incorporation of a new "breed" of sportscaster who was *knowledgeable* about sport, *presentable*, and able to *articulate* his (and occasionally her) knowledge of the event. More important, the sportscaster had to incorporate an experienced expert (usually a former athlete) into the role of "colourman" (Cantelon and Gruneau, 1984).

Individualization was strikingly apparent in the British studies. Buscombe's (1975) experience was that British experts were openly critical of the West German team-oriented visuals as crude, archaic sports coverage. Peters (1976:13) noted the placement of cameras, strategically located so that the audience would experience the fairness of competition (the start of the race) but, above all, participate in the triumph of the individual ("The winner of a race, the gold medalist, after breaking through the tape, could often be seen vignetted in the surround of a crowd shot"). As already noted (Whannel, 1981), the 1980 Olympic coverage was dominated by Coe and Ovett, as if they epitomized Olympic competition. But even in the Colley/Davies coverage of the F.A. Cup, an obvious team game, there was an individual fetish. Goals, controversial decisions, or unusual incidents were always covered from the perspective of the individual.

3. *The narrative.* Although there have been attempts to televise sport with no audio portion other than that rising from the contest itself (crowd noise, player and coach exhortations, etc.), these have noticeably failed. As already noted, the right verbal cues can turn a one-sided contest into an exciting spectacle. Also, many sports require the narrative to realize their potential as television events. For example, the delineation between play and non-play segments varies considerably between hockey and football. Hockey action often continues for over thirty seconds before a break in game action while, in football, periods of action are shorter (usually under eight seconds from snap of ball to the tackle). Consequently, hockey, with its more continuous action, conceivably could utilize less narrative than football in order to hold an audience (Cantelon and Gruneau, 1984). Sports such as downhill skiing are disadvantaged without narrative, however, because of the nature of the event and the similarity of equipment worn by each competitor. The narrative informs the audience whom it is to watch.

Alpine skiing is also a good illustration of how the theme question "who will win?" is posed. The narrative typifies the particular verbal codes which produce a selective image of sport. Anyone who has actually witnessed a World Cup downhill competition realizes the difficulty in (a) identifying individual competitors, and (b) actually knowing who has the best runs. These difficulties are inherent in the nature of the sport. Competitors wear similar helmets and wind-resistant ski suits and are often sponsored by the same commercial enterprise, and the speeds reached all but rule out catching glimpses of insignia identifying competitors as Austrian, Canadian, Swiss, etc. In short, the narrative is essential for televised ski-racing.

In posing the theme, the narrative builds on the hierarchization and personalization aspects to create a particular story.

Peters' (1976) analysis of the 90-metre ski jump competition at the 1976 Winter Olympics illustrates both. The commentary included verbal "masks" with which the audience identified the competitors: "Here comes the truck driver from Ohio"; "the New Zealander who's only got one eye"; "last year's World Record Holder"; "the 1972 Olympic Runner Up Champion." The audience also receives a brief personal vignette of the competitors which underpins the promise that even truck drivers or one-eyed New Zealanders might compete for (and win) an Olympic Gold Medal. However, spectators are especially encouraged to watch those who have proven their athletic excellence in past years.

Narrative is essential to win and hold the audience, but it need not necessarily focus on the athletic prowess of the competition. The 1981 F.A. Cup final included a wide selection of "humanizing" dialogue, about the height and weight of the players and their occupations away from football, as well as "inside" gossip about nicknames, personal quirks, and superstitions. But the authors note, "the players' wives shown in long shot as a collection of look-alike Cindy dolls, were not permitted to attain this doorstep of humanity" (Colley and Davies, 1981:8). Nor are such pronouncements unique. The objective is to teach the marginal viewer, who is attracted by the expert's explanation of what is happening, that "anyone" can compete and that stereotypically attractive women do continue to watch "their men" play the game.

4. *Placing the event in a broad frame of reference.* The final aspect which Whannel (1981) has identified is, as argued earlier, a necessary step in linking the production of sport to wider issues of political economy. When commentators talk about "our" competitors, "an honest footballer," "mother of two," and so on, they are clearly preferring dominant notions of nationhood, the family, and appropriate social values within the citizenry (see Clarke and Clarke, 1982). In the authors' view it is this final aspect which needs further development. The only quarrel one might have with the analyses cited in this chapter is that they do not sufficiently pursue the ideological and political implications of the specific production of televised sport. What kind of an image does narrative help to consolidate? How is sport naturalized and dehistoricized by the telling of particular types of stories? What kind of hero is created by television's narrative structures? How do hierarchy and personalization dramatize the ideology of meritocracy? These are all questions that need to be answered more fully.

Concluding Comments

Culture is a process created in the context of enabling and constraining structures. These structures operate through the differential (unequal) capacities possessed by some groups and classes to effectively define the rules which govern political and legal processes, economic relations, and cultural production, within the scope of limited access to particular resources. It is not simply that television is biased. Rather, various constraints built into television's multiple contexts of production and consumption work to create some images and meanings and not others. This occurs in ways that mask the process of preferred selection, so that television transmission appears "objective." These constraints occur at all levels and, in the particular case of television, include professional ideologies, work practices, editing routines, technological developments, and various combinations of wider social and political forces.

An image, and the codes underlying its production, can work either for or against particular groups in society. It can work for those in power by masking fundamental contradictions and problems and by favouring dominant meanings in social life. Images become ideological by either naturalizing or dehistoricizing cultural forms and their relationships with other forms and broader social formations. On the other hand, images often have their ideological character undermined because (a) the encoding of a message or sign is not a determined process but indeed is often an unconscious phenomenon (Nichols, 1981:26), and (b) audiences are often able to reject or ignore the encoded message. The television images which represent western sports forms are often shot through with contradictions. They celebrate heroic qualities of human endeavour that have little to do with commerce and the dominant culture. But they do so in ways that naturalize the current dominant social definition of sport. Understanding how this occurs necessarily involves analysis of the changing production and coding of images on television, and such analysis must always be closely tied in with the politics of audience consumption and the political economy of mass communications.

Suggested Readings

There is a substantial body of media studies literature dealing with many aspects of popular entertainment. Ed Buscombe (Ed.) (1975), *Football on Television*, British Film Institute, is interesting as one of the first attempts to look at the production of sport for television. For an analysis of the relationship between televised sport and ideology, see Alan Clarke and John Clarke (1982), "Highlights and Action Replays — Ideology, Sport and the Media," in Jennifer Hargreaves (Ed.), *Sport, Culture and Ideology*, Routledge & Kegan Paul. Susan Birrell and John Loy (1981) utilize a model based on Marshall McLuhan's theory of media in "Media Sport: Hot and Cool," in John Loy et al. (Eds.), *Sport, Culture and Society*, Philadelphia, Lea & Febiger.

Chapter Ten
Active Women, Media Representations, and Ideology

Margaret MacNeill

"Four, three, two, one . . . and take it to the right, left, right, left . . . ooouh you're lookin' good." Across North America, millions stretch and bounce to the tune of the *20 Minute Workout*. Now switch the channel to CBC; *Sportsweekend* is covering the 1985 Women's World Bodybuilding Championships. Someone in the audience yells, "Hey, where's the beef?" Then the hooting and whistling begins. How different are the oiled bikini-clad bodybuilders from the aerobic dancers in high-cut leotards? Are these images progressive or do they stereotype female activity? Initial conceptions of active leisure pursuits often locate aerobics within a "female" realm of activity while placing bodybuilding within a "male" sphere. These arbitrarily defined boundaries between "male" and "female" activities are cultural constructs.

Since the 1970s, growing numbers of women have been attempting to liberate themselves through physical activity. Some would argue that this expansion is primarily individual and has led to changing ideas of femininity. Others would argue that the movement can be attributed to larger social forces. For example, the fashion industry foresaw the potential of increased profits by developing a line of women's sportswear. Entrepreneurs soon realized the business opportunities in women's fitness clubs and other services. The federal government also had an interest in promoting physical activity; its Participaction campaign was aimed at reducing health-care costs and improving the productivity levels of the Canadian work force (Labonté, 1982).

The (re)production of these structural considerations through the mass media, specifically televisual representations,

is the central focus of this discussion of active women, media representations, and ideology. An episode of the *20 Minute Workout*
and *Sportsweekend*'s coverage of the 1985 Women's World Bodybuilding Championships are examined in order to investigate the
changing patterns of female physical activity. The discussion
locates both aerobics and bodybuilding within the locus of
dominant hegemonic relations and ideologies.

Ideology and Hegemonic Relations

The concept of hegemony allows one to examine agency-structural
ties with specific attention to the linking of work and leisure
spheres. What women do in their free time, and the media representations of this activity, cannot be examined independently of
the external constraints that direct individuals into various patterns of social organization; reciprocally, one must not ignore the
capacity of human agency to create change.

Hegemonic relations are so effective because they are
legitimated; moreover, they are not based on economic considerations alone — moral, political, and intellectual power are vital
determinants as well (Mouffe, 1979:183). Hegemonic power so
saturates the common-sense reality of humans that people rarely
act or think in ways alternative to those that are legitimated. In
other words, in their lives, people operate within a relatively
narrow range of practices and beliefs. Alternatives to this range
are either never considered or dismissed as inappropriate, that
is, they are marginalized. Hegemonic relations are thus "silently"
maintained without coercion.

For instance, the everyday practice of sending young girls
to figure-skating lessons while their brothers go to arenas to play
hockey is an example of hegemonic relations. Without ever being
taught or told, children learn that certain activities are more
appropriate for girls and others are more suitable for boys.

One should not equate hegemony with the absence of
change, however. Hegemonic relations are dynamic in that they
must be continually reaffirmed and renegotiated. Without this
dynamic component, relationships would remain static. We know
that some young girls play hockey and that some boys figure skate.
This dynamic nature of hegemony is described by Raymond
Williams (1980) as a residual/dominant/emergent set of tensions
(see Gruneau's discussion in Chapter One).

The role of human agency is important in the residual/ emergent areas to initiate change. For example, although active leisure for most women was unthinkable in 1886 and was a counterhegemonic (or emergent) practice for those few women who were active, in 1986 such activity was more acceptable. This acceptance of particular forms of female physical activity (such as aerobic classes) is now being challenged by the women's body-building subculture. The emergent notion of the muscular female image is being negotiated in many ways. What is "appropriate" female muscularity? How can bodybuilding competitions, which were an exclusively male domain, be feminized? How can activity be best marketed? All these emergent views are challenging the dominant notions of what is proper female activity.

Sports hegemony in Canada includes specific socialization practices. Although there are obvious differences between individual families in the upbringing of their children, Canadian families have much in common, including notions that result in, reflect, and maintain *gender* stratification. Residual patriarchal ideologies concerning the "inferiority" of feminine practices seem to be at the basis of female socialization.

Research concerning female physical activity often uncovers gender differences in game and sport orientation due to polarized socialization processes for males and females. Further, the history of female opportunities is one of expansion and contraction. For example, in the "Golden Era" of women's sport between the two World Wars, women were indispensable for wartime industry. Attitudes became more liberal and women moved into essential jobs and expanded their leisure opportunities as well. However, attitudes can be just as quickly reversed and the longer history of women's oppression has been accompanied by the channelling of women into expressive, aesthetically pleasing sports such as gymnastics, dance, and figure skating (Cochrane et al., 1977). Duquin (1978) and Hall (1982) note that boys are socialized into *instrumental* activities that teach qualities such as competitiveness, teamwork, and co-operation to aid their later integration into the labour force. Boutilier and San-Giovanni (1983) similarly argue that females are inadequately socialized into sports roles, since the institution of sport in Canadian society embodies the "masculine" values of hard work, competition, and deferred gratification. Sports behaviours are therefore defined as male gender roles.

Socializing women into selective roles in active leisure serves to legitimate the dominant ideology of patriarchy, that is, the system of power relations based on male domination. The problem for women in assuming healthy athletic roles is based on the cultural definitions of the masculine/feminine dichotomy. Aggressive and competitive patterns of behaviour learned through play are considered appropriate for males and inappropriate for females (Hall, 1982). Most sports, therefore, offer few positive status or prestige incentives for females. To socialize girls and women into a wider spectrum of play, games, and sport, a redefinition of the positive aspects of masculine/feminine and athletic traits into *androgynous* traits (that is, neither male nor female) needs to be accepted (Hall, 1981, 1982).

The degree of self-expression located in media representations of active women provides clues to the extent of patriarchal ideology. The next question to be addressed is: how is the dominant ideology reaffirmed through the medium of television?

Active Women on Television

Sportsweekend's televised presentation of the Women's World Bodybuilding Championships and Orion Entertainment's *20 Minute Workout* are, first and foremost, productions constructed by humans. In order to understand how the dominant ideology is reaffirmed through television the theory of semiology must be briefly considered. Specifically, it is necessary to discuss three terms: the signifier, the signified, and the sign. At every level of understanding, semiologists argue, there are signifiers (a physical form) and a signified (the meaning attached to the signifier), which together create a sign. Through the examination of both levels, the physical form and the meaning can be distinguished from each other to display the conventionality of human communication.

For example, the letters w, n, o, a, m are physical forms (the signifiers). Arranged in a particular way they become signified to represent (in the English language) the sign for woman. By combining the physical forms in this particular way, an item of knowledge is denoted. But the sign carries with it a cultural meaning as well as a representational one. The sign "woman" also involves cultural images of what a woman is, what she does, how she looks, etc. Thus a television image of a woman engaged in physical activity may embody the notion of femininity if she is an aerobic dancer, or masculinity if she is a bodybuilder.

The following analysis will deal with two basic categories of communicative modes: visual and auditory signs. For research purposes it is possible to separate the former from the latter but it should be noted that both modes of representation are broadcast simultaneously, and for the most part are received by the audience as a package. However, from this artificial separation, a series of subcategories of popular production techniques emerges. Among the visual signs which could be examined (camera angle, framing, scan and zoom, focus, dissolves and wipes, special effects, lighting, background, body language), only some have been singled out for analysis. A similar selection has been made from the numerous auditory signs (auditory noise, music, commentator's verbal speech, and instructors'/competitors' verbal speech). Those which have been selected provide a good illustration of how the cultural meanings of active women are constructed.

Visual Signs

The Camera Angle
The camera angle is a common method of lending a particular meaning to the visual. In the *20 Minute Workout*, the models are surveyed from all angles except directly underneath. In the episode examined, 18.28 per cent of the 257 shots were aerial. This highly distortive angle of aerobic movements accentuates "cleavage" shots of the women, in their low-cut leotards, exercising on a rotating stage. The limb movement of criss-crossing arms and the spinning bodies arranged in various line and triangle formations create an interesting human kaleidoscope for the viewer but do not permit the audience to perform aerobics with ease. To maximize participation the camera should be directly aimed at the instructors, thus providing a standard frame of reference for the active viewer. This direct vantage point was displayed in only 36.63 per cent of the shots. The majority of the shots, 47.08 per cent, were from an upwardly tilting angle, usually whenever the women were bent over from the waist. In addition, the cutting rhythm of these shots increased in speed. Thus, the predominance of aerial and upwardly tilting camera angles helps create sexual images rather than images of physical activity.

Sportsweekend's production of the Women's World Bodybuilding Championships employs a very different distribution of angles. Of the 69 shots from the routines, 76.6 per cent displayed the bodybuilders through a non-tilted camera. Downwardly tilted shots from behind the stage curtains accounted for 25.37 per cent, and 11.94 per cent of the shots tilted up from the side stage exit. These side stage angles are employed occasionally to capture the entrance and exit expressions of the competitors, and to permit the television audience to closely survey their bodies. Downward tilts from behind the stage are used sparingly. The direct angle is the simplest angle to capture the event without having to contend with other extraneous factors. It allows an audience that is unfamiliar with the sport to view female bodybuilders with little angular distortion; as well, it accentuates the physical rather than the sexual.

The Framing of the Image

The framing of aerobic images differs significantly from that of women's bodybuilding. The camera determines the borders of the image seen by the viewer. For the most part, the bodies of the instructors from the *20 Minute Workout* are fragmented. Rather than capturing complete visual images of the whole body in exercise, 62.75 per cent of all shots, in the episode examined, were close-ups and medium shots (half body). Predominantly, the midsection (hips, thighs, buttocks) was centred on the screen. The tendency to focus on this part of the anatomy further objectifies an image of the "sexually active" female body.

Conversely, the camera coverage of women's bodybuilding frames the entire body of the competitors for most of the show. Since bodybuilders often flex muscle groups in the lower and upper body concurrently, and since sports broadcasting has not yet standardized the presentation of the new sport of women's bodybuilding, the long shot framing is more appropriate. In total, 37.25 per cent of the shots were framed as long shots, 32.39 per cent as medium. Close-ups of facial features during pre-taped personal interviews with the competitors accounted for the remaining 30.36 per cent of the framing. Overall, the sexually oriented (some would say pornographic) nature of the *20 Minute Workout* is absent in the coverage of bodybuilding. The objectification and orientation, in a sexual way, of the female bodybuilder is largely the product of the judging criteria, the women's posing, and the verbal analysis by the commentators.

Camera Techniques

The use of scan and zoom is common to both the body-building competition and the *20 Minute Workout*. However, like the camera angles, their use denotes disparate images of women. In the bodybuilding competition the zoom is used most often to focus on the poses that display back muscularity and during the final "posedown." In the *20 Minute Workout*, a disorienting zoom and scan occurs continuously. In fact, 32.79 per cent of all aerobic shots zoomed in or out. In addition, the audience is titillated by the constant visual caressing of the female body created by the rotating stage and camera angles.

Like the camera angle and the zoom and scan, the use of the focus transmits a very clearly defined image. In the "cooldown" section of the *20 Minute Workout* the softly focused women wiggle their hips, sway their arms overhead, and look "groggy-eyed" to intensify the significations of sensuality. The bodybuilders, always in sharp focus while performing on stage, are softly focused during interviews, when the women are carefully "made-up" with cosmetics. The other exception to the bodybuilding sharp focus occurs in brief shots of the women "psyching up" in the "pump-room," which create the illusion that the audience is quietly intruding on this preparation.

Body Language

Body language (locomotion patterns, stances, gestures, and facial expressions) is created by the aerobic instructors and the bodybuilding competitors themselves. The sexually oriented physical gestures in both cases are projected towards the television audience only. The only connections made to other women in either aerobics or bodybuilding are externally constructed by the television viewer or the judges' narrative.

Although it is the women who position and manoeuvre themselves on stage, their choices of body language are not absolutely "free" choices. The locomotion patterns of both activities are founded in dance. The *20 Minute Workout* is choreographed by the lead instructor Bess Motta, with every episode following the same repertoire. Instructors of fitness classes across North America are quickly adopting this procedure, thus presuming that dance is the basis of aerobics. Similarly, although the bodybuilding poses are borrowed from the male counterpart and carry the muscular/masculine connotations with them, female competitors must include a dance transition between poses. These transitions tend to blur muscular definition.

The sexual stances and wiggles help to sell aerobics and bodybuilding to particular audiences. Through the choreography and the directions of the production crew, the aerobic instructors are positioned within an eighteen-inch range (defined as intimate in kinesic theory). In some instances, they are positioned so closely that their legs overlap in the open-legged stances and their buttocks touch in bent-over triangle formation, though there is sufficient room on the stage to space the women further apart. The proximity of the women, the erotic pulsing, and the arched backs unobtrusively sell sex appeal rather than fitness development. The bodybuilding poses separated by dance transitions are also sexualized through bodywaves, arched backs, hand movements, and constant wiggling.

Finally, the facial expressions in these productions are a further visual portrayal of feminine sexuality. While active men in televised sports are usually presented in a serious aggressive manner, women in both aerobics and bodybuilding smile, kiss the camera, and create seductive looks. This sexualization of women's physical activities through the choice of certain signs forces a closure on other possible definitions of female athleticism and activity.

Auditory Signs

As noted above, the auditory signs (music, verbal commentary), along with the visual, are important carriers of dominant ideologies.

The Use of Music
The "female" activities of aerobics and bodybuilding, with their underlying dance orientation, are always performed to pre-recorded popular music. During the *20 Minute Workout* the movements co-ordinate exactly with musical phrases. In the dynamic cardio-vascular section, the music is fast and loud to complement the happy faces and energetic actions of the women. Later, in the cool-down, the music softens in volume and tone to relax participants and enhance the sexual hip sways. The bodybuilders also choreograph their routines to match the style and phrasing of the music. The main difference between the effects of the music in the two shows is that the aerobic instructors talk exactly to the 4/4 beat in a choppy monosyllabic fashion, whereas the verbal

commentary of bodybuilding follows the rhythms of normal sentence flow more closely.

The Commentary

The primary role of the commentators is auditory rather than visual. It is their job to introduce the show, describe the activities to educate the audience, provide technical facts concerning fitness or bodybuilding judging criteria, and conclude the show. An important aspect of this narration is the personalization of the show; the commentators talk to "you" rather than "everyone."

Aerobic participants are told "you want to look good so com'on let's see you move." The female bodybuilding commentator looks directly at the viewer and suggests that "maybe in five years you'll find yourself on the bodybuilding stage." During the *20 Minute Workout* the commentator is never seen. She is an outside authority whose every word is simultaneously reinforced by written graphics across the screen. Her clear enunciation and correct sentence structure starkly contrast with the blurred tones and choppy speech rhythms of the models leading the class.

Because *Sportsweekend* is presented as a live event, the commentators are rarely seen during the performance. They make their appearances before, between, and after major segments to analyse and discuss the proceedings. Carla Dunlap, the "expert colour commentator" by virtue of her three-time world bodybuilding championship record, supplements her "inside scoop" on what it is like to compete with technical knowledge about women's bodybuilding. This knowledge confirms her presence as the authority and allows Vic Rauter, the co-commentator, to ask Dunlap those questions "we all have": "Is this a show or a sport?"; "Do these women have to be feminine?" Vic Rauter plays the role of student; he goes on a learning experience with the audience in viewing women who are muscular. The voice-overs are positive but the audience never sees Rauter's actual facial expressions and reactions to the women as they compete. He appears only in the pre-taped segments in which he asks Dunlap the aforementioned general questions.

Again, it is important to reiterate that members of the audience individually interpret the images of aerobic dancers and bodybuilders. However, it can be argued that the structured verbal mediation also affects the audience's reception of female activity. Whereas the aerobics commentary is presented as factual, the bodybuilding expert is required to defend the activity. In other words, the hegemony of patriarchy intervenes in the auditory encoding of "muscular" women. Aerobic dancers reaffirm their femininity, their sexual attractiveness to men; the muscular frame of the bodybuilder is still an area of contestation.

The television viewer is not permitted to individually decide his or her feelings towards this new active image. Decisions are made within the constraints of patriarchy. For example, the eventual winner of the bodybuilding competition, Mary Roberts, is confirmed as a woman as well as a bodybuilding competitor. Rauter mentions that she is a mother, while Dunlap responds, "See, women can have children and still look this good." This exchange guides the audience's interpretation of the image. Rather than concentrating on her muscularity, the commentators present Roberts as still being able to fulfil the traditional female sex and gender roles. Four of the five finalists are congratulated for "softening" their posing through dance, that is, enhancing their femininity. At the same time as the narrative provides examples of the residual, there are examples of emergent notions of the female image. Rauter notes that Deanna Panting is very "thin in the upper body in comparison to the other competitors." Paradoxically this new image is also situated in the male/female sexual mediation:

> Rauter: "Look at the lats; even I'm getting into this."
> Dunlap: "It's very sexy." (They both chuckle.)
> Rauter: "It's showbiz . . . and a little wave to the crowd,
> and there's her boyfriend."

The viewer "learns" that, like Mary Roberts, Deanna Panting, despite her muscularity, can still attract men.

Discussion

However, the question must still be asked: "to what extent are these activities counterhegemonic or emergent?" In the historical context, both aerobics and bodybuilding are counterhegemonic to the notion that intense physical activity for women is harmful. But, as noted above, hegemonic relations must be continually reaffirmed. As such, these relations vie for supremacy with emergent ideas. In the case of bodybuilding and aerobics, both contain, within their structure, patterns of the dominant, residual, and emergent. They are emergent in that they symbolize the increased opportunities for physical activity which are opening to women. They are also emergent in that physical activity of different sorts (such as bodybuilding) is increasingly seen as a socially accepted part of female social life. On the other hand, aerobics and body-building are also sites of residual and dominant relations in that they reproduce patterns that subjugate women. Physical activity, yes, but in a form that stresses a preoccupation with beauty, glamour, and sex appeal as status symbols. The fitness boom chan-nels women into traditional but revamped areas of "female" public space; simultaneously, the entry of men into aerobics and the possibility of developing men's bodybuilding beyond a few static poses are prevented by these same ideological barriers.

To leave the analysis at this point overemphasizes agencies/individuals making decisions that are either constraining or enabling. It must also be remembered that structure limits those decisions that can be made. Thus, not only is the range of "common-sense" choices a woman considers severely ordered by the "follow-the-leader" style of aerobics or the rule-bound nature of bodybuilding, but it is also limited by wider-reaching structural constraints.

Initially, the contemporary fitness and sport-related activ-ities for women did contain counterhegemonic or emergent impulses. The fitness boom of the 1970s in some ways symbol-ized the radical notion of freedom from the constraints of waged and domestic work, and liberation from sedentary lifestyles. Being physically active was a visible, concrete display of the discontent with the dominant ideology of femininity. Aerobics and, perhaps to a greater extent, bodybuilding are counterhegemonic activities that eventually may emerge as a reaffirmed dominant hegemony. Yet aerobics is also being reintegrated into the dominant patriar-chal and capitalistic modes of life. A greater differentiation from the "norm" is displayed by the female bodybuilders through their musculature and their heavy training program. However, this, too, is not counterhegemonic in the fullest sense because bodybuilders reaffirm their femininity through the dance-like posing and the degree of controlled muscle development. Repeatedly, commen-tator Dunlap mentions how many of the finalists have "softened" their look or style of posing. The less static posing ensures that the viewer does not see the full extent of muscle definition of which the competitors are capable. In other words, the posing ensures that female bodybuilders do not too closely approximate their male counterparts. Furthermore, the judging criteria for "assessing the female physique" state that:

> ... first and foremost, the judge must bear in mind that he or she is judging a woman's bodybuilding competition and is looking for the ideal *feminine* physique. Therefore, the most important aspect is shape, a feminine shape. The other aspects are similar to those described for assessing men, but in regard to muscular development, it must not be carried to excess where it resembles the massive muscularity of the male physique. (my emphasis) (International Federation of Body Building)

The "ideal" feminine shape is rooted in the patriarchal notion of femininity. It ensures that the distance between male and female muscularity is maintained and the continued common-sense notion that men have a greater biological potential for muscularity is continued. Female physicality has been intentionally obscured. More important, the "choices" for bodybuilders are also tied to the structured judging criteria. With rules and subjectivity of judging that deter full muscle development, bodybuilders must balance their training between an adherence to the sport through muscle development, and the demonstration of "female qualities."

While the rules of competition make it clear how limited the choices are for bodybuilders, even more significant is the way dominant power relations reproduce hegemonic knowledge and practices. Consent and loyalty to the common-sense conceptions constrain the degree to which active women can negotiate new forms. Female involvement is a "partial penetration" because it does not threaten the dominant hegemony. In other words, an active and emergent leisure counterculture is gradually stripped of its radical impulses. Moreover, the concessions granted to allow for activity also neutralize the more radical counterhegemonic impulses. The dominant hegemony affirms women's rights to adopt an active lifestyle but within a strict social context. Thus, women move back into positions of inferiority by accepting the common-sense notions of a "female" bodybuilding or by participating in aerobics less for reasons of fitness and personal freedom and more for reasons that reaffirm the patriarchal notions of femininity (i.e., to lose weight, to improve sex appeal). The reattachment of patriarchal values defines aerobics as a "female" activity and consequently not as important as "masculine" leisure; and because it is so popular among women, aerobics marginalizes other active leisure possibilities.

But not only is there conformity in the choice of "appropriate" leisure forms, there is also a conformity in the styles and fashions in which the activity takes place. All over North America, active women are wearing mass-produced bodysuits to aerobic classes taught by instructors who copy the *20 Minute Workout* style of teaching, movements, and fashions. Similarly, bodybuilding is gradually becoming more acceptable as the dance-oriented style of posing becomes more pronounced and the "ideal feminine" shape is mass-marketed as the form of champions. Generally, the styles of both these leisure forms are packaged within the music, the fashions, the gestures, and facial expressions. Through conformity to these patriarchically grounded styles, gender differences are upheld and alternatives are not considered. Even the lead instructor on the *20 Minute Workout* cannot think of any forthcoming changes in aerobics. The only differences between the first and second year of production were stated as "new faces, new music, new colours for the leotards . . . there are not too many ways to make the show different" (Motta, cited in Taylor, 1984). Obviously, ingenuity and imagination have been suppressed during the process of style reification.

The combined influences of media, service, and commodity industries leave little room for personal initiative to mould the styles. These have become quickly institutionalized into hegemonic rituals for women. Ritualization occurs when the articulation of a particular style becomes reified. For example, across North America each episode of the *20 Minute Workout* attracts a million and a half viewers in ritual motion. The show format follows prepackaged standard instructions and motions.

The intent to "feminize" aerobics in the mass media generally is acknowledged by the lead instructor. Bess Motta considers aerobics

> . . . a women's medium because it's soft and very flowing and graceful, and men would look a little klutzy. We could get terrific guys but they'd just look a little funny doing aerobics. (cited in Taylor, 1984)

Because of this ritualization, the presence of aerobics and bodybuilding does not fundamentally reduce the domination of men over women in patriarchal society. Indeed, they complement other roles that are also experienced through femininity. Aerobics and bodybuilding are performed to music in the same way as the "feminine" sports of dance, figure skating, and gymnastics are experienced. Aerobics helps to uphold the feminine values of non-aggressiveness, non-competitiveness, and gracefulness. Thus, the feminine "self" is learned, developed, and personified in aerobics. Bodybuilding develops the feminine "self" in the graceful sexually oriented dance transitions. It is, however, more competitive by the nature of the sport. Also, given the muscular development of the participants, it contains greater capacity to create new definitions of the feminine self.

As already noted, the production of the World Bodybuilding Championships and the *20 Minute Workout* objectifies female instructors and competitors. One of the reasons for the immense popularity of aerobics is that it caters to the voyeur through the sexualization of the images. The earlier textual analysis of the show demonstrated that the *20 Minute Workout* is produced in such a way that it emphasizes the sexual rather than safe and proper exercise. Similarly, the commentators of *Sportsweekend* noted how "sexy" one competitor's back appeared and yet it was later noted that her upper body musculature was underdeveloped in comparison to that of other competitors. Thus, the television viewer is situated in the role of voyeur capable of exerting domination over the image of active women. Women are voyeurs also, looking through "male eyes" to determine what the "ideal" female body is and to rank themselves according to standards set by the media.

It was also noted that, in the *20 Minute Workout*, the female body is constantly objectified into parts. Entire bodies are rarely framed in the *20 Minute Workout*. This tends to fabricate pornographic and erotic myths about how activity is to be experienced, and what an active woman should look like. The instructors are arranged in carefully planned positions that are intended to arouse. There are no fitness purposes being served through lingering "crotch" shots as arm exercises are being performed. The dehumanizing fragmentation of women into sexual objects is a repressive practice which is tied to the commodities market. "Sex" is marketable and promotes both male and female viewer identification with shows. Commercials describe "how to liven up your afternoon with the 'beautiful' instructors on the *20 Minute Workout*" rather than mentioning "fit" or "professional" instructors. Similarly, the closing comment for the bodybuilding championships noted that "one thing we all have to agree on is that those are very nice swimsuits those girls are *almost* wearing."

Unlike that of the aerobics dancers, the objectification of the female bodybuilders also contains a muscularity component. The objectification creates internal contradictions for the women who must display sensuality to be successful while still developing muscularity. To display maximum muscle definition, the women diet to a dangerously low level of body fat. This process, while enhancing muscle definition, tends to eliminate the ideal curves or "female shape" for which the judges must look "first and foremost." To balance muscle and sex appeal, some contenders are undergoing silicone breast implants to artificially meet the criteria. Dunlap is one of the first bodybuilders to publicly admit this. It goes without saying that, like aerobics, the sport does not have a health-oriented or fitness/bodybuilding-oriented base.

Indeed, these leisure activities have become new forms of the traditional beauty contest. The *20 Minute Workout* instructors are paraded on a revolving merry-go-round before the audience. Over the past two years aerobic competitions, such as the popular Etonic National Championships (U.S.A.), Coppertone Tanercise, or Crystal Light Aerobic Championships, have emerged. These competitions are similar to Broadway auditions based on routines consisting of moves such as leaps and gymnastic poses.

Bodybuilders are also paraded before judges and a very critical audience. Mary Roberts eventually won the 1985 World Championships because of her "perfect combination of round, massive, voluptuous muscles, aesthetic symmetry, balanced proportions and exceptionally sharp muscularity" (Reynolds, 1985:179). These activities have become an extension to the traditional feminine preoccupation with beauty; they are a form of cosmetology or "bodywork."

Throughout this chapter it has been argued that leisure is a site of contestation. Women's participation is presenting new ideas of physicality while reaffirming some of the established ones. Although some redefinition always occurs (such as the place of leisure in the female world), it is evident that residual patriarchal notions are difficult to alter.

In addition to the patriarchal infrastructure that objectifies a particular notion of femininity, capitalism plays an important part in the commodification of the feminine style. The range of commodification includes clubs, fitness classes, testing, and active lifestyle counselling. Clothes for aerobic classes, casual wear with the aerobic "look," published materials on the subject (videos, books, periodicals, and records), exercise equipment, and non-related products such as diet aids are all marketed.

Patriarchy is thus reproduced in a newly negotiated form that attracts women to buy the range of narcissistic commodities. This exploits women by creating "needs" that are in reality only wants. Furthermore, the champion bodybuilders and the *20 Minute Workout* instructors are commodities in themselves. They are used to sell boats, condominiums, clothes, and memberships at racquet-ball clubs. Just as female sexuality and glamour help sell physical activity to women, the sexuality and glamour of these active women help to sell unrelated products.

Advertisers gain the consent of particular groups of people by reproducing and legitimizing various ideologies and types of social organization. In particular, advertising is a major impetus in the acceptance of the aerobic ritual and its style as "feminine." Because it reproduces dominant ideologies, there is no need to coerce women into aerobics. Women learn through the narrative of advertising the "appropriate" social behaviour: "develop your figure as it was meant to be — radiant, fit, alluring" . . . "the joy of cooking" . . . "fitness mate" . . . "fit to be eyed" . . . "exercite-ment." Physical activity for women is often associated with diet food and beverages, fashions, and beauty aids, just as alcoholic beverages, cigarettes, cars, and computers are the products asso-ciated with active male leisure activities. Similarly, men learn the vocabulary of physical fitness: "excel in every direction" . . . "win-ning is a state of mind — competitive, determined, first" . . . "game-plan for life." Thus, economic forces suggest the direction of leisure and the degree of control that agents have in producing social transformations.

Conclusions

Media representations of active women, as this case study of aero-bics and women's bodybuilding has shown, are aligned with domi-nant hegemonic relations. While the activities seem divergent because of the nature of aerobics and bodybuilding, they both serve to produce and reproduce images of active women engaged in "feminine" activities. For women to be *active* is an innovative and emergent notion in comparison to earlier periods in Canadian his-tory. However, the alliance of physical activities with motifs of sexualized and feminized participation suggests that the liberating impulses are being reincorporated into residual/dominant hege-monic tendencies. The ideological politics surrounding the pre-sentation of the female body in motion reinforces and perpetuates the patriarchal subordination of women. Thus, patriarchy serves as a major structural determinant of these cultural forms as they develop in North America.

As a critical method for analysing how the mass media orchestrate hegemonic relations, semiology enables us to better understand the various types of signs transmitted to mass audiences by revealing that representations of human social and material life are not neutral or natural. It forces people to question how and what they communicate and suggests the cultural meanings associated with communication. This questioning must necessarily lead to a deeper understanding about how power relations enable us to think, experience, and interact, and how these same relations and practices restrict access to a wider range of possibilities.

Suggested Readings

Two excellent sources dealing with the interrelationship of gender and sport are Mary Boutilier and Luciana SanGiovanni (1983), *The Sporting Woman*, Illinois, Human Kinetics, and Paul Willis (1982), "Women in Sport in Ideology," in Jennifer Hargreaves (Ed.), *Sport, Culture and Ideology*, London, Routledge & Kegan Paul. For literature dealing with television and cultural representations, see John Fiske and John Hartley (1978), *Reading Television*, London, Methuen, and Umberto Eco (1976), "Articulations of the Cinematic Code," in Bill Nichols (Ed.), *Movie and Methods: An Anthology*, Berkeley, University of California Press.

Chapter Eleven
English-Canadian Sports Novels and Cultural Production

Robert G. Hollands

Culture, Cultural Production, and the Novel Form

The successful production of recent journals, such as *Arete: The Journal of Sport Literature*, and the organization of conferences on sports fiction (Jenkins and Green, 1981), point towards a burgeoning interest in the relationship between sport, culture, and literature. While the affiliation between sport and literature is hardly new, it is only recently that this subject has received any serious scholarly attention.

Sports fiction, in conjunction with the production of sport through other media (i.e., television, radio, newspapers, magazines), forms an essential component of our western culture and identity. This chapter will look at the sports novel as a specific form of culture.

The novel is an historical combination of a number of genres, and is also a relatively new cultural phenomenon (Stevick, 1967:1–2). Although numerous attempts have been made to understand the general characteristics of the novel form, little consensus on the exact list of characteristics has been reached. From a sociological standpoint, there are obvious structures inherent in the production of the novel, and in the novel form itself, which obliquely reflect the revolutionary transformation from feudalism to a capitalist mode of production. Swingewood (1975:3–4), for example, has suggested that the industrial middle class, along with its corresponding ideology of individualism, has favoured the notion of the hero in conflict with the social order.

Raymond Williams (1965), in his discussion of "Realism and the Contemporary Novel," has argued that, since 1900, the history of the modern novel can be understood best as an increasing polarization into the social and personal. However, in emphasizing the importance of the individual hero in the novel, it is possible to lose sight of the close interdependence which exists between the individual and society generally. Much earlier, Ralph Fox (1945:37–38), in his book *The Novel and the People*, noted the limitations of the individual/social order separation:

> In short, capitalism, which created realism as a method and gave it its perfect form in the novel, capitalism, which made man the center of art, also in the end destroyed the conditions in which realism can flourish and only permitted man to appear in art, particularly in the novel, in a castrated and perverted form.

In other words, Fox notes the tendency in modern literature to separate or estrange the individual (or in the case of the novel, the hero) from social forces and social structure. The individual, rather than being understood as a social being, is portrayed as an autonomous entity defined solely in terms of personal or biological characteristics.

As well as maintaining the individual/social order connection, any analysis of the novel form must take into account the process of production and the specifics of publishing, distribution, and patronage. By recognizing these structural factors, one gains an appreciation of the constraints with which writers contend when writing a novel. All literature is affected to some degree by broader social forces and relationships. One very obvious condition is the production of fiction entertainment as a commodity. As one literary critic has stated:

> Books are not just structures of meaning, they are also commodities produced by publishers and sold on the market at a profit. . . . Writers are not just transposers of transindividual mental structures, they are also workers hired by publishing houses to produce commodities which will sell. (Eagleton, 1976:59)

The essence of this argument is that the writer must be sensitive to the forms of popular novels which will sell, and understand what literary elements are necessary to increase sales and to more widely distribute the book. Certainly the notion behind series story production is motivated partly by hyper-consumption, and such literary devices as simple plots and stereotypical characters all help to contribute to this particular phenomenon. Consider, for example, the production of Canadian sports novels, particularly those written in English.

The Cultural Production of Canadian English-Language Sports Novels

The Sports Novel as Commodity

In the production of any sports novel there is a strong connection between the book publishing industry, the sports merchandising business, and professional sport (in Canadian society, mainly professional ice hockey). In the instance of the Canadian novel, National Hockey League teams and famous players — all playing with brand-name sports equipment — are included in the stories. Whereas the connections influence the story line of the novel, there are other factors which affect the publication process itself. One of the more important factors is the pervasive economic interests of the United States. This pervasiveness is felt in two ways. First, there is a strong American presence in the Canadian publishing industry generally. This is not to imply that there are no independent Canadian publishers, but simply that American parent companies wield a great deal of power. Second, the indirect effect of the strength and size of the American market influences Canadian literature to take on an internationalist (that is, American) writing style, suitable for consumption in the United States (Cappon, 1978:10–32).

American economic interests translate into cultural domination through channels other than the book publishing trade, however. As Cappon argues, the liberal ideology, which undergirds these institutions of Canadian literary production and criticism (for example, the universities), consolidates American interests in Canadian literature and intellectual life as a whole (Mathews, 1969). One would assume that the Canadian sports novel would highlight a national-cultural type of independence because of the strong connection between our national heritage and the game of ice hockey. Although some recent hockey novels have made some reference to American influence and cartel control of the professional game, ironically, authors realize that success relies on distribution to markets in the United States.

Authors, Hegemony, and Sports Literature

In addition to considering constraints created by American economic structures and the commodity market of the publishing industry, it is also important to examine the social relationship between authors and the way in which their work is created for distribution. A truly dialectical analysis of literature must respect the agency component of literary selection, while at the same time realizing that it is not separate from broader social processes. Literary conventions do not evolve autonomously but are chosen by human agents acting within the limits created by their social structure. The real question is, why are some forms and conventions chosen instead of others, and to what extent is their choice supportive of the dominant social values and practices of the particular society?

As a general theoretical starting point, Gramsci's concept of hegemony is useful. With regard to the production process of the news, one prominent theorist argues:

> Hegemony operates efficiently — it does deliver the news
> — yet outside consciousness; it is exercised by self-
> conceived professionals working with a great deal of
> autonomy within institutions that proclaim the neutral
> goal of informing the public. (Gitlin, 1979:18–19)

The key phrase "professionals working with a great deal of autonomy" also is applicable to a discussion of hegemony and the novel form. For example, it is fair to assume that authors go about their work in a fairly autonomous fashion. At one level the choice of topic, plot, characterization, or setting can be attributed to an author's particular style and preference. But to assume that style is chosen from an infinite variety of possibilities is simplistic. First, this assumption overlooks the fact that there are limited, and fairly standardized, conventions already accepted within the writing community. Second, such a view tends to assume that all existing conventions and forms are equally *valued* and *accepted*. There is absolutely no notion of power here. The fact is that, through the hegemony of power and influence (that is, *resources*), certain forms come to be seen as more meaningful and acceptable by editors, publishers, and even the writers themselves. To more fully understand the production of the novel form, one must take into account the particular power relations surrounding its production and continued maintenance. The major conventions and forms used in the construction of novels must be examined and linked with broader ideological and material arrangements.

The Canadian sports novel, for example, originally adopted literary devices very similar to those used in its American counterpart (Evan, 1972). As noted above, this is partially explained by the broader, more general economic and cultural dominance the United States exercises over Canadian society, and while recently there has been a departure from the American sports formula, this can be explained with reference to the hegemonic. For example, while more recent works such as Scott Young and George Robertson's *Face-Off*, John Craig's *Power Play*, and R. J. Childerhose's *Winter Racehorse* have all been relatively critical of American domination in professional ice hockey — in addition to *not* producing the typical sports success story in their plot — they fail to elucidate the fundamental contradictions of the wage-labour relationship. The departure from the American norm is only attitudinal. They suggest that, although corporate dominance is bad for hockey, there was a golden age when both players and owners were gentlemen, the game was less violent, and hockey was the cultural glue that held Canada together. This position becomes a pseudo-criticism rather than an alternative. It ignores the fact that professional hockey has existed in near monopoly conditions since the Second World War (Kidd and MacFarlane, 1972:58; Jones, 1976).

It can reasonably be assumed that both editors and publishers have an impact on the selection of what elements are to remain in a story and those that are to be deleted. Also, editors and publishers may unconsciously instruct or steer the writer into adopting certain standard plots and stereotypical characters, in order to ensure a particular volume of sales. Alternative notions concerning human possibilities may be edited out for seemingly realist reasons, when the decision to cut material may actually be due to latent ideological preferences.

Writers also play an active role in this process by imposing limitations on their own work. Many early Canadian sports novelists were closely connected to the sports they were writing about (i.e., as journalists, sports writers, broadcasters, ex-athletes, statisticians). It is clear that self-imposed censorship is exercised in much the same fashion in sports journalism as it is in journalism in general. Although the copy or story is read by a number of different individuals (that is, editors), very little material is edited out on objectionable grounds (Smith, 1975). Gitlin (1979) pointed out this effect of hegemony on autonomous professional journalists. Sports writers know what they can write about and criticize (and how far), before even submitting their work to a newspaper editor. They also realize the symbiotic relationship existing between the sports industry and newspaper circulation. The former needs the news media for free advertising and promotional "hype," while the newspaper recognizes that status quo or pseudo-critical sports news sells newspapers. Brian MacFarlane put it bluntly when he stated: "most hockey writers and broadcasters are simply press agents for the owners of professional hockey" (quoted in Kidd and MacFarlane, 1972:149).

This is not to say that sports writers have not attempted to press against the boundaries protecting the fundamental contradictions of professional sport, nor does it mean that the style of sports writing has remained the same. There is a degree of autonomy for the writer. Indeed, the very success of the hegemonic or dominant value system of liberal democracies depends on this apparent flexibility. However, the outer limits of such a system are only too real. Stan Fischler, a hockey critic and syndicated columnist, has publicly admitted that the owner of a hockey magazine, *Hockey Pictorial*, "was constantly warning me — and I mean constantly — not to get anybody mad, because in hockey it's not done. In hockey, you have to write nice things" (quoted in Kidd and MacFarlane, 1972:152). Other sports columnists, such as Dick Beddoes and Scott Young, have faced threats, been ostracized, banned from dressing rooms, and even dismissed from their positions because they were too critical (Kidd and MacFarlane, 1972:151–159).

What *is* being suggested is that elements of this hegemonical process (ranging from editing practices to self-imposed limitations regarding the type of literary devices used) are carried over into the writing of a hockey novel. The next section of this chapter addresses the major characterization devices used in Canadian English-language sports fiction to represent the dominant values of masculinity and individual heroism found in the wider society. It demonstrates the inscription of the dominant ideological and political structures of Canadian society into a literary product. The case study material discussed in this section is derived from a careful reading of over thirty Canadian sports novels, written between 1948 and 1980.

Characterization, Masculinity, and the "Positive" Sports Hero

Character development, through the linkage of subjective experience to social structure, is one of the most important aspects of the novel form. Moreover, the manner in which characters are revealed and typified is the most important literary device to be exploited (consciously or unconsciously) in a hegemonic way by an author. The mode in which a character is presented also represents the writer's social philosophy and corresponding assumptions concerning human nature. Therefore, it is important not only *what* the character is like but also *how* he or she is presented.

Character development in the Canadian sports novel is particularly revealing in this regard. The usual formula is to include secondary characters but to always introduce a main character or hero around which the entire novel revolves. This main character, not surprisingly, is almost always a male figure. Even R. J. Childerhose's 1973 novel *Hockey Fever in Goganne Falls*, although a community-oriented story, has a primary male character through which the plot is organized. Given the pervasiveness of this formula, it is appropriate to discuss how the sports hero is constructed and revealed.

Constructing the Sports Hero:
Physicality and Masculinity

Canadian sports novelists have adopted an interesting method of representing the main masculine hero which underdevelops the *social* component of mental, emotional, and psychic factors. Instead, there is an overdevelopment of physical and biological features as a basis upon which the reader forms his or her initial impression of the main character. For example, the hockey heroes Bill Spunska in Scott Young's *Boy on Defence* (1953:16) and Les Burton in John Craig's *Power Play* (1973:13) are introduced in the following manner. Spunska is:

> . . . big all over, big as a man, wide shoulders, bulging thighs, strong jaws.

> Les Burton was thirty-five. He had dark, short-cut hair beginning to grow a little thin. His complexion was clear and quite dark, and a long scar ran from one corner of his mouth to just below the right ear. He was tall for a hockey player, strong through the shoulders, well conditioned down through his flat stomach and tight body, and a little thin in the legs to have the power of a really strong skater.

These are only two examples drawn from hundreds of similar statements in the sports fiction genre. It is not uncommon for any writer to introduce characters by describing them physically. But the over-reliance on this method by Canadian sports novelists is telling. This literary device, in connection with other characteristic devices, promotes a socio-biological theory of personality and masculinity, and is grounded upon a philosophy of "methodological individualism." In simple terms, this philosophy asserts that any understanding of social phenomena can only come about through the *exclusive* study of individuals and their actions (O'Neill, 1973).

Although physical stature and biologically based character traits are paramount in the sports novel, the physicality of the hero is tempered in comparison to other elements. In actual fact, the "man-of-steel," natural-athlete prototype occurs in its pure form only in a select number of cases. Even though characters are described graphically in physical terms, it is their strong will, and tremendous desire and dedication which make up the bulk of the heroic constitutions. For instance, in R. J. Childerhose's *Hockey Fever in Goganne Falls* (1973:1), Andy, the major figure, is portrayed as follows:

> . . . as an athlete he was of the workhorse variety. That
> is to say, he weighed more than most boys his age, was
> notably fleet of foot. But an athlete.

There are numerous examples of this athlete dedication phenomenon. Les Burton in *Power Play* (1973), Joe Johannsson in *Winter Racehorse* (1968), and Bill Spunska in *Scrubs on Skates* (1952) immediately come to mind. Burton is an aging hockey star whose inner drive and determination guarantee his position on the team, while Bill Spunska symbolizes the immigrant making good in a system (whether it be hockey or capitalism) designed to produce a winner out of anyone who is hard-working, dedicated, and who, of course, possesses some natural talent. Similarly, Joe Johannsson compensates for his poor skating ability with an incredible wrist-shot, developed by religiously shooting two hundred lead-weighted pucks at a target every day. Whether it is a natural God-given talent or the sheer desire to succeed, both are seen to be embedded in the genetic code of the athlete involved.

In his discussion of American sports fiction written in the 1950s, Walter Evan (1972:110) has noted a similar pattern of characterization. It was quite common, argues Evan, for American sports authors to construct a boy hero who was a remarkable athlete, not only in the physical sense, but because of a correct balance of "physical coordination, courage, intelligence, and a propensity for hard work." The relevance of this approach is understandable in view of the North American ideology of success. If the hero was a completely natural athlete there would be little room left for fortitude, determination, and those other qualities that constitute the typical North American success story. Such characterization (as noted above) also reveals something about the authors themselves. This revelation can occur either through the mouths of the characters or in narration; for example,

> I believe a lot of people can get to be about ninety per-
> cent of whatever is possible for them all by themselves
> (Craig, 1973:192)
> In any contest between human beings, everybody has a
> chance (Young, 1952:49)
> If you took him apart to analyse him, you'd have to come
> right down to it, he was all drive, all spirit (Young,
> 1952:133).

These comments are not just being made about the characters in the novel; they also suggest the author's assumptions about the world and how humans are constituted within that world. By creating heroes with small deficiencies and hardships which must be overcome, the author reproduces the notion that the individual alone is responsible for his or her own success in North America.

Although the biological/physical dimension is dominant in the sports novel, the hero or main character is introduced in other ways as well. Yet even when he is described in mental or emotional terms, these are assumed to be entrenched, natural, individual qualities. In other words, the hero's personality is viewed as strictly individual rather than socially constituted. This does not mean that the hero is portrayed as lacking any social relations with other characters (i.e., as a brother, son, lover, friend), but that these relations and corresponding behaviours *flow* from a pre-disposed personality structure; and while social events and happenings do occur in most of the fiction (mainly limited to the game situation itself), the hero's actions and reactions reveal already existing personal traits. For example, in Sheldon Ilowite's novel *Centerman from Quebec* (1972), the main character is described as a boy with a quick tongue, a critical attitude, and a rude and peppy spirit. All these traits can be seemingly explained by his French-Canadian temperament and heritage. In fact, his hockey talent and physical skills are also attributed to his ethnic status. Even after social situations assist in changing him into a more co-operative team player, his entrenched (biological) French-Canadian passion still remains.

Similarly, R. J. Childerhose's hero, Joe Johannsson, in *Winter Racehorse* (1968) is portrayed as a naturally uncaring and unco-operative personality, rather than as a young man reacting violently to an historically constituted social and cultural situation (that is, being treated as a commodity in a professional hockey cartel). The point is that, in reality (and there is no doubt that these novels attempt to be realistic), the development of personality traits is inextricably linked with social structure, social movements, and historical modes of action and behaviour — which are always social in nature. What Canadian sports novels fail to capture are the social and political components of human action.

The Sports Hero as "Positive" Hero

Rather than being the problematic hero characteristic of much of our twentieth-century literature (Lukacs, 1964), the Canadian sports hero is usually portrayed as an integrating force in the novel, that is, the positive hero (two exceptions being found in Young and Robertson, 1972, and Childerhose, 1968). Instead of being estranged from the society in which he finds himself, the sports hero is both strong and powerful enough to adapt the external world to fulfil his needs and desires. The demonstration of this capacity need not be unduly criticized. However, any depiction of human beings in action must show how an individual's inner meaning and overt behaviour are connected to the social rules and resources that are available in a given society. In the sports novel the theory of human agency or action has been taken out of the social context (Lukes, 1977). Instead, the hero overcomes external situations and obstacles by the exertion of non-social, personal qualities. In addition to the strong elements of individualism and voluntarism found here, a normative component is also present. Problems are not only resolved by the hero individually, but also by his choosing a *morally* correct response (being honest, ethical, or hard-working). This conflict/resolution pattern invariably takes place between the hero and events occurring in the story. Secondary characters are rarely, if ever, directly involved.

In novels without a sports story line, the positive hero is usually defined in much the same way as the sports hero with regard to physical appearance, strength, and superior physique. As Sattel (1977) states:

> . . . it is as if the author wanted to impress on the reader that the hero must be understood in terms of biological or ethnic inheritance; that the individual's personality and social life are primarily reflective of intrinsic biological factors over which little control or change is possible.

Moreover, he (because, like the sports hero, the positive hero is almost always a male) is depicted as a producer, a man of action, or a statesman. The positive hero embraces hard work and all forms of mundane labour, however tedious, and naturally accepts the necessity of disciplined leadership while retaining leadership qualities himself. In addition to this, he "takes on his opponents" (note the sport metaphor) by expressing his anger through appropriate channels (primarily retributive punishment to fit the crime). Finally, although unassumingly religious, the positive hero has an undying faith in an ordered belief system. The sports novel is the positive hero novel with a sports theme.

The Positive Hero and His Foil

Sattel (1977) also develops his notion of the positive hero by contrasting him with his major antagonist. These latter individuals are usually bureaucrats, non-producers, or men who are willing servants of the system. They are not *necessarily* evil, just weak individuals who have gone wrong by subordinating themselves to the dictates of society (opportunists, Communists, etc.). Antagonistic foils are commonly stereotyped and usually receive little attention with respect to character development. Similarities between the positive hero/sports hero and the antagonist sports bully are easily identifiable. As already mentioned, the main character (the sports hero) is developed in biological and physical terms. Because of these innate factors, he is "a man of action" able to personally alter any social force or institutional structure which confronts him. The task then is to create a confrontation between the positive hero and his foil. The climax of the story is the resolution of the conflict. Depending on the novel, the sports hero may be embroiled in various conflicts, always solving the crisis by applying his individual will to the situation at hand. This particular formula closely approximates the early American sports story plot described by Evan (1972). In Evan's words, the formula is attack $\longrightarrow$ proof of positive hero and antagonist $\longrightarrow$ bully regeneration $\longrightarrow$ apotheosis (happy ending).

An example may serve to clarify this approach. The author situates his characters clearly in the role of hero or antagonist. Thus, note the contrast between the boy sports hero Bill Spunska and his chief antagonist Benny Moore in Scott Young's *A Boy at the Leafs' Camp* (1963). Spunska is honest, hard-working, polite, and self-disciplined — the all-Canadian boy. The antagonist, Benny Moore, is brash, overconfident, and more confused than naturally evil. As the term suggests, in the bully regeneration stage the antagonist realizes the error of his ways and repents. This realization normally comes about through some form of punishment, usually retributive in nature, handed out by the positive sports hero (in this particular case, it is a solid, bone-crunching, but *clean* body-check). Again, the expression of anger by the positive hero and the "taking on of opponents" by the sports hero are uncanny parallels to the ideology of discipline and hard work.

The sports hero, as already noted, maintains an undying dedication to hard work and discipline. Work, whether it is in sport (for example, the practising of sports skills) or in the workplace, is taken on with relish and devotion. With the possible exception of Billy Duke, the super-talented hero in Scott Young and George Robertson's *Face-Off* (1972), the majority of Canadian sports heroes are characterized by their affection for hard work during team practice sessions. Off the ice rink or sports field, this enthusiasm spills over into the workplace, whether the job is creative or mundane. Notable for their capacity to work hard both on and off the ice are Danny Dooner in *Hockey Wingman* (1967), Bill Spunska in *Boy on Defence* (1953), Buck Martin in *Buck Martin in World Hockey* (1966), Andy MacFarlane in *Hockey Fever in Goganne Falls* (1973), and Sam Shurtliff in *The Calgary Challengers* (1962). Dooner and Shurtliff are both grocery boys, Spunska works for a tobacco warehouse, Martin works in an accounting office, while Andy MacFarlane makes extra money chopping wood. As if work and sport were not enough, all of the above characters are enrolled in school as well (either high school or university).

For the most part, almost all of the early Canadian sports novels present the hero as an individualist, yet someone who realizes the value of external guidance in addition to self-discipline. The coach's word is heeded, whether it is due to his technical knowledge, conventional wisdom, or simply because of his authoritative position. Heroes in more recent novels, such as Joe Johannsson in *Winter Racehorse* (1968) and Billy Duke in *Face-Off* (1972), are such extreme individualists that, although they possess some measure of self-discipline, they only accept external constraint out of necessity (that is, in order to keep their jobs in professional hockey). While Billy Duke appears to bend all the rules and authoritative conventions of professional hockey, in the end he chooses to return to the very structures that oppressed all of his personal relationships. Submission to authority and belief in hierarchical social arrangements are still very much part of the sports creed and are reflected clearly in most sports novels.

A final comment should be made about the sports hero's relationship both to the social environment and to other characters. Following Raymond Williams' (1965) argument, the sports hero can be analysed in terms of the "lack of totality perspective."

In other words, the hero is not adequately connected to the totality of institutional arrangements and social relationships which characterize a particular historical time period and way of life. He is neither developed nor constituted as a social being, surrounded and engaged in a vast number of social situations. Instead, the hero is narrowly defined and developed only in the context of his sport or in sports-related activities. There is little, if any, characterization revealed in the hero's other possible capacities such as a lover, child, son, worker, or student. It is as if all of these varying roles which human beings experience and which form the totality of everyday life are non-existent or subordinate to the monolithic importance of the sports contest. This is not to say that personality development does not occur through participation in sport — the question is, what kind of personality? (see Brohm, 1978, for an alternative viewpoint). However, it is only one facet of an individual's social life. By greatly overemphasizing the sports role as the major defining factor in the character development of the hero, Canadian sports novelists distort reality.

Conclusion

Central to this chapter has been the argument that the production of Canadian English-language sports novels is the result of a complex series of determinate conditions and arrangements. The conditions range from the economics of fiction publication to the hegemonic selection of various literary devices — such as characterization — which, in turn, limit the presentation of sport realities and experiences. The case study outlined earlier attempted to show how some of these broader processes and decisions become inscribed into the very text of sports literature by limiting the many ways heroes can be represented in society. The case study demonstrates the power of masculine and conservative forces in society and how they also limit the characterization of sports heroes.

It must be recognized that, taken in isolation, studies of sports literature are of little use. Theorists of cultural production and social reproduction remind us that culture is a whole social process which must not be divided or compartmentalized. With respect to sport and literature, it is clear that the study of sports novels would benefit greatly from additional analysis of the entire sports entertainment media (i.e., television, radio, newspapers, magazines, the leisure industry, etc.). Similarly, sports production as a whole could be compared and contrasted with other aspects of cultural life. Finally, the study of the sports novel provides a good indication of the dominant notions concerning sport, its participants, and the accompanying philosophy.

Suggested Readings

In order to more fully appreciate the development of the positive hero in the Canadian sport novel, one should read several of the following: R. J. Childerhose (1968), *Winter Racehorse*, Toronto, Peter Martin; R. J. Childerhose (1973), *Hockey Fever in Goganne Falls*, Toronto, Macmillan; Scott Young (1952), *Scrubs on Skates*, Boston, Little, Brown and Company; Scott Young (1953), *Boy on Defence*, Toronto, McClelland and Stewart; Scott Young (1963), *A Boy at the Leafs' Camp*, Boston, Little, Brown and Company.

Chapter Twelve
Employee Fitness: Doctrines and Issues

Pierre Brodeur

Health and Work Efficiency Through Physical Activity

In 1976, in a series of articles entitled "Fitness and Work," the Montreal newspaper *La Presse*, under the headline "Business Begins to Take Interest in Employee Fitness," stated that "it was not until three or four years ago that Canada began to consider the health of workers. The idea of sport at work first appeared in the branch plants of large American companies" (December 8, 1976). Three years later, the newspaper reported, under the headline "Fitness Aids Productivity," that in the preceding years, 150 Canadian companies had established programs for their employees (March 21, 1979). Even the business columnists stressed that "getting managers to jog is profitable for business. Numerous tests show that the results obtained in employee fitness programs far exceed the investment required" (*La Presse*, September 1981).

These examples show the steady progress of a phenomenon that is relatively new in form, i.e., physical activities for fitness purposes related either to the work environment or to the duties, and hence to the health, of the various categories of workers. It is a revived formula that dates back to an historical development analysed earlier by Ronald Melchers (see Chapter Three).

In the present context, not only have large Canadian companies, following the example of their American counterparts, begun to develop such programs specifically for their personnel, but the Canadian state has openly assumed, through physical activity, the role of agent of change, both on the ideological level and in relation to habits associated with health and productivity.

In their study on sport and the state, Harvey and Proulx have used the classification of the motives for state intervention in sport developed by the political theorist Jean Meynaud. Among these motives was the improvement of productivity, about which he noted:

> Although it may be a part of a general concern for well-being, this tendency should be mentioned separately because, in a society dominated by the profit motive and the private ownership of the means of production, it can lead to measures that are clearly more beneficial to the employers than to the workers. From this point of view, the encouragement of physical education and sport may be part of a policy of social diversion. . . . In any case, it is a fact that the state is concerned today with improving physical fitness for the sake of productivity. . . . This concern can only become more obvious when the state institutes a national health service, because it then has a direct financial interest. . . . (Meynaud, 1966:135)

Beyond any moral judgement, this passage merely confirms the convergence of the state's motives, objectives, and strategies with those of the social groups made up of owners and managers of the means of production of goods and services.

It is important to note the following: it is a question of physical and sports activities linked not to recreation, but to preparation for work; it is not a matter of entertainment, but of fitness; the recreational aspect is less important than the health aspect; pleasure is of less concern than work. The traditional view of free time and popular participation in physical activities and sport no longer means anything in this professionalized universe.

In this area, and increasingly over the past few years in areas where business is too small or underdeveloped to be able to afford its own specialists and generate programs tailored to its needs, the state has assumed the task of promotion and encouragement, for which it has diversified and specialized its own governmental institutions.

In this context new fitness and physical productivity professionals have appeared, the latest generation of experts concerned with the productive body, in the footsteps of Taylor, Ford, and industrial psychologists; their actions will help to define the troubles in the "social body" and to rationalize and professionalize the battle for health, welfare, and good working conditions.

This probably means new work prospects for physical educators, kinanthropologists, recreologists, and the like, who have had few career opportunities in the schools and municipalities over the past few years. For the moment, however, this aspect seems much less important than the extent of their role as health ideologists and physical efficiency technicians in the unions' fight for health and safety in the workplace, a shorter work week, and a right to time off.

Whatever their intentions, these new "agents of change" rarely escape their role as "state clerks at the service of the dominant groups, performing the low-level functions of social hegemony and political government" (Gramsci, 1977:607). Though they are not yet very numerous, their actions are not inconsequential. After having defended their point of view on the benefits of physical activity and sport, and the need for their own professional intervention, for several years, they have now joined forces both with business — employers, medical services, and business management services — and with the political institutions — ministers, public servants, and technocrats — in order to develop and administer the appropriate programs.

Starting from a legitimate position, which is that physical activity is, in principle, good for one's health, they have been led by their social perspective to promote their practice independently of the interests involved. This has "naturally" prompted them to woo business leaders, who are seen as having the power to act. Moreover, since physical educators are still seeking professional status in the social division of labour, the tendency to propose something positive becomes overwhelming, and this also leads them to reproduce the dominant doctrine and to seek alliances with dominant groups in order to prove their social usefulness. In this context, aside from the fact that certain factions in these professions have quite conservative leanings, underestimating the social issues related to physical fitness in business has caused these new specialists to tailor their practice to the interests of business owners.

In recent years, provincial authorities have more or less imitated the federal government, which is still taking the lead today, as we shall see later.

In British Columbia, Action B.C. was created and various programs were set up, including the Industrial Fitness Program, which was designed to provide operational, administrative, and educational support (for example, *IF*, an information letter on physical fitness training in the workplace, an advisory service to assist in setting up and organizing programs, and so on) to physical fitness programs in businesses.

In Ontario, Fitness Ontario/En forme has published pamphlets entitled *Fitness and the Working World* and *Promoting Employee Fitness and Recreation in the Workplace*. It also distributes the *Employee Fitness Resource Kit*, and provides financial assistance to businesses that request it.

In Quebec, the Comité national sur la condition physique et le milieu de travail (National Committee on Physical Fitness and the Workplace), which operates the program Kino-Québec pour la santé des Québécois par l'activité physique (Kino-Quebec for the Health of Quebeckers through Physical Activity), has just sent to its regional officers a complete kit for the establishment of such programs.

It would be wrong to treat lightly or as a marginal phenomenon the development of these policies and programs in co-operation with business. All of this material illustrates another instance in which the state reveals itself through a "set of practical and theoretical activities by which the ruling class not only justifies and maintains its domination, but also succeeds in obtaining the active consent of the governed" (Gramsci, 1977:556).

This is our starting point for a socio-political understanding of physical activity in the context of work and the intervention of the political apparatus. While the specific characteristics and dynamics of provincial programs also need critical examination, we will confine ourselves to the Canadian situation as a whole.

By tracing the main phases of the strategy pursued by the Canadian political apparatus in setting up these new physical activity programs in the economic sphere, we will be in a better position to judge the strategy's ideological and practical orientation and at the same time to identify the social issues behind it. We feel this is a necessary step to understanding how liberal democracies exert educational pressure on individuals when they wish to obtain the consent and collaboration of these individuals and to make necessity and constraint appear to be "freedom."

The Canadian State and the Fitness of the Productive Body

Over the years, the state has not been restrained in its efforts to encourage business to establish physical activity programs. Under the cover of a concern for the health and welfare of the population in general, the federal government has gradually developed a coherent strategy whose ideological and economic impact must be taken seriously.

As early as 1941, medical checkups and physical ability tests revealed the low fitness levels of Canadians likely to be drafted into the armed forces. With a world-wide conflict raging at the time, the Canadian government in July 1943 passed the National Physical Fitness Act, with the aim of promoting physical education, sport, and athletic activities.

In 1961, the Canadian government took action again, introducing Bill C-131, which drew a significant distinction between fitness and amateur sport. About ten years later, Partici-paction was born.

From Participation in Sport to Physical Activity in the Workplace

In 1972, the stage was set, or almost set, for the state to begin refining its thinking, diversifying, and specializing its interventions, thus moving closer to its real objectives.

Participation in physical activities and physical fitness exercises was now incorporated into the policies of the Canadian state and was considered a determining factor in the health of all Canadians, whatever their material conditions of existence or their place in the social structure. According to this doctrine, health is no longer a social product, but rather the result of the choices and habits of each individual, whom the state quite rightly takes responsibility for informing and educating.

Thus it is not surprising that, in *A New Perspective on the Health of Canadians*, published in 1974 by the Minister for National Health and Welfare, the twenty-three recommendations for a health promotion strategy mainly concerned information, awareness, and attitudes to be developed regarding "nutrition, driving, health education, mental health"; nor is it surprising that half of the recommendations (twelve out of twenty-three) dealt directly with individual participation in physical activity for physical fitness (Lalonde, 1974:71, 72, 73).

Clearly, in the Minister's view, all this was justified by the fact that health-care costs were climbing steadily and that they might become an excessive burden for our economy: "If there were additional money to invest. . . , it [would be] better used to encourage changes in lifestyle and in the environment and to improve the lives of people generally" (Lalonde, 1974:45).

The ideas of the Minister of Health, presented in 1974 at the First National Conference on Employee Fitness in Canada (whose keynote speech was given by the Minister of Industry,

Trade and Commerce), were characteristic of an ideological doctrine that had been widely disseminated by political society. This
doctrine was aimed at erasing an awareness of the class conditions under which individuals lived and offering a functional solution to problems that had been distorted and redefined by the ruling
groups. In other words, the Minister was addressing lifestyles in
order to avoid questions about modes of production.

This national conference was organized in 1974 by the
Department of National Health and Welfare to encourage the creation of employee physical education programs and to develop
guidelines and appropriate policies.

Furthermore, it seems clear that the "health" objective
was not the only motive for state intervention. For the former president of the National Advisory Council on Fitness and Amateur
Sport, the issue was much broader:

> Our task is to discover and promote outlets for actively
> getting rid of people's tensions. . . . The evidence is
> mounting that Canada is coming up against serious prob-
> lems of stress in the workplace and that this stress is
> explained in part by the absence of physical activity. . . .
> We must combat the physical inertia of Canadians at
> work and at play. (De Gaspé Beaubien, unpublished
> document, 1974:11–12)

The whole thrust of state doctrine is crystal clear if one
considers the following points:

(a)   For economic reasons related to the costs of providing collective health services, it was necessary to revise and adjust
health policies in the direction of individual responsibility for
lifestyles. This whole strategy was aimed ultimately at making the
working classes accept a reduction in the share of social production allotted to collective health services, in order to increase the
profits of private enterprise and hence of the owners of the means
of production.

(b)   Reinforcement was given to the ruling classes' idea
that the population of Canada constituted a relatively homogeneous
whole, in which differences were only individual ones between
legally equal people, and health or fitness depended on the degree
of "laziness" of each person in choosing healthier lifestyles, among
which physical activity should constitute a larger part. This political doctrine would seem logical only if one agrees to jump from
"collective health" to "individual fitness," which is seen to have
its origins in physical conditioning, which in turn is based on participation in sports and physical activities on a regular basis. Thus
the issue of the "system" was avoided and replaced by a focus

on the individual, who was confronted with the necessary, inevitable evolution of the means of production, to which he or she had to adapt.

(c) Finally, political and economic motives converge when one attempts to fight inertia at work while at the same time seeking to regulate social tensions generated by the content and organization of work. In both cases, physical activity programs for workers offer the advantages of a credible stopgap measure without the need to attack the root causes or problems (tasks, organization, and conditions of work and/or class structure).

The 1974 conference marked another important step in the expansion of state policies, since it established the ideological and political bases for systematic, justified intervention in the working environment of employees and employers.

Clearly, programs designed to maintain and improve the physical health of the population in general and of workers in particular would be advantageous in all respects: "(1) they are less costly than cures; (2) they maintain the work force more efficiently; (3) they make it possible to control the people's leisure time; (4) they open up new markets (profits on goods and services); (5) they respond to demands for a better quality of life" (Jamet, 1980:64).

Contradictory Interests Reconciled by the State

One of the problems is that the individual who was made for intense physical work in the Stone Age must now adapt to a world of technological innovation . . . we have a great deal of free time. . . . We must give part of it to active leisure [because], by nature, humans are rather lazy animals, players who take great risks. (Direction générale, 1975:5)

Technological constraints, individual irresponsibility, a civilization of leisure, the problems of a society of abundance, employer-employee co-operation: these themes returned constantly and were used consistently by the state to explain the collective health problems of human beings, who had passed too rapidly from the Stone Age to the Industrial Age and the demands of modern life.

In this Canadian government publication on health and fitness, there was a chapter entitled "The Human Body as Machine" — an evocative title to say the least, which gives an idea of the level of concern and the relationship with the body that is presented. It was no longer necessary to invoke national defence or national pride, not even the collective quality of life. The new objective, supported by ideological rhetoric, directly concerned the human machine, which had to be maintained like a tool or even improved to fit in with the new technology. In other words, economic competition between capitalists not only required a reduction in collective health and welfare services, but also obliged each and every person to become more efficient and more productive. The improvement of the human machine now had to be "incorporated" into the process of improving the machine of production.

In another important document intended to serve as a list of, and guide to, employee health and fitness programs, the Minister, Mrs. Campagnolo, discussed the question in detail, making sure to note the convergence of the economic and political interests of the ruling class:

> Recent studies indicate that participation in employee physical health programs not only benefits employees, but also contributes to an increase in work efficiency. . . . I am happy that physical activity is being brought back into the workplace, since technological evolution has left less and less room for overall physical activity. (Unpublished government document, 1977:6)

It could not have been said better. This passage is a synopsis of remarks intended for both employers and employees, which professionals on the subject could use. But there was more:

> Certainly the blame for this situation cannot be placed on the quality of medical care, but much more on the lifestyle of the average Canadian worker. . . . There is no doubt that well-directed physical health programs succeed in improving the physical health of employees. More than that, however, the employer should note the effect an employee physical health program has on the financial balance. The following question should be asked: is the physical health of employees a philanthropic enterprise on the part of the employer or an investment intended to protect the human resources of a company or enterprise? (Unpublished government document, 1977:6)

It was not by accident that the 1978 Canadian Conference on Employee Recreation and Fitness was aimed primarily at providing representatives of industry and government with an opportunity to explore the specific potential of employee recreation and fitness services, to bring information up-to-date, and to divide up responsibilities for the consolidation of the programs. It is worth noting that the principal parties — workers, unions, and grass-roots associations — were "absent" from this conference and others.

The view favoured by the Minister of Fitness and Amateur Sport was echoed in another major document involving the state apparatus, entitled *Toward a National Policy on Amateur Sport*:

> Business corporations are using sport to improve morale, work attitudes, performance and days-on-the-job. (Campagnolo, 1977:2)

What was remarkable in this phase of the state's long-term strategy was the dissemination of a two-sided official doctrine. First, the working classes had to be convinced of the truth of this viewpoint on worker health, in order for their ideological and political support to be won, as well as their active participation — this is what the Participaction program had been trying to do for several years. Second, a concerted effort was made to inform and persuade the most conservative members of the ruling classes, who were slow to recognize that this was in their interest, not to mention profitable for them.

"Well-being" and personal benefits for one side, "surplus value" and private profits for the other — this was the two-sided doctrine that the Canadian state put forward while cleverly hiding the basic contradiction between capital and labour. Not only did the state succeed in sidestepping the problem, but it even managed to transform it into a reciprocal relationship: each side was likely to gain equal advantages, such as lower health costs, higher tolerance of working conditions, and higher productivity.

The state as educator, seeking to manage in the most efficient manner possible, succeeded here as elsewhere by making leaders better prepared, by occupying the areas of least resistance, and by obtaining the consent of the ruled or governed.

Diversified, Specialized Intervention by the State

In the past few years, intervention by the Canadian state apparatus has not been limited to rhetoric and the periodic circulation of inspirational leaflets and manuals such as *Action Break, Exercise Break*, or *Exercise at the Office*.

In 1977–78, the Employee Fitness and Lifestyle Project was conducted in two large Toronto insurance companies, in response to recommendation 12 of the 1974 conference, which called for the creation of research programs to evaluate employee physical fitness programs and analyse the "costs and benefits" to the employer. This project was also to be used to develop a model for intervention in business and to measure the effects on job satisfaction, health costs, absenteeism, and productivity for 1125 people. The University of Toronto received $191 841 from Fitness Canada (part of Fitness and Amateur Sport) to observe an average productivity increase of 4.3 per cent and to report that 63 per cent of the employees said they were more relaxed, more patient, and less tired.

An awareness project co-ordinated by the Canadian Public Health Association (CPHA) was also conducted in fifty-one businesses scattered among the five regions of Canada.

This was followed in 1981 by a new, two-year project, at three large Canadian companies in Nova Scotia, Quebec, and Manitoba, co-sponsored by Fitness Canada and the CPHA, to design, implement, and evaluate fitness and lifestyle programs, this time in an industrial setting, to provide instructions and applicable models, and chiefly to "prove" that the quality of life in the workplace could be improved through such programs (CPHA, 1984). This is a clear case of "political" association, from which each side benefits, both the social group (the professionals of the CPHA) and the state (political society).

Beyond these few examples, what was important at the political level was not only the wide acceptance of these interventions, but also the visibility of state action and the results that showed its effectiveness.

In June 1980, the *Financial Post* published a "Special Advertising Feature" consisting of about ten pages. Under the headline "1980: Fitness Goes to Work," it praised, for the benefit of business managers and executives, the educational effect of Participaction and its programs of intervention in the workplace:

> Essentially it is an educational program for the individual employee. . . . Participaction's goal is to effect a fundamental improvement in life style . . . also the program makes fitness a very personal matter for each individual and I feel that is the way in which fitness should be addressed. . . . It's a pleasing prospect: Participaction, the company that made fitness a national issue in the '70s.
> (*Financial Post*, June 1980, 2, 3, 4, 10)

In other words, this intervention was not coercive and respected individual commitment within an educational context. In this sense, the work of the federal-provincial Conference on Physical Fitness, held in the spring of 1985, which was the setting for the first presentation of awards to the most deserving businesses for their commitment to employee physical fitness programs, showed clearly that, while the state could tax and punish, it could also reward and value hard work. It is worth noting that representatives of all the provincial governments (except Quebec, which wished to remain distinct and politically autonomous) were present at the head table for the event, which was co-chaired by the federal Minister of Fitness and Amateur Sport and the president of the Canadian Chamber of Commerce.

It was no longer 1943. The content of the preceding pages and these last examples show that the situation had changed considerably. They also show how the strategy of the state had evolved to this point. First, the state laid the groundwork by disseminating a doctrine and particular practices regarding health and welfare and by reinterpreting the issues involved in health and work in its own political and economic terms, in order to find solutions compatible with the interests of the dominant classes. Second, the state tailored its doctrine to the various social groups, whose fundamental interests were different, and associated itself with "public interest" social groups in order to avoid charges of "statism" in a liberal society. Finally, the state went beyond doctrine and actually intervened in practice to demonstrate the correctness of its strategy and to propose plans of action that the government had prepared under the cover of the neutrality of the state. From this point, there was a more or less obvious conversion of part of the national health budget into grants that went straight to the economic sector under the control of private enterprise to change the organization of working hours and improve the efficiency of workers.

In short, the state in effect acted as an educator inasmuch as it sought to modify habits and lifestyles, which are matters of culture. In the economic sphere, the state also became an instrument for rationalization, for acceleration of the development of the means of production, and for the Taylor system, i.e., scientific management in the workplace. In the end, all of the state's educational action can only be understood in relation to the economic interests of the social groups in power.

The Issues of Physical Fitness Programs in Quebec Business

In Quebec, the interest in physical fitness in the workplace was destined to play an increasingly important role in the mission of Kino-Quebec.

In order to evaluate and certainly to encourage intervention by Quebec business in the physical fitness of their
employees, the Haut-Commissariat à la jeunesse, aux
loisirs et aux sports (HCJLS) (the High Commission for
Youth, Recreation, and Sports) [later the Ministry of
Recreation, Hunting, and Fishing] ought to know how
many firms act to encourage employees fitness. (HCJLS,
1977:17)

In an initial survey that the HCJLS commissioned the
Fédération des jeunes chambres de commerce du Canada français (Federation of French-Canadian Junior Chambers of Commerce) to carry out, 32 per cent of businesses stated that they had
"sports activities for their employees." Of these, 83.9 per cent held
sports activities at least once a week. These sports "programs,"
however, reached less than 20 per cent of the employees. It was
also learned that only 3.1 per cent of these businesses had physical fitness programs at least once a week, and participation in them
was less than 10 per cent. Finally, all these activities were funded
by joint worker-management plans in 80 per cent of the cases, by
management alone 11 per cent of the time, and by the employees
in 8.43 per cent of the cases.

As an illustration of Kino-Quebec's planned commitment
in this matter, regional co-ordinators were given, at a meeting in
November 1979, the objective of increasing the proportion of businesses providing physical fitness services to their employees by
25 per cent by January 1985 (Landry, 1979:24). Shortly afterwards,
in the 1980–81 Kino-Quebec National Action Plan, the target population assigned first priority for action was that of labour force
participants aged 18 to 35.

In 1983, faced with the scant number of studies on the
subject and the weak flow of information on experiments in the
workplace, the Recreation and Holidays Committee of the Confederation of National Trade Unions (CNTU) gathered information from some fifty CNTU locals and drew the following
conclusion: about one-third of businesses had some sort of
organization for physical, recreational, or socio-cultural activities,
usually called a "recreation committee," which had little to do with
physical fitness programs. Less than 10 per cent of the businesses
had been contacted directly by Kino-Quebec representatives or
physical educators promoting a physical fitness or sports activities program. The majority of respondents nevertheless said they
were ready to meet with a Kino-Quebec representative to discuss
the development of a physical fitness program (CNTU, 1984).

At the same time, a survey of recreation programs in the workplace commissioned by the Ministry of Recreation, Hunting, and Fishing revealed that 57 per cent of Quebec businesses with one hundred or more employees had one or more recreation programs and that physical fitness programs existed in 8 per cent of these businesses. It was also learned that the latter programs were most common in the public service.

Moreover, while 70 per cent of the sports and recreational programs were run by employee associations, 60 per cent of the physical fitness programs were run by management. This is a rather significant observation, not only on the needs to be met, but also on the dynamic of the two fields of involvement. According to this study, 12 per cent of the businesses had been contacted at that point by a representative of Kino-Quebec. Finally, 11 per cent of the businesses paid for physical fitness programs outside the workplace.

Encouraged on all sides and present in all spheres of social activity (such as education, health, hygiene, recreation, shopping, and advertising), the wave of enthusiasm for physical activity and physical fitness certainly left no one indifferent.

> Testimony from the workplace indicates that there exists currently a favourable attitude among workers making them receptive to interventions which would seem at first glance to be directed at an improvement in their physical and mental well-being. This is the crux of the matter. (CNTU, 1984:54)

One cannot oppose virtue. It is evident that the new programs had something attractive in them and adequately met the particular needs of certain categories of workers, given the characteristics of their work and their living conditions.

However, while empirical data issued by the agents of the state have some credibility, it should be noted at the outset that there are no simple answers to a problem as complex as health in the workplace. This is what Merwin and Northrop (1982) concluded in their analysis of health programs in the workplace:

> (a) Multiple variables have multiple effects; causes cannot be reduced to a single magic variable.
> (b) In the workplace, the environment is determined by specific human and material conditions and characteristics.
> (c) Each environment has its own dynamic, affecting the eventual application of programs, which do not operate in a vacuum; the average worker and the typical environment are abstractions of technocrats. (1982:76)

It is also worth noting that, while the model comes from large firms, it is a fact that, in the United States for example, 68 per cent of individuals work in companies with 250 or fewer employees, and 42 per cent in companies employing 50 or fewer. Yet, up to now, the large firms have been leading the way in the health field. We are far from a social policy of health for all, at work or otherwise.

There is more, though. What matters here is not simply a criticism of the method or the means used. No one would deny the beneficial effects that physical or sports activities have on the participants. What is more important on the social level is the incorporation of these activities and this doctrine in the social relations of production and exchange, as well as the determined use that the ruling classes make of them politically and economically.

> By focusing on the individual instead of the economic system, the ideology performs its classical role of obscuring the class structure of work. Lack of health in the workplace is blamed on individual shortcomings. . . . Holding individual workers responsible for their susceptibility to illness, or for an "unproductive" physiological state, reinforces management attempts to control absenteeism and enhance productivity. Job dissatisfaction and the job-induced stress, principal sources of absenteeism and low productivity, will become identified as life-style problems of the worker. (Crawford, 1981:499)

In short, it is once again the victim who is wrong. Accordingly, it is not surprising to find, in a report on physical fitness in a Bell Canada company newsletter, the statement that "one gets the heart one deserves" (November 19, 1979).

Crawford's analysis of medicine and the social production of collective health confirms what has been demonstrated in the preceding pages. With that in mind, we need only contemplate the current use of physical efficiency tests and evaluations (already being carried out in a number of areas, most often on a voluntary basis) to foresee, if it is not already a reality, the spread of programs to screen employees according to their vulnerability or resistance to the hazards of particular jobs.

Unions that recently began denouncing any approach that sees physical activity programs as a reform element in the organization of work in business certainly cannot be accused of "negativism":

> We are currently fighting against forms of work organization that deprive workers of their trade and make them

cogs in the complex machine of business profitability.
We also refuse to let physical activity be used in such
a process. . . . We must make every effort to increase
workers' control over their work. Physical activity in
business should be part of this approach and not its opposite. We wonder as well about physical fitness programs
in business whose primary function is to adapt the worker physically to a job that is too difficult. (Auger,
1981:3–4)

In this context, for the unions, "it would be an adultera-
tion of health" to try to solve the problems of health and security
in the workplace through physical activity (*La Presse*, June 5, 1976).
What state ideologists present as causes — nutrition, recreation,
and buying habits which can be changed through information and
advice — the unions instead view as effects, determined by the
organization of work and society.

Obviously, there are statistics that show the substantial
differences between social groups with respect to sports, recreation, nutrition, buying, hygiene, and health habits. Yet it is necessary to agree on what these statistics mean and how to interpret
them politically, although unanimity is, of course, impossible since
what a person thinks depends on where he or she comes from.

It is true that man is what he eats to the extent that food
is one of the expressions of social relations as a whole
and that each social grouping has a basic food, but in
the same way it can be said that man is his clothing, man
is his living quarters, man is his particular means of
reproduction, that is, his family, because it is precisely
food, clothing, housing, and reproduction [here we
would add recreation and physical activity] that are the
elements of social life where the complex of social relations are manifested in the most obvious and widespread
fashion. (Gramsci, 1977:181)

Thus, when researchers such as Labonté and Penford
undertake a systematic study of the relationship between living
conditions, on the one hand, and health and work, on the other,
they have to overcome a major obstacle. The publication entitled
Indicateurs sanitaires (Health Indicators), which assembles data
on health, provides no information on the links between the state
of health and such variables as income, social category, or occupation. "The fact that this type of information has not been
gathered clearly shows that income and social category are not
considered significant variables as far as health is concerned"
(Labonté and Penford, 1981:7).

However, information gathered elsewhere points to one fact, namely, that physical fitness is first and foremost a condition of class and cannot be isolated from the physical conditions of daily existence.

For unions confronted with the new health and fitness programs introduced by the state and business, it is unacceptable to dissociate them from working conditions, the organization of work, and the specific relations established in the workplace.

> At the basic, local level, workers as a group are the real experts on their own fitness. Workers accumulate in their bodies the daily effects of their working and living conditions — recreation, pollution, housing, food, in addition to work. . . . Workers within their unions must put forward the measures suitable to them. . . . Fitness therefore is not something which can be reduced to a few quick exercises in the office, under the benevolent gaze of Kino-Quebec. (CNTU, 1984:55)

In any case, there can be no doubt that these programs are not tokens of the generosity and understanding of employers towards those who sell their labour and often their health. As such programs invade the workplace, it should surprise no one to see more or less open resistance by employees and unions, who have other priorities or who want effective control over the contents, effects, and functions of activities organized in the workplace (the battle over health and safety at work and the organization of work).

Aware of the need to respond in accordance with the collective interests of its members, the Confederation of National Trade Unions has drawn up its own strategy on this whole question. First, the introduction of specialized physical activity programs in business must be negotiated with the unions. Second, the content of the programs should meet the real expectations of the workers and not the requirements of production. Finally, the workers must have control of the programs.

Suggested Readings

For an introduction to the description and analysis of the structures and functions of sport at the national and international levels, see Jean Meynaud (1966), *Sport et politique*, Paris, Payot, and Michel Jamet (1980), *Les sports et l'État au Québec*, Montréal, Éditions coopératives Albert Saint-Martin. For specific reference to physical fitness see Jean Harvey (1983), *Le corps programmé ou la rhétorique de Kino-Québec*, Montréal, Éditions coopératives Albert Saint-Martin, and Jean Harvey (1986), "The Rationalization of Bodily Practices," in *Arena*, X, I.

Part Four
The Social Determinants of Sports Participation

In this part, Raymond Boulanger, Suzanne Laberge and David Sankoff, and Bruce Kidd examine, in different ways, the myth of the democratization of sport. One of the fundamental, common ideas of advanced capitalist societies is that individuals receive all the social and economic benefits to which their efforts entitle them. Similarly, the growth of the capitalist economy creates an increase in collective wealth that is redistributed more and more equitably. With respect specifically to sport, these common ideas have led to a debate about whether sport is a mass phenomenon or a class phenomenon.

Gruneau (1976a) has already analysed these two positions. Those who assert that sport has been democratized adhere to the view of sport as a mass phenomenon. Their arguments take the following form. Although certain types of discrimination have prevailed throughout certain periods of history, contemporary sport provides freedom of access for all, regardless of race, ethnic origin, or sex. Furthermore, since there is more widespread access to economic advantages in modern Canadian society, individuals have more opportunities to participate in sports and recreational activities.

Those who support the other position recognize that advantages are more evenly distributed than before. However, even though the blatant discrimination of earlier eras has disappeared, democratized access to participation in physical activity is by no means assured. According to those who hold this second position, access still depends on differences in class, ethnic origin, and gender. This is the view maintained by the authors of the chapters in this part of the book.

With data from several major national surveys, Boulanger uses a classification of cultural forms to paint a general picture of the chief social determinants of sports participation in Canada. This classification shows how cultural models are specific to each class or class segment, producing "choices" of sports activities that conform to those models. Based on a few surveys conducted over a number of years, Boulanger's analysis questions the contemporary myth of the democratization of access to sports activity.

Laberge and Sankoff focus on the sports activities of women and show how they are linked to other physical activities. Using the analytical framework developed by Pierre Bourdieu, they make a detailed analysis of the statistical correlation between different activities and socio-economic parameters, and attempt to explain these activities by disclosing the differences in perception and judgement between the various classes and class segments with respect to these activities. They reveal the systems of selecting sports activities by incorporating them into various physical practices, the systems themselves arising from the living conditions of the social agents.

In other words, the agents' living conditions and their respective positions within the division of social classes create systems of perception and judgement of cultural choices which structure the sports in which they will actually engage. Moreover, these activities fit into systems that cover all physical practices and therefore provide an understanding of sports choices as part of the lifestyles that govern the relation that individuals have with their bodies (Boltanski, 1971:225).

The final chapter highlights the social constraints with which those who have chosen to perform in high-level competitive sport must live. Kidd notes that some athletes, who were receiving financial support from state or private sources, in order to uphold amateurism and other dominant values, had to face poverty, racial or sexual prejudice, the dictates of federation officials and coaches, or the whims of the sports press barons.

Kidd also recognizes the complex nature of the democratization of sport. He shows the constraints that exist in employer-employee relations when the wage earners are not unionized, as was the case with professional athletes prior to their unionization. He shows how the restrictions imposed on athletes affect decisions with respect to their training.

Kidd advocates collective bargaining, which might result in greater democratization between the employer (the Canadian state) and athletes funded by the state. Finally, this chapter reveals the contradictions between personal accomplishments, public attention, and the social constraints which are the daily lot of high-performance Canadian athletes.

Chapter Thirteen
Class Cultures and Sports Activities in Quebec

Raymond Boulanger

The study of sports activities and those who engage in them leads in very different directions depending on which of these two, the activity or the participant, the researcher starts with. For example, studying the "typical" sports participant or the various types of sports participants, based on the intrinsic characteristics or the internal logic of sports activities, takes us ultimately to the psyche, to the person. On the other hand, by examining the social nature of sport, the sociologist is led to analyse the influence of the social structure on the orientation and choice of sports activities.

We shall follow the latter course here. Hence, no classification of sports based on attributes proper to the activities being studied will be proposed, nor will this be a sociological study of a particular sport. The approach centres on the social position occupied by individuals, which is used to identify the similarities and differences between social classes in the social arena of sport. The analysis that follows flows from the general hypothesis that the social classes, by the very nature of their respective positions in the social order, engage in different sports activities and behaviours. Of course, the ideology conveyed by the sports media, sports institutions, and sports professionals (such as journalists, physical educators, sports clubs, and the Olympic Games) holds that sports participation is democratic and universal. However, not everyone has the same financial, social, and cultural resources, nor even the same "cultural goodwill" (Bourdieu, 1984) to pursue official or "legitimate" sport. If there are different ways of seeing, thinking, acting, and feeling among the different groups that make up a society, we should be able to observe them in sport just as we can in other areas such as recreation (Lalive d'Epinay et al., 1982), housing, health, and shopping.

   To that end, we shall resort to secondary analyses of data from surveys conducted for state recreation and sports organizations (Kirsh et al., 1973; Statistics Canada, 1978; David and Gagnon, 1983). Before the actual analysis of the results can begin, however, it is necessary to examine the chief influences on sports since the 1960s in order to determine the main models of behaviour promoted in the sports market and the cultural behaviours embraced by various social classes in relation to those models.

Sport and Cultural Models

Two main concepts of sport have been dominant in Quebec since the 1960s. In fact, as the data in Table 6 show, the thesis developed here could probably be applied generally to Canada as a whole. One of these concepts, mass culture, is linked to the capitalist mode of production. The other, professional culture, which entails scientific and technical expertise, has developed principally within the Quebec state (Levasseur, 1980, 1982). These two cultural forms dominate the type of sports promoted, clearly influence the social conception of sport — as much in the connotation that the term takes on as in the norms of sports participation — and contribute as well to the definition of a new field of activity (Levasseur, 1982; Jamet, 1980; Harvey, 1983).

Mass Culture

   Mass culture refers to domination by a few producers who use the principal channels of distribution (such as television, radio, press, commerce, advertising, and recreation centres) to present to the mass of consumers (predominantly the working class) many different, but homogeneous, sports products for use during their free time. As consumers, these workers are offered spectacles of all sorts (including hockey, football, baseball, and automobile racing), a wide variety of goods and equipment, and numerous activities (such as aerobic dance, bodybuilding, tennis, and windsurfing). In short, the concept of mass culture underscores the destruction of community lifestyles through the establishment of mechanisms for the cultural integration of the masses by this minority of producers and distributors. Social relations are founded on relations of cultural domination which are reflected in the reduction of the individual to the role of consumer and in the influence exerted on sports activities by industries, which shape them to suit their own interests.

Nonetheless, the concept of mass culture does not imply that sports activity is uniform. On the contrary, it is largely determined by social level, socio-economic status, position in the social hierarchy, "a result of class relations and the ruling class's control over social organization as a whole" (Levasseur, 1980:119). In other words, mass culture leads to inequality in sports participation, which varies according to social stratum.

Professional Culture

Overlying the concept of mass sport is a concept based on the actions of professional groups and individuals who claim that they are capable of ensuring the "quality of life" and even the "health" of individuals and society. Sports professionals such as physical educators and organizers "infest" the media, especially television, and pressure the state to intervene in the field of sport to promote and improve sports participation by the general public. Their self-imposed mission is to raise the level of people's physical and sports activity by disseminating inspirational messages ("getting back to health," for example) and by getting people involved in organized activities, such as courses in hockey, golf, physical fitness, and yoga (Levasseur, 1980, 1982). The themes of democratizing sport ("everyone can play outside") and decentralizing access to sport ("everyone in every region of Quebec can play outside") are the *leitmotivs* of sports "specialists" who take it upon themselves to make accessible all the sports activities that they promote.

Like mass culture, professional culture is a dominant culture: sports professionals shape and influence the needs and activities of individuals by representing the professional as the sole possessor of the technical know-how and skill necessary to introduce individuals and groups to sports activities (Levasseur, 1982; Jamet, 1980; Harvey, 1983). Hence sports professionals have things their own way in this area. This is the same phenomenon as we saw in mass culture — the cultural integration of the masses. In the case of physical culture, this integration is effected by defining and determining, for everyone, what sports activities consist of and even how they should be pursued. To play hockey today, it is no longer sufficient for a group of individuals to split up into two teams equal in number and strength and determine each team's respective territory; rather, each team must have the proper number of players, equal in age and category, and the game must be played on a regulation-size rink, preferably covered, and be presided over by officials — all this for a simple game of hockey. The same is true for most other sports activities, whatever the age of the participants.

Sport, Social Integration, and Social Participation

Mass culture and professional culture do not constitute two opposing, or contradictory, facets of sport, but two forms of mass social integration:

> When one opposes high culture (considered as liberating) to the mass media, this is only the defence of an aristocratic conception of society which reinforces a hierarchized style of consumption. When one opposes the organization of leisure activities to free time, one is only proposing a different form of social integration — as oppressive, and sometimes more so. (Touraine, 1971:225)

These minority-produced cultures nevertheless remain dissociated from the daily existence and activities of individuals, who are asked to limit their social participation to that of consumers of sports activities established by agents of the upper classes, such as sports industries and businesses, physical educators, and state administrators. These models of sports activity, presented to society in general, give rise to heterogeneous cultural behaviours in various social strata.

Depending on the stratum, the behaviour consists of the following: resisting, affirming, or challenging the dominant models; imitation; or cultural and social differentiation. Finally, cultural retreat can be seen as reflecting the extreme social and cultural isolation of marginal groups and individuals in a society.

The first three cultural behaviours can be linked to three social classes. The upper classes, who " . . . define themselves less by property or money than by education and managerial roles, that is, by cultural characteristics" (Touraine, 1971:206), pursue social and cultural differentiation. This behaviour is exemplified by their infatuation with "new" or "fashionable" sports and by their ownership of "private preserves" (golf courses, tennis courts, and riding clubs).

The middle classes, who also identify themselves by cultural traits (education and a high-ranking, but not top-level, job), often adopt imitative behaviour. Influenced by cultural models presented in the media, sensitive to social hierarchies, and with above-average incomes, the middle classes see sport as a favoured means of identification with the upper classes; this social positioning is effected through activities such as swimming, jogging, and cross-country skiing.

Finally, the working classes, characterized by their low incomes, a level of education seldom above secondary school, and low-level jobs, rarely participate, as a general rule, in sports. They prefer the warmth and intimacy of the family home and intense social relations — to be "entre soi" (Hoggart, 1958) — conditions that they do not find in sports participation. Only activities that are traditional in character (such as hunting and fishing) or which afford "togetherness" (walking, for example) are of any interest to them. Consequently, neither dominant model — mass culture or professional culture — ever has a solid grip on the working classes. That is why the dominant theories are constantly being reworked.

Now that we have outlined, in broad terms, the major influences on sport in Quebec and the main cultural behaviours of the social classes in relation to those models, let us see to what extent an analysis of empirical data will demonstrate the relevance and validity of our original propositions.

Sport as an Expression of Social Discrimination

First, it should be noted that this study is based on a secondary analysis of data from three surveys carried out for the Secretary of State, Health and Welfare Canada, and the Quebec Ministry of Recreation, Hunting, and Fishing, in 1972, 1976, and 1981, respectively. Only those data which relate to sports activities in Quebec will be analysed here. Readers interested in methodology and the representativeness of the samples should consult the reports published by the agencies (Kirsh et al., 1973; Statistics Canada, 1978; David and Gagnon, 1983).

The data from each survey were subjected to correspondence factor analysis (Benzécri et al., 1973). With this descriptive statistical method, data on all the sports activities and all the characteristics of the population being studied can be taken into account simultaneously with a view to establishing the most significant correlations between them.

In very general terms, the objective is to show that sports participation tends to conform to the organization of the social structure reflected in the different cultural behaviours of the social classes. Accordingly, social characteristics that are indicators of

Table I

Sports widely practised but unevenly distributed among the
social categories, population of Quebec aged 15 and over, 1972,
1976, and 1981 (percentage of participants)

Social categories		Population in the labour force Male				
Sports and year		B	W	P	Mn	I[2]
Play sports in general[4]	(1972)	29.1	35.0	50.5	39.1	22.2
	(1976)	70.3	76.4	86.5	83.0	68.8
	(1971)	86.4	90.3	94.4	91.0	—
Walking	(1972)	36.9	46.1	52.6	39.9	30.7
	(1976)	35.2	40.4	46.9	40.1	30.1
	(1981)	54.4	58.1	58.4	51.1	—
Sports events	(1972)	27.0	32.0	36.5	37.3	27.6
	(1976)	20.8	28.7	27.9	27.1	19.8
	(1981)	38.2	44.4	44.9	47.8	—
Swimming	(1972)	15.6	23.3	28.6	24.3	15.3
	(1976)	14.9	18.9	28.4	21.6	14.1
	(1981)	31.9	38.7	44.4	40.2	—
Exercise on foot	(1981)	29.3	26.6	40.4	32.6	—
Fishing	(1981)	41.4	32.3	36.5	33.7	—
Cycling	(1981)	16.9	16.1	19.1	25.0	—
Physical fitness exercises	(1981)	15.9	16.9	19.1	19.6	—
Gymnastics	(1976)	10.2	17.7	16.1	14.7	12.4
Hunting, fishing	(1972)	26.3	23.7	19.9	22.1	18.8
Snowmobiling	(1972)	19.9	16.4	10.3	12.5	20.6

1. This category was divided among the others in 1981.
2. This category is 99 per cent male.
3. These categories were included in the "other" category in 1976.

this structure (occupational category, income, and level of education) were selected, while other social attributes were included
to test the relevance of the above hypothesis. It is quite possible,
as some current theories on sports and physical exercise suggest,
that sports participation is determined by other social factors, such
as the size of the city of residence, being single, being male, or
being an anglophone.

All sports activities identified as such in the questionnaires
were selected, excluding "other" but including attendance at sports
events. Regular activity was used as the criterion in calculating
participation rates. This criterion varied according to the reference
period and the limits imposed by the time frame of the survey.
In the case of bicycling, for example, the criterion was "once a
week" in the 1972 survey, "four times or more in the past month"
in the 1976 survey, and "three times or more in the past six
months" in the 1981 survey. This problem applies, with a number of variations, to thirty-four different sports activities. This variability in the choice of activities and the criteria for regular
participation suggests that great caution should be exercised in
comparing the surveys, and this chapter was written with that in

| Population in the labour force | | | | | M or F | Not in the labour market | | | Other | | |
B	W	Female P	Mn	I[1]	Fa	Students M	F	H[3]	M	F	Total
21.1	32.6	42.7	24.4	16.9	22.3	63.2	61.0	20.5	10.1	6.2	31.6
61.4	75.3	85.3	87.2	76.4	56.6	—	—	—	71.8	62.7	71.9
83.4	92.2	93.3	90.5	—	63.9	76.8	95.1	80.2	80.8	71.1	85.2
40.9	50.4	60.0	39.9	38.5	21.5	60.8	67.4	44.0	45.3	32.4	45.6
35.5	42.7	53.2	58.6	42.1	30.4	—	—	—	46.6	39.5	40.3
70.2	69.4	69.8	47.6	—	30.6	52.3	56.1	69.4	57.5	58.4	61.6
19.7	25.5	27.7	18.0	16.4	17.8	49.0	49.1	14.1	8.3	3.1	25.3
12.5	17.7	17.5	17.5	13.7	11.2	—	—	—	13.8	10.4	18.2
26.5	27.5	27.3	19.0	—	22.2	42.1	32.9	20.2	17.2	10.4	28.6
12.4	23.1	31.8	22.8	6.3	8.4	39.3	40.2	11.0	4.0	6.8	18.8
11.1	19.1	26.3	31.0	14.3	8.0	—	—	—	17.9	13.2	17.1
39.1	45.3	46.7	61.9	—	11.1	55.1	61.0	24.2	16.9	15.6	32.5
29.1	31.8	46.7	47.6	—	33.3	35.5	24.4	26.3	24.5	20.2	29.5
17.9	28.2	16.0	9.5	—	19.4	45.8	15.9	13.5	29.1	12.1	25.0
20.5	25.2	25.3	23.8	—	8.3	38.3	37.8	14.4	10.0	14.5	18.3
15.2	19.0	21.3	9.5	—	8.3	50.5	31.7	14.6	10.3	13.9	17.2
12.7	17.7	18.7	28.5	17.6	6.5	—	—	—	21.1	14.4	15.0
6.6	6.3	8.7	10.3	6.0	21.6	24.2	4.0	6.1	12.1	3.4	14.2
13.3	12.4	9.9	12.4	16.6	27.0	20.6	24.0	9.0	5.0	-6.4	14.1

4. These three indices cannot be compared with one another, for example, to illustrate growth in overall sports participation between 1971 and 1981, since the indicators used to construct them varied from survey to survey.
Legend: B = blue-collar worker; W = white-collar worker; P = professional; Mn – manager; I = industrialist, merchant, craftsperson; Fa = farmer; H = homemaker; M = male; F = female.
Sources: 1972 = Kirsh et al. (1973); 1976 = Statistics Canada (1978); 1981 = David and Gagnon (1983).

mind. Regularity criteria also vary from sport to sport. For example, it is difficult to compare regularity in jogging with regularity in horseback riding. Moreover, the meaning of this criterion has widened considerably for some sports, owing to their recent arrival in the market (windsurfing, for example). Nevertheless, these sports are very useful indicators of the upper classes' propensity for seeking out novelty.

Sports Activities

Few sports activities were practised by a significant proportion of the population (more than 15 per cent), including attendance at sports events. Furthermore, only one activity, walking, can really be considered common: between 40 and 60 per cent of the total population, depending on the year of the survey, regularly engaged in it. This participation rate was far higher than that recorded for any other sport, no matter how popular. All sports, regardless of their relative popularity, showed differences linked to position in the social structure, between producers and non-producers, managers and subordinates, men and women, and women working inside and outside the home. In other words, participation, even in the most popular sports, was not equal or proportionate in all social categories (see Table 1).

It is also noteworthy that blue-collar workers attended sports events proportionately less often than members of other occupational categories, especially managers, who had the highest attendance rate. This observation contradicts the conventional view that the working classes are over-represented among sports spectators. In fact, the data show that the higher the level in the social hierarchy, the higher the frequency of attendance at sports events, especially among men — a trend similar to the one observed for sports participation in general. This means that being a spectator and being a participant are not opposite or incompatible attitudes towards sport, as we are too often led to believe, but rather complementary tendencies.

On the other hand, some less popular sports (under 9 per cent) can justifiably be called common inasmuch as they were distributed fairly evenly among the occupational categories (see Table 2). The fact that hockey was one of those sports is hardly surprising; in view of the appeal that hockey has for crowds, it seems natural that members of all occupational categories, especially men, would be equally tempted to lace on a pair of skates. Cycling, bowling, and pétanque (a form of lawn bowling) were also practised by all occupational categories, probably because of the familial, social atmosphere surrounding them, which makes them seem like games. This hypothesis appears all the more reasonable since the expressions "cycling to keep fit" (1976 question) and "bicycle trips" (1981 question), which refer to two of the more upscale forms of cycling, reveal biases based on occupational category. Lastly, the presence of canoeing/kayaking in this group of common activities is surprising, especially in view of the distances that must be travelled to pursue it, the attendant expense, and the setting, which provides little in the way of social contact or community life. It probably means that this sport, in spite of the isolation of the natural environment in which it is practised and its highly technical and competitive form, has kept or regained a traditional quality in the advanced, urbanized society that Quebec is today. This, however, is merely an avenue of research that would have to be explored in a more detailed study of canoeing/kayaking.

Finally, certain sports, such as weightlifting, hockey, hunting, and softball, appeared typically male, while yoga and walking were more popular among women. The data also reveal contrasts between groups of sports: for example, in 1972, snowmobiling, hockey, hunting, and fishing attracted a very different population

Table II

Sports infrequently practised but evenly distributed among the social categories, population of Quebec aged 25 to 64, 1972, 1976, and 1981 (percentage of participants)

Social categories	Population in the labour force										M or F(2)	Not in the labour force			
	Male					Female							Other		
Sports and year	B	W	P	Mn	I	B	W	P	Mn	I	Fa	H	M	F	Total
Bowling (1981)	7.5	6.6	6.7	6.8	—	6.3	8.5	8.0	5.0	—	2.9	5.9	4.2	9.7	6.8
Hockey (1972)	11.5	10.7	11.2	9.9	9.8	1.9	2.8	1.0	1.3	0.7	5.4	2.4	1.8	—	6.2
Canoeing– Kayaking (1981)	8.1	3.8	8.5	6.8	—	6.3	4.5	6.6	5.0	—	8.6	2.7	4.2	8.1	5.5
Cycling (1972)	4.7	4.8	3.6	6.1	3.5	4.0	5.6	6.7	8.3	2.0	5.0	4.2	1.3	8.9	4.6
Pétanque (1981)	3.2	4.7	3.7	4.5	—	6.3	2.5	2.9	—	—	2.9	3.1	1.7	1.6	3.2

1. This category was divided among the others in 1981.
2. This category is 99 per cent male.
Legend: B = blue-collar worker; W = white-collar worker; P = professional; Mn = manager; I = industrialist, merchant, craftsperson; Fa = farmer; H = homemaker; M = male; F = female.
Sources: 1972 = Kirsh et al. (1973); 1976 = Statistics Canada (1978); 1981 = David and Gagnon (1983).

from that which participated in downhill skiing, curling, tennis, swimming, and golf (see Figure 2), and in 1981, indoor tennis, sailing, and windsurfing appealed to a different population from that which engaged in fishing, hunting, and softball (see Figure 4).

In short, even though sport reached all levels of society, its distribution was not uniform, but appeared more like a mosaic of activities distributed among different social groups. Few sports practices, in effect, are generalized or common to the broad social strata, in the same way as the overall rate of participation in sport varies broadly with the social categories. Let us look now at the distribution of these sports as a function of the social structure.

Social Determinants of Sports Participation

Sport reflects very clearly the differences that stem from position in the occupational hierarchy and, more generally, in the social structure. Young, well-educated males who belonged to professional or managerial categories and had high incomes were the most likely to participate in at least one sport. Conversely, the groups who were most likely to be non-participants in sport were those whose position was not defined by their jobs, excluding students (notably homemakers and persons who had retired because of age or disability, those who had low-level jobs [especially blue- and white-collar workers], those who did not have an education above the primary level, and women).

An Activity of the Young

Sport is unquestionably an activity of the young. The 15- to 24-year-olds participated in all sports in proportionately larger numbers than they represented in the samples. Even though participation in sports declined progressively with age, not all age groups had the same effect or the same weight in this relationship. On the one hand, there was a very sharp contrast between 15- to 24-year-olds and those in the other five age groups; the difference was so great that the former seemed to consist entirely of participants and the latter of non-participants. On the other hand, there was very little difference in the level of participation of the four middle groups; the contrast between the two extremes, the 15- to 24-year-olds and those 65 and over, was the most pronounced (see Figure 1). In fact, when the population between the ages of 25 and 64 is analysed, age proves to be only a secondary factor in sports participation. The key elements are the social structure characteristics, primarily occupational category, income, and education, and to a lesser extent, gender.

An Activity of Non-Manual Workers

Labour force participation was the primary determinant of sports participation. On the whole, those who were not in the labour force were inactive in sports. They were not linked with any particular sport, and seemed to be simply excluded from the sports market. Although we cannot determine the origin of, or the reason for, this exclusion, we can say that the social categories in which this group belonged were at the margins of the social structure and were identified not by job but by occupation (basically homemakers and persons who had retired because of age or disability).

On the other hand, the fact that employed people (blue- and white-collar workers, salaried professionals, and senior managers) were, by and large, participants in sports does not mean that they formed a homogeneous class. Those who belonged to the higher occupational categories attempted to distinguish themselves from members of the lower categories by making investments in sports that expressed their class difference. This social distancing was based on occupational skills and leadership roles.

A Reflection of Occupational Skills

There is a difference in behaviour between blue-collar and white-collar workers on the one hand and salaried professionals

Figure 1

Sports activity and social categories, population of Quebec aged 15 or over, 1976 (Axes 1 and 2)

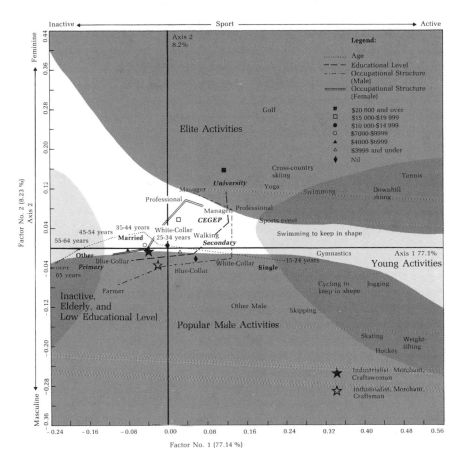

and managers on the other. What separates these two groups are occupational skills: the former perform operational tasks requiring few skills, while the latter, who have duties demanding special capabilities, have great professional autonomy. These occupational skills are also reflected in the important cultural capital (usually university-level education) and above-average incomes enjoyed by salaried professionals and senior managers.

This points to a split in sports participation: downhill skiing, tennis, jogging, and waterskiing, for example, are privileges of the middle and upper classes, both men and women (see Table 3).

Table III

Sports that discriminate on the basis of occupational skill, population of Quebec aged 25 to 64, 1972, 1976, and 1981 (percentage of participants)

| Social categories | | | | | | | | | | | M or F | |
| Sports and year | | Male | | | | | Female | | | | | |
	B	W	P	Mn	I	B	W	P	Mn	I	Fa	Total
Swimming (1972)	13.1	19.1	28.0	24.2	15.3	9.7	19.6	30.3	23.1	6.5	12.2	15.6
Swimming (1976)	10.6	13.0	27.9	22.4	11.7	6.7	16.2	20.9	31.9	9.6	3.1	13.9
Downhill skiing (1972)	4.4	5.3	17.3	17.4	3.3	3.1	7.9	19.4	13.9	4.9	3.6	6.5
Tennis (1972)	1.6	2.6	8.3	6.7	1.0	0.5	2.2	6.3	6.5	—	—	2.5
Tennis (1976)	1.5	3.7	9.0	9.6	1.3	0.8	2.3	5.0	4.8	—	—	2.9
Cross-country skiing (1976)	5.2	6.4	14.4	10.6	4.3	3.5	8.3	10.1	12.8	4.9	5.0	7.2
Jogging (1981)	10.6	13.2	23.8	20.5	—[1]	8.0	8.5	10.9	—	—[1]	5.7	10.4
Water skiing (1981)	6.3	5.7	9.1	9.1	—[1]	2.7	3.5	4.4	5.0	—[1]	—	4.0
Horseback riding (1981)	4.1	1.9	7.3	9.1	—[1]	3.6	5.0	7.3	10.0	—[1]	3.6	4.1

1. This category was divided among the others in 1981.
Legend: B = blue-collar worker; W = white-collar worker; P = professional; Mn = manager; I = industrialist, merchant, craftsperson; Fa = farmer; H = homemaker; M = male; F = female.
Sources: 1972 = Kirsh et al. (1973); 1976 = Statistics Canada (1978); 1981 = David and Gagnon (1983).

It would be rash to attribute the under-representation of the working classes in these sports solely to the cost of participating. Snowmobiling, for example, an expensive sport, was more popular among blue-collar and white-collar workers (see Table 4). Softball too can be quite costly if its social context is taken into account; the friendly get-togethers that follow games are to all intents and purposes an integral part of the sport. In short, although low incomes can be an obstacle to participation in sport, higher incomes do not remove all the barriers. It is probable that the working classes, who perceive work and leisure as two separate spheres of social life, participate in sport less for the challenge and personal fulfilment than for their attachment to collectively experienced values (Hoggart, 1958). By contrast, life seems less compartmentalized to the middle and upper classes and more open to individual interpretation; thus they seek in sport the equivalent of what they have at work.

A Sign of the Upper Classes

In many respects, salaried professionals and senior managers are similar; the latter, however, through their leadership function within organizations, readily identify with the upper classes and thus distinguish themselves from the salaried professionals. This role differentiation is also observable in the area of sport. Certain activities, though not exclusive to the upper classes,

Table IV

Sports characteristic of blue- and white-collar workers, population of Quebec aged 25 to 64, 1972 and 1981 (percentage of participants)

Social categories		Population in the labour force										M or F	Total
		Male					Female						
Sports and year		B	W	P	Mn	I	B	W	P	Mn	I	Fa	
Snow-mobiling	(1972)	17.6	13.4	10.0	11.4	20.9	9.3	8.2	9.2	13.3	17.0	24.0	12.1
Softball	(1981)	14.0	17.0	15.9	12.5	—[1]	3.6	2.5	0.7	—	—[1]	5.7	7.4

1. This category was divided among the others in 1981.
Legend: B = blue-collar worker; W = white-collar worker; P = professional; Mn = manager; I = industrialist, merchant, craftsperson; Fa = farmer; M = male; F = female.
Sources: 1972 = Kirsh et al. (1973); 1976 = Statistics Canada (1978); 1981 = David and Gagnon (1983).

arc more popular among them; such is the case, for example, with indoor tennis, sailing, windsurfing, and golf (see Table 5).

It is interesting to note that the upper classes switch to "new" sports as other social categories move into the older ones. For instance, in 1981 golf apparently no longer played the differentiating role it had played in 1972 and 1976; at the same time, the upper classes had become comparatively much more active in most of the sports that had come onto the market recently or had seen a renewed popularity, notably indoor tennis, sailing, and windsurfing. Tennis is interesting in that the indoor game is more appealing to the upper classes than the outdoor game. This is no doubt because outdoor courts are much more accessible than indoor courts. In other words, discrimination in sport relates not only to the exclusiveness of the activity, but also to the place where it is played.

Influence of Other Social Characteristics

Sport is without doubt a male activity: in general, women's participation rates were lower than those of men. Nonetheless, insofar as we are concerned specifically with the behaviour of women, we note that the higher they were in the social hierarchy, the more they erected barriers based on their occupational category, just as men did. In short, women who were at the margins of the social structure, primarily homemakers and female blue-collar workers, took little part in sports, while those who held the highest-level jobs participated considerably more (see Figures 2, 3, and 4).

Self-employed refers to those who derive their principal income from the exploitation of the means of production that they own: industrialists, merchants, and craftspeople. This category,

Table V

Sports characteristic of the upper classes, population of Quebec aged 25 to 64, 1972, 1976, and 1981 (percentage of participants)

| | | Population in the labour force | | | | | | | | | | M or F | |
| | | Male | | | | | Female | | | | | | |
		B	W	P	Mn	I	B	W	P	Mn	I	Fa	Total
Golf	(1972)	5.4	10.5	13.3	20.3	8.6	2.1	4.3	3.3	4.2	1.4	—	5.9
Golf	(1976)	2.2	4.8	4.7	11.4	3.9	0.3	1.3	2.0	1.9	—	0.5	2.5
Golf	(1981)	4.3	9.4	17.7	15.9	—[1]	1.8	3.5	5.1	—	—[1]	—	4.6
Indoor tennis	(1981)	1.4	0.9	5.5	9.1	—[1]	4.5	1.5	1.5	20.0	—[1]	—	2.0
Sailing	(1981)	2.5	4.7	6.1	8.0	—[1]	1.8	3.5	7.3	10.0	—[1]	—	3.1
Wind-surfing	(1981)	0.5	—	1.8	4.5	—[1]	1.8	1.0	2.2	5.0	—[1]	0.3	1.0

1. This category was divided among the others in 1981.
Legend: B = blue-collar worker; W = white-collar worker; P = professional; Mn = manager;
I = industrialist, merchant, craftsperson; Fa = farmer; H = homemaker; M = male; F = female.
Sources: 1972 = Kirsh et al. (1973); 1976 = Statistics Canada (1978); 1981 = David and Gagnon (1983).

though apparently heterogeneous, since it is impossible to separate the owners who usually operate their businesses alone from those who profit by exploiting the labour of other workers, is nevertheless stable from a socio-cultural and socio-economic point of view. In fact, most people in this category have no post-secondary education and have incomes comparable to those of blue-collar workers. The sports behaviour of farmers, too, to the extent that they have free time at their disposal, is like that of blue-collar workers. We can only conclude that, regardless of the control they have over their work activity, people in these categories are subject to living conditions analogous to those of blue-collar workers. Having a similar relationship to the world, farmers and self-employed workers express it, in sport, through behaviour similar to that of blue-collar workers: activities such as hunting, fishing, snowmobiling, and softball, for example, were particularly popular with them (see Figures 2, 3, and 4).

Although an activity-by-activity analysis might reveal correlations between participation in certain sports and other social factors, such as marital status, mother tongue, census metropolitan area, and municipality size, these diverse variables, as a whole, had little or no effect on sports participation. In short, the differences between married and single people, between residents of large cities and residents of small towns, and between anglophones and francophones, were so tenuous and applied to so few activities that these characteristics played almost no role in establishing a significant relationship.

Figure 2
Sports activities and social categories, population of Quebec aged 25 to 64, 1972 (Axes 1 and 2)

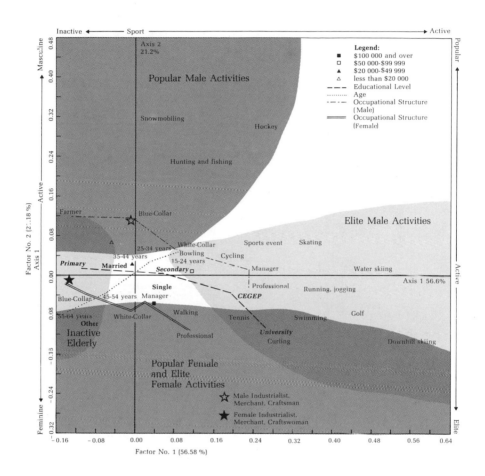

Towards Democratization in Sport?

Far from being democratized and universal, as current ideology would have it, sport appears to bear the stamp of the sports production apparatus (state and capitalist) and the uses that the social classes make of it. These classes perceive sport differently according to the position they occupy in the social structure; each one reinterprets, in its own way, the signs, models, and styles conveyed by the sports apparatus and assigns them a meaning determined by its own particular social experience.

Figure 3

Sports activities and social categories, population of Quebec aged 25 to 64, 1976 (Axes 1 and 2)

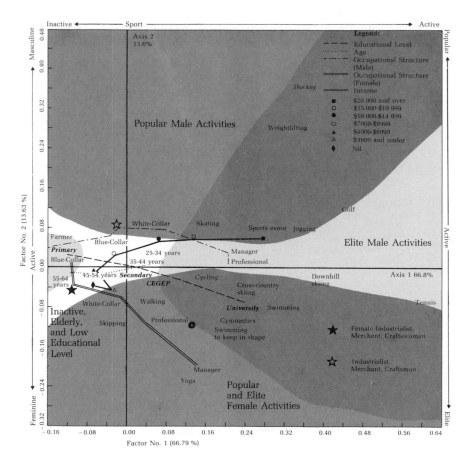

The working classes, who have a very clear feeling of being a group apart, of being "the people," take little part in the values of capitalist industrial society. Their attitude towards sport is thus consistent with the sense and meaning that they confer on their way of life and their daily existence, which centre on family and community life. In other words, they participate in sport to the extent that it is integrated into their lifestyle and allows activity or participation by the whole group.

The middle and upper classes, who participate to varying degrees in the development of the values that are propagated

Figure 4

Sports activities and social categories, population of Quebec aged 25 to 64, 1981 (Axes 1 and 2)

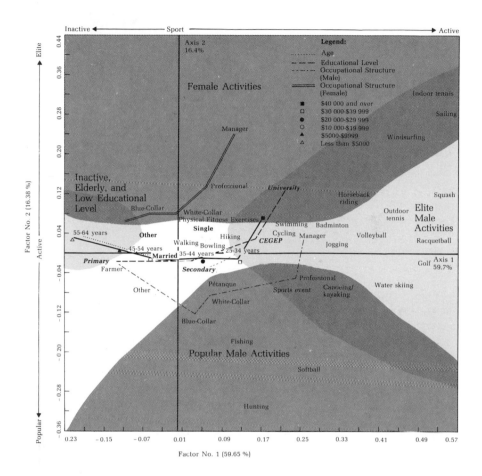

throughout society, see sports activity as a means of identifying themselves with these values and expressing socially preferred behaviour. The upper classes are the true initiators of new ways: they bring "new" sports onto the market and are at the same time the first to take them up. As a corollary to this, they tend to keep certain activities out of reach or to raise barriers to insulate themselves from the other classes when they engage in activities that are not limited to them. It is in this sense that the upper classes have distinctive social and cultural behaviours. The middle classes, who are more dependent on institutions, especially the state, to

Table VI
Comparison of sports participation in Quebec and other provinces

	Population aged 15 and over		Population aged 25 to 64	
Sports	Quebec (%)	Others (%)	Quebec (%)	Others (%)
Sports events	18.2	22.4	17.0	18.8
General sports activity*	71.9	74.8	68.8	72.2
Walking	40.3	38.7	36.8	34.7
Swimming	17.1	20.8	13.9	17.2
Gymnastics	15.0	18.0	10.6	13.6
Cycling for fitness	10.1	9.2	7.2	7.0
Jogging/running	9.6	12.9	7.0	7.4
Cross-country skiing	7.4	2.0	5.7	2.0
Swimming for fitness	6.4	5.3	4.8	4.4
Skating	6.2	7.4	3.5	4.4
Hockey	4.8	5.6	2.9	3.1
Tennis	4.8	6.9	2.6	4.2
Downhill skiing	3.4	3.2	2.5	2.0
Weightlifting	3.4	5.0	2.2	2.6
Golf	2.4	5.2	1.7	5.4
Yoga	1.6	2.6	1.5	2.5
Skipping	1.5	2.0	1.1	1.5

*This index was constructed on the basis of the following questions: "Have you exercised in the past month?" and "Have you taken part in sports or physical recreation activity in the past twelve months?"
Source: Statistics Canada (1978).

satisfy their needs, follow new cultural models more often than they create them. This is why their behaviour is considered to be imitative.

In spite of all the efforts and all the programs initiated by governments to encourage participation in sports, the results presented here indicate that sport was not democratized between 1972 and 1981. The observed increase in sports participation led to mass sport, but this does not mean that the various activities spread uniformly to all classes. On the contrary, the classes continually invent new ways of differentiating themselves and putting distance between themselves and others in order to mark their positions in the social structure. If sport is no longer, as it was in the recent past, the exclusive privilege of the upper classes, neither is it today a universal, democratized activity.

Suggested Readings

For an in-depth analysis of leisure and sport as cultural models in Quebec, see Roger Levasseur (1982), *Loisir et culture au Québec*, Montréal, Boréal Express, Michel Jamet (1980), *Les sports et l'État au Québec*, Montréal, Éditions coopératives Albert Saint-Martin, and Jean Harvey (1983), *Le corps programmé ou la rhétorique de Kino-Québec*, Montréal, Éditions coopératives Albert Saint-Martin. On class culture, see Christian Lalive d'Épinay et al. (1982), *Temps libre. Culture de masse et cultures de classes aujourd'hui*, Lausanne, Éditions Pierre-Marcel Favre, and Pierre Bourdieu (1984), *Distinction. A Social Critique of the Judgement of Taste*, Harvard, Routledge & Kegan Paul.

Chapter Fourteen
Physical Activities, Body *Habitus*, and Lifestyles

Suzanne Laberge and David Sankoff

The Socio-Cultural Approach

The analysis we present here follows the socio-cultural approach and is based on the theoretical framework set out by Pierre Bourdieu (1978, 1984). Our starting point in this approach is to question the "naturalist" postulate, according to which participation in physical activities responds to a natural need to move and choices of, or preferences in, physical activities are relatively arbitrary or innate (determined by genetic inheritance and morphological and physiological characteristics). We also assume that functionalist theories stating that physical activities correspond to social functions of "physical relaxation," "self-betterment," and "diversion" (Dumazedier, 1977), which are characteristic of our industrialized societies, can be challenged.

A model whose objective is the understanding of participation in physical activities or of the unequal "popularity" of these different physical activities between social classes, sexes, or age groups must of course take into consideration such determining factors as: economic capital (more or less necessary depending on the physical activity — for example, golf requires a greater monetary investment than jogging does); cultural capital (that is, knowledge essential to participation, also more or less essential depending on the physical activity — for example, sailing compared with cycling); and free time (often dependent on economic capital). Nevertheless, these factors, however necessary they might appear, are not sufficient. A model that fails to go beyond them misses an essential dimension: the different concepts and perceptions that social classes or class segments have of the various physical activities, and whether they engage in them or not. Thus a sociological understanding of participation in physical activities cannot ignore certain aspects of reality: (a) for certain social classes, participation in diversified, regular physical activity is part of a certain ethic or custom, while for others it is a waste of time; (b) certain classes see physical activity primarily as an expenditure of energy, while others choose to regard it as an information-processing activity; and (c) certain classes seek originality and freedom in their activities while others prefer a framework of some sort.

Class Habitus

The systematic variation in attitudes, perceptions, and appreciations among the various social classes and class segments is the cornerstone on which Bourdieu builds his theoretical framework. He postulates the existence of a schematic system (a set of schemes forming an organic whole) of dispositions, perceptions, and appreciations specific to each social class or class segment. The affinities observed in the nature, properties, or characteristics of the various practices of a given social class (such as rules of etiquette, interior decoration, choice of clothing, type of food, and type of recreational activities) provide the grounds for establishing the existence of such a schematic system. Bourdieu defines "class *habitus*" (1984:101) as that generating principle of tastes, likes, and dislikes which determines choices in the form of consumer practices which constitute a lifestyle.

The Latin word *habitus* was first used by Marcel Mauss in his study of body techniques published in *Sociologie et anthropologie* (1966:365–386). Mauss chose it because he was looking for a specific term to identify the shaping of the individual by the community and because it conveyed better than "habit" the idea of having been acquired. Whereas Mauss used *habitus* only with reference to physical demeanour or behaviour, Bourdieu broadened the notion and developed it into a concept that represented a generating principle of the totality of habits that make up lifestyles and are characteristic of the social classes.

It is important to point out here that class *habitus*, as defined by Bourdieu, is an "internalized form of the class condition and the conditionings it entails" (1984:101). Hence, if we wish to understand the origins of physical activity practices, we must go back to the different conditions of existence that produce different *habitus*, which themselves produce different lifestyles (see

Figure 1
Conditions of Existence, *Habitus,* and Lifestyles

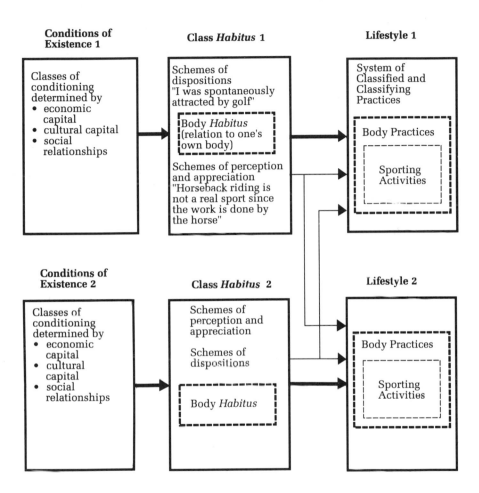

Conditions of Existence 1

Classes of conditioning determined by
• economic capital
• cultural capital
• social relationships

Class *Habitus* 1

Schemes of dispositions
"I was spontaneously attracted by golf"

Body *Habitus* (relation to one's own body)

Schemes of perception and appreciation
"Horseback riding is not a real sport since the work is done by the horse"

Lifestyle 1

System of Classified and Classifying Practices

Body Practices

Sporting Activities

Conditions of Existence 2

Classes of conditioning determined by
• economic capital
• cultural capital
• social relationships

Class *Habitus* 2

Schemes of perception and appreciation

Schemes of dispositions

Body *Habitus*

Lifestyle 2

Body Practices

Sporting Activities

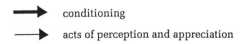 conditioning

acts of perception and appreciation

Figure 1, which shows the relationship between conditions of existence, class *habitus*, and lifestyle). Conditions of existence determine the multiple conditionings that characterize daily life, such as type of work (which depends on position in relation to the means of production and the division of labour between the sexes), greater or lesser distance from the constraints of economic necessity, knowledge acquired from educational and cultural capital, and type of family ties. These conditions of existence, which vary from one social class to another, determine *habitus* that reproduce the differential separations between the classes. In turn, the *habitus* give rise to lifestyles, sets of practices whose properties express the differences objectively recorded in the conditions of existence.

By way of illustration (inevitably stereotyped and incomplete), the preferences of blue-collar workers for collective sports (such as softball and hockey) can be seen as the carry-over of disposition schemes conditioned by directed work, which often involves a special relationship with the group, into sports activity. These preferences contrast with those of executives and professionals for sports played individually or in pairs, which embody the disposition schemes produced by jobs that emphasize autonomy and individual initiative (Le Pogam, 1979:77). Class *habitus*, then, is both the internalization of the conditions of existence and the practice-generating principle of social agents. It effects the indispensable mediation between class conditions on the one hand and structured practices (that is, lifestyles) on the other.

Body Habitus

In order to comprehend more fully the specific character of participation in physical activities, however, a fundamental aspect of the class *habitus* must be taken into consideration — the body *habitus*. Boltanski, who applied this concept heuristically in an analysis of the use of medical services in France, defines it as a system of implied schemes governing the relation to one's own body (1971:225). Bourdieu too recognized the theoretical necessity and the explanatory value of this concept in his article "Sport and Social Class":

> . . . it is the relation to one's own body, a fundamental aspect of the habitus, which distinguishes the working classes from the privileged classes, just as, within the latter, it distinguishes fractions that are separated by the whole universe of a life-style. On one side, there is the *instrumental* relation to the body which the working classes express in all the practices centred on the body,

whether in dieting or beauty care, relation to illness or medication, and which is also manifested in the choice of sports requiring a considerable investment of effort, sometimes of pain and suffering (e.g. boxing) and sometimes *a gambling with the body itself* (as in motor-cycling, parachute-jumping, all forms of acrobatics, and to some extent, all sports involving fighting, among which we may include rugby). On the other side, there is the tendency of the privileged classes to treat the body as an *end in itself*, with variants according to whether the emphasis is placed on the intrinsic functioning of the body as an organism, which leads to the macrobiotic cult of health, or on the appearance of the body as a perceptible configuration, the "physique," i.e. the body-for-others. (1978:838)

This implies that the body *habitus* characteristic of male members of the working classes would translate, in their physical activity practices, into the use of the body as a means or instrument of playing sports, while the body *habitus* of male members of the middle classes would tend towards participation in "sports for the body," with their aesthetic or health connection (physical fitness, disease prevention). The gender specification is important here also: as we will see later, women of the various social classes have their own specific body *habitus* which reflect the particular social relations between the sexes in the different classes.

It is important to stress that the relation to one's own body cannot be identified with or reduced to "body image" or "body concept," which essentially consists of objective representation of the body produced and transmitted back by others; a body *habitus* is made up of all the dispositions one has towards one's body, themselves determined and conditioned by the material conditions of existence. Body *habitus* is revealed by the manner in which the body is carried (upright or listless), groomed, nourished, and cared for; the differences among the various social classes in their relation to the body show up in all these areas.

The adoption of this theoretical framework for the study of the social significance of participation in physical activities implies the necessity of recognizing the body *habitus* present in a given social structure and of relating these body *habitus* to the various class *habitus*. Obviously such a research project presents a number of methodological problems. First, the very concept of *habitus* cannot be pinpointed directly with immediately accessible empirical data. *Habitus* are essentially unconscious; they are experienced like anything else that is natural (Bourdieu, 1962:100). Nevertheless, they are expressed through products, that is, through the activity of those whose activity they govern. Hence, it will be possible to identify practice-generating schemes through observation, analysis, and comparison of the body practices and lifestyles of members of the different social groups. These schemes will be deduced both from the relations between the practices of a single group (disposition schemes) and from the relations with the practices of other social groups (perception and appreciation schemes).

Another methodological problem is to identify sociologically relevant body practices; since it is not realistic to attempt to consider all the daily acts and all the elements that characterize a lifestyle, it is necessary to make a selection based on prior ethnographic observation and sociological analysis.

Women and Participation in Physical Activities

Hypotheses and Objectives of the Study
The data analysed here are from a survey on the broader topic of the socio-economic determinants of participation in physical and sports activities by women living in Montreal. Women are considered social agents with a specific position in the social structure, given the particular conditions of existence imposed by their social relations with the male agents of their social class. One of the main objectives of the study was to understand the *social significance* of participation in physical and sports activities by women of different socio-economic milieux by relating this participation to other physical behaviours and other recreational activities.

Two fundamental hypotheses were formulated, based on the theoretical framework described above. The first is that participation in physical activities is consistent with other physical behaviours in that it is determined by the same generating principle — the relation to one's own body or the body *habitus* that varies systematically with the social conditions of existence. The second is that the various body practices are an integral part of the lifestyles characteristic of the social classes.

The specific aim of this study is, initially, to identify the structure of the relations, in terms of both common and distinct properties, between concepts, perceptions, and behaviours concerning the body that seem relatively independent, as described by women from different socio-economic milieux; this should highlight the distinctive body *habitus* that characterize them. Subsequently, the aim will be to situate these behaviours and concepts within a larger set of activities — in this case leisure activities, which are characteristic of lifestyles — in such a way as to reveal the different social logics that give rise to them.

Methodology

The target population consisted of married (or formerly married) female francophones who were neither athletes nor students; this choice was based on sociological evidence that female students and unmarried women have different lifestyles and that ethnic origin is a determining variable for certain activities. The general objectives of the research project justified the selection of a sample stratified by socio-economic level (five strata). A total of 180 women, ranging in age from 20 to 70, were interviewed. The data are taken from responses to a questionnaire containing 108 semi-open questions on four main subjects: (1) participation in physical activities; (2) opinions and perceptions regarding various physical behaviours; (3) cultural consumption and leisure practices; and (4) socio-demographic information. In order to obtain additional ethnographic observations and qualitative and spontaneous commentary, complementary to the quantitative results and essential to the explanation and interpretation, interviewers were instructed to visit the respondents in their homes and to record their answers personally, along with any additional comments, on the questionnaire form. Only information relevant to our present concerns will be used in the analysis conducted here.

A two-stage statistical process was used to discover the structure of the relations between the various practices studied. First, the Pearson correlation coefficient was calculated for each pair of practices or variables. This provided a matrix of correlation coefficients which, in stage two, were subjected to a multidimensional scaling analysis by means of the INDSCAL program (Carroll and Chang, 1970). This statistical procedure translates the configuration of weak and strong correlations into a two-dimensional display of the practices. Hence, with the results of stage two, it was possible to locate each practice spatially and identify configurations or structures of relations. The principle behind this procedure is that practices most often associated with one another in the target population will appear closer together on the display, while those least often associated will be farthest away from one another. It is important to note that the axes do not necessarily represent interpretable dimensions or variables; they serve only as mathematical points of reference for the construction of the display. The underlying premise in this analysis is that the spatial configuration obtained is sociologically significant and is representative of the schemes of concepts and perceptions that characterize the classes and class segments making up the sample.

Participation in Physical Activities and Body *Habitus*

First of all, we wanted to relate the regular participation (on a monthly basis) of women in physical activities to various aesthetic or ethical perceptions and consumer practices related to the body. This meant studying the variation in the mode and form of attention to, and interest in, their bodies and attempting to identify their sociological significance in terms of body *habitus*. To do this, we considered the responses to seventeen questions about opinions, concerns, and behaviour regarding the body, health and beauty care, and hygiene, such as "Do you smoke?", "Have you ever been on a diet?", and "Do you go to the doctor to prevent as well as to cure illness?" The answers to each question corresponded to a particular value on an ordinal variable defined as a function of characteristics most likely to be associated with regular participation in physical activities. It follows that the relations identified in the analysis arise within a set of practices that have an inherent sociological consistency (for example, non-smoker, dieter, and participant in physical activities) and not among incompatible elements (for example, smoker/non-smoker or active/sedentary).

The diagram obtained (by applying the spatial representation technique to the matrix of 136 correlation coefficients, calculated over the 17 variables) reveals four main groupings, some of which partially overlap (see Figure 2). Each group was labelled with a name reflecting the distinctive features common to its members — *discipline*, *cosmetics*, *health*, and *luxury*. Even though these are groupings of variables, each of them necessarily corresponds to a more or less well-defined group of individuals who tend to have a number of these variables in common.

Discipline
In this group there is a concern with abstinence from tobacco, the "pleasures of eating," and fast food. This concern is typical of women who check their weight almost daily and rigidly

Figure 2
Physical Activity and Body *Habitus*

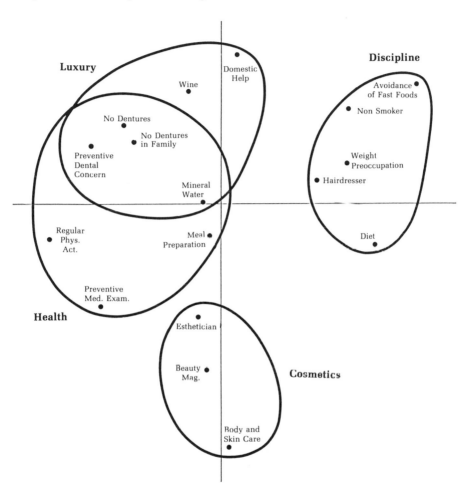

adhere to the "norms" of a particular concept of "healthy maintenance of the body." For instance, there was a primary-school teacher (who by the objective standards of physical activity professionals would be considered very slender) who told us she restricted her food intake whenever she was more than a kilo above her usual weight and who defined a "tasty" food as a "healthy" one. This ascetic outlook contrasts with the view of working-class women we met, whose weight gain limit before they started a diet was as high as ten kilos; being considered "fat" has more to do with the cultural system to which one belongs than with the actual percentage of body fat. Moreover, many working-class women prefer smoking to dieting as a means of reducing their appetite and say that they like the taste of a "good hamburger from the fast-food place on the corner."

Bourdieu associates disciplinary ethical and aesthetic attitudes with the middle classes. Thus, he states:

> Everything seems to suggest that concern to cultivate the body appears, in its most elementary form, i.e. as the cult of health, often implying an *ascetic exaltation of sobriety and dietetic rigour*, among the middle classes, i.e. among junior executives, clerical workers in the medical services and especially primary-school teachers. (1978:838; emphasis added)

Cosmetics

Cosmetics are defined here as the set of all practices involving the use of beauty and health products for the body. Far from, or even opposed to, the previous grouping is a cluster of at least three variables representing concerns and consumer practices that centre on care for the appearance. This relates to a concept of body aesthetics that has to do with the techniques of using make-up or beauty care products and with following the current fads in this area. This concept is characteristic of women who are attracted by beauty magazine products trumpeting miracle "cellulite remover" or "wrinkle remover" products; these products are obviously rejected by the group with the disciplinary ethos, who basically consider the only valid treatment of skin and body to be that due to "healthy nutrition."

Health

On the left side of the display appear two groupings that partially overlap: one shows a group of traits or practices typical of a preventive attitude towards physical problems that we have labelled "health"; the other also includes certain practices that are socially classified under the heading "luxury." In particular, regular participation in physical activities (as measured on the basis of frequency per month for the current year) appears to be statistically associated with behaviours that are consistent with the preventive-care precepts characteristic of the thinking of most health professionals today. In his study on the use of medical services in France, Boltanski observed that "the percentage of social subjects willing to submit to the demands of preventive medicine

was larger in the upper classes than in the working classes"
(1971:221). This is due, in part, to the fact that obeying the rules
of preventive medicine does not depend on individual responsibility but is determined by the material conditions of life. Boltanski
points out that the objective conditions under which members of
the working class live, especially economic insecurity, force them
to internalize an ethos and an attitude regarding time that pro-
hibits them, *a fortiori*, from adopting a preventive attitude towards
illness (1971:222).

It seems sociologically valid to consider the drinking of
mineral water and the amount of time spent preparing meals compatible with concerns about preventive health care; for those who
see the chemical additives and preservatives used in commercial
preparations as a threat to their health, investing time in the preparation of "home-cooked meals" is a necessity. By the same
reasoning, the preference for mineral water can be traced to a
certain disdain for tap water.

Luxury

We have included semi-annual preventive dental checkups
and the absence of false teeth in the subset of luxury dispositions
because of the special position of dental care within the health-
care system. Dental care is not covered by the state health insurance program, and in view of the high fees charged by dentists,
not having false teeth is a form of luxury. As well, in contrast with
the custom in France, drinking wine at meals is seen, in North
America, as a luxury typical of a certain middle-class style. Lastly,
avoidance of housekeeping chores is another "body-saving" attitude associated with luxury; doing housework oneself or paying
someone else to do it comes from the same principle which opposes
"forced necessity" to luxury as a "statement of distance from
necessity" (Bourdieu, 1984:254).

If we now look at the positions of the various sets of practices in relation to the axes, we can obtain some information about
the contrasts between the body *habitus*, which are represented by
spatial separation: (1) on the one hand, the practices associated
with a luxury ethos contrast with cosmetic concerns and atten-
tions; (2) on the other hand, a disciplinary disposition towards the
body — surprising as it may seem — is distant from both the preventive health-care ethic and the rules of cosmetic behaviour. The
system of relations between these *habitus* could be interpreted as
the opposition between, on the one hand, acceptance of and con-
fidence in (or dependence on) "professionals" (doctors, dentists,

beauticians, physical educators, and other specialists) (Harvey, 1983) and, on the other, preference for self-directed or self-controlled care of the body.

Participation in Physical Activities and Lifestyles

To achieve fuller understanding of the sociological aspect of the body *habitus*, we must locate them within the larger framework of the class *habitus*. Considering our empirical approach, it is methodologically necessary that our access to *habitus* be through the study of lifestyles. The leisure activities of women have been used as indicators of lifestyles. We believe that it is possible to discern the typical lifestyle of a social group through its use of free time.

The same mathematical process described above was applied to 36 variables (including the 17 already indicated). The Pearson measure of correlation was calculated for these 36 variables taken in pairs, which produced a matrix of 630 correlation coefficients. This new matrix was then subjected to multidimensional scaling analysis in order to produce a two-dimensional display of the relations among the various practices (see Figure 3).

The results once again formed four major groupings. Overall, although there are some changes, variables that are near each other in the first graph remain associated. Since these variables are now part of a larger matrix, however, the application of scaling analysis has realigned them, causing the observed changes. The scaling analysis has also produced groupings that are more representative of the different lifestyles. We have labelled them by social class, relying on subjective knowledge of the community being studied (Bourdieu, 1962:108) and not on correlations with the socioeconomic data (income, education, and occupational category) of the sample. We shall now analyse these groupings and see how the underlying logic characteristic of each social class, as well as the dynamic of social relations, can add to our understanding of the body *habitus* and participation in physical activities.

The Middle Class
The highest frequency of participation in physical activities seems characteristic of the lifestyle of women of the middle class (such as primary-school teachers, secretaries, nurses, and librarians). The most common daily activities are basic exercises,

Figure 3
Physical Activity and Lifestyles

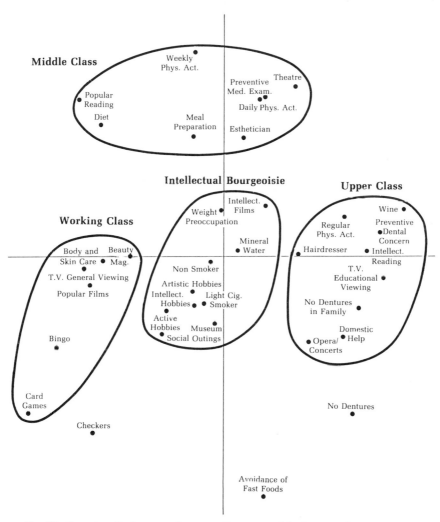

or "callisthenics," done at home. On a weekly basis, the most popular physical activities are swimming and aerobics, "jazzercise," or "workout" exercises. This is a perfect example of the phenomenon of prestige imitation (Mauss, 1966:369), that is, copying the behaviour of those one admires. This frequent physical activity is statistically associated with preventive health-care behaviour (but not in the luxury category — preventive dental checkups are a feature of the upper class), as well as with an obvious desire to be "slim"; these women follow strict diets and willingly spend a great deal of time preparing low-calorie meals. The preferred leisure activities of this social group are reading "popular" literature (bestsellers, usually American books translated into French) and attending the theatre (by subscription). For this group, going to plays is not a matter of gratuitous aesthetic pleasure but a self-imposed rule of behaviour. In their own words, "one must nourish the mind as well as one nourishes the body." Thus, even the way they spend their free time seems to obey a logic conforming to prestige models and to norms of the dominant classes.

One might ask what the rationale is that prompts these women to invest so much in terms of effort (participating in physical activities), deprivation (dieting), and time (preparing meals) in their physical appearance. It might be assumed that the amount invested is proportional to expected material or symbolic profits. These women profit from their investment all the more since their professional "success" is largely a function of their "image" or their appearance. By virtue of their position in the labour market, these middle-class women have no choice but to submit, to some degree, to the dominant norms. This forced conformity is a source of tension. As a consequence, they are intimidated, underrating their own physique and spending more time on beautifying activities (in the never-fulfilled hope of improving the body) than do women of other classes, including the upper classes. In fact, they appear to be as dissatisfied with their bodies as working-class women do with theirs, but perhaps this has to do with their knowledge and acceptance of the dominant ideal of "physical excellence" (Bourdieu, 1978:51–54).

The Working Classes

Contrasted with this ethic or stringent morality requiring care of the body is the set of practices characteristic of the working classes. First, participation in physical activities is not one of those practices. Government agencies promoting physical fitness regularly complain about the low rate of participation by these women. It is important to note, however, that only those activities which conform to a normative or "dominant" definition of physical activity are considered and that this particular picture of reality would be markedly different if other types of physical activity were taken into account (Laberge, 1983). Second, middle-class and working-class women have sharply contrasting concepts of physical appearance. In the former group, the dominant concept centres on an "internal causality" of form (dieting and frequent, regular physical activity) along with a preoccupation with preventive health-care (medical checkups), whereas in the latter group, the dominant concept is based on cosmetic factors, stressing the alteration of surface details or external traits. In fact, the material conditions of existence of working-class women and the unlikelihood of their getting jobs that require conformity to the "legitimate" model account for their disinclination to "change nature"; when there is no possibility of "correcting the problem," one can only "dress it up." This is perhaps not dissimilar to the idea of "working-class realism" discussed by Bourdieu (1984:200), which leads people to "be what they are" rather than "kidding themselves." This line of reasoning explains, in part, the distinctive preferences of these women with respect to cosmetic products and beauty magazines. Moreover, it may be assumed that reading beauty magazines ("mostly for the pictures," one informant told us) is consistent with an escapist attitude that is also manifested in leisure practices — "popular" films (the label we have used to represent films with an entertainment or romantic content rather than an "intellectual" one) and "popular" television programs (soap operas and variety shows). Finally, card games and bingo are leisure activities that stigmatize and are uniquely characteristic of the lifestyle of working-class women.

The Intellectual Bourgeoisie

Some people would be surprised to find no evidence of participation in physical activities in this class segment. However, we should point out that we did not include in the "participation in physical activities" variable such activities of the "anti-exercise" style as the "Thérèse Bertherat technique," "body expression," "psycho-physical therapy," yoga, relaxation techniques, and "body awareness through movement" techniques. (These activities were noted in the supplementary qualitative information.) The women of this social group expressed dislike for the intense physical effort required by "physical conditioning" or any other type of aerobic exercise, which they considered more "dangerous" than "beneficial," maintaining, for example, that "the body is not meant for that," or that "it's stressful for the body." Rather than this ethic of physical effort, they preferred the "gymnastiques douces" which are based on a different system of precepts that is just as stringent but in a completely opposite way. Designed to substitute relaxation for tension, pleasure for effort, "creativity" and "freedom" for discipline, and communication for isolation, they favour a treatment of the body that consists of "listening," "rediscovering," "centring," and "liberating." Bourdieu describes this anti-ascetic ethic as follows:

> The new ethical avant-garde urges a morality of *pleasure as a duty*. This doctrine makes it a failure, a threat to self-esteem, not to "have fun," . . . pleasure being not only permitted but demanded. . . . The fear of not getting enough pleasure . . . is combined with the search for self-expression and "bodily expression" and for communication with others ("relating" — *échange*), even immersion in others (considered not as a group but as subjectivities in search of their identity); and the old personal ethic is thus rejected for a cult of *personal health* and *psychological therapy*. (1984:367)

This passion for activities involving physical expression can be linked with a new ethic of some upwardly mobile segments of the middle class who favour liberalism in educational affairs, in relations with authority, and in sexual matters, contrasting it with ascetic rigour, which they denounce as "repressive."

This "anti-repressive" ethic may also prevent them from dieting even though they consider themselves "too fat" and are concerned about their weight. Instead, they tend to buy natural products, which is why they are popularly branded as "granola intellectuals." Moreover, they either do not smoke at all or else smoke "light" cigarettes.

The activities favoured by these women of the "new middle class" involve a large cultural investment (taking courses or training). However, the profits they expect to derive from that investment are of a more symbolic or socially distinctive nature than economic or material. This "cultural distinction" logic may explain the large number, diversity, and type of leisure activities preferred by this class segment. A total of six leisure activities (or at least twice as many as in the other classes) are statistically associated here: intellectual films (such as Bergman and Pasolini), artistic hobbies (such as photography, painting, playing musical instruments, and singing), active hobbies (doing odd jobs, gardening, travel), intellectual hobbies (conferences, literary writing, politics, genealogy), social outings (visiting or dining out with friends), and visits to museums.

The lifestyle of this class segment also shows evidence of the phenomenon of prestige imitation; the model in this case, however, is Paris or London. This European-oriented prestige imitation is deliberately antithetical to everything "American," to everything mass-produced or mass-consumed. Thus their dislike of the group pantomime of a Jane Fonda workout, which is so popular in the middle class, is comprehensible.

The Upper Class

The last grouping we identified, the farthest from the working classes in its practices, corresponds to a lifestyle characterized by luxury. In this group, people employ housemaids, have preventive dental checkups (and therefore do not have false teeth), attend concerts (classical music, of course) and operas, and regularly drink wine.

Physical activities are engaged in regularly as measured on a monthly basis. Preferred sports are golf, tennis, and downhill skiing, activities often pursued at private clubs. The typology of social logics developed by Baudrillard (1969) may help us to understand the different *habitus* governing participation in physical activities. Baudrillard believes that "the social logic that governs the use of objects according to class is inseparable from that of the ideology of 'consumerism' underlying their use" (1969:60–64). The "logic of sign-value" (the activities most highly prized socially are appropriated by the subjects and serve as an expression of distinction) influences both participation and the mode of participation in physical activities by the upper class (the liberal professions and the business establishment). At the same time, the "economic logic of exchange-value" directs women of the middle class towards frequent participation in physical activities in the expectation of benefitting professionally from it, owing to the importance of physical appearance in their area of work. This logic of sign-value, which directs the choice of physical activities among upper-class women, is associated with a desire to accumulate social capital. This can be seen in the fact that participation in physical activities often serves as a pretext for specific get-togethers and constitutes a means of social contact serving to broaden and to "improve" their network of "acquaintances." The time required for these "après-sport" get-togethers limits the frequency of participation compared with the "excessive" frequency of middle-class women, who go directly home or to work after their activity.

Finally, participation in physical and leisure activities by upper-class women is characterized by family activity (Le Pogam, 1979:131–133), a feature that does not show up on the graph. Women in this class segment seem to attach considerable importance to the transmission of cultural capital. Hence they seek and prefer activities they can engage in with their husbands and children (the father is presented as a model and it is hoped that the son will follow in his footsteps: father is a doctor, son is a future doctor; father is a lawyer, son is a future lawyer).

We shall now summarize the main points arising from our analyses. Frequent participation in physical activities seems primarily characteristic of women of the middle class. Their specific position in the labour market, where great importance is attached to physical appearance and to representational roles, accounts to a large extent for the desire, demonstrated in their physical consumption practices, to conform to the dominant norms that define what the outward configuration of the body should be.

This class segment contrasts with what we call the intellectual bourgeoisie. The activities favoured by this second group reflect both the balance of power in the struggle for the definition of legitimate physical activity and the opposition between two views of the world, two antagonistic philosophies; women of the intellectual bourgeoisie seem to value "physical awareness" over "physical form" (or "physical fitness"), the search for "harmony with the body" over the search for "control of the body," the acquisition of "cultural knowledge" over the acquisition of will and strength of character (the second term in each of these contrasting pairs represents values belonging to the middle class).

Women of the intellectual bourgeoisie take up the latest physical activities supplied by the production market, on the one hand because of their new and rare character which gives them much of their value, and on the other hand to be able to disqualify and discredit the values of activities that at one time were considered legitimate and which are now popular with the middle class. Once these "new activities" become widespread (obeying the producers' and suppliers' logic of popularization), they are gradually deserted by this social group because they lose an essential part of their value (Pociello, 1981:220). This process relates to the historical perspective inherent in any social phenomenon. Although we have not been able to develop this aspect in the present cross-sectional study, we must stress in passing that the social significance of physical activities is essentially determined by evolution and the historical context in which they are situated. For example, the massive influx of women into the labour market, in jobs involving appearance and representation, is a determining factor in the expectations of women of this new class segment with regard to physical activities.

Taking advantage of their freedom from necessity, upperclass women show their "class comforts" through the diversity of areas in which they invest their time (in relation to the variables proposed in this study): intellectual (reading and television programs), socio-cultural (concerts and opera), aesthetic (hairstyling), health (preventive dental checkups), and sports (regular physical activity as measured on a monthly basis). Their class comforts go hand in hand with a search for distinction expressed in the consumption of luxury items (domestic help, regular consumption of wine, and absence of false teeth). The manner in which upper-class women behave with respect to physical activities is connected to a sign-value imperative in the choice of activities and to a social capital accumulation logic and a cultural capital transmission (through family activities) in the types of activity.

The relative absence of participation in physical activities by working-class women, as defined by the norms, may be due to the fact that they see no advantage in it. In view of their specific position in social space (determined by sex and class), the contribution that participation in physical activities could make to changing the conditions of their lives is probably quite small. Thus their material conditions of existence would encourage a sort of "realistic" or "critical" awareness when they look at the hygienic (health), professional (physical appearance and "keeping trim" are not keys to success in manufacturing or factory work), and aesthetic (physical activity does not change one's external traits) benefits that physical activity could bring them. Cosmetic products, which produce "immediate" and perceptible surface changes, are therefore the best way of responding to their aesthetic concerns.

In conclusion, it seems that the structure of the relations between various physical practices, different types of attention to the body, and various leisure activities provides information about the social meaning of participation in physical activities, that is, about the social logics that govern these activities and the balance of power between the different classes and class segments with respect to the definition of legitimate physical activity. It is important to note that our analysis is only valid for women, because each class and each class segment attributes to each sex a specific position in the system and the dynamic of social relations.

Moreover, it appears that the variation in participation by women in physical activities according to social class depends not only on the different capacities of women with respect to time and money, but also on the variations in the perception and appreciation of the profits, whether immediate or long-term, that the various physical activities could bring them, perceptions and appreciations that are essentially determined by the class *habitus*.

Suggested Readings

Besides the books and articles mentioned in this chapter, all of which are fundamental theoretical works, the closest reference to our type of analysis is Christian Pociello (Ed.) (1981) *Sports et société*, Paris, Vigot. This book contains several studies which use the socio-cultural approach developed by Pierre Bourdieu. In particular, for an account of women and sports, readers should note the chapters of Catherine Louveau and Jacqueline Blouin–Le Baron. For a comparative analysis of the sporting practices of two opposed groups, see Yves Le Pogam (1979), *Démocratisation du sport: mythe ou réalité?*, Paris, Jean-Pierre Delarge.

Chapter Fifteen
The Elite Athlete

Bruce Kidd

Introduction

Athletes are often aware of the perspective which informs this publication — that modern sport is deeply structured by society and history — because they experience it in both rewarding and conflicting ways.

I think back to my own career as a runner in the 1960s. My teammates and I developed a tremendous sense of our own power, pushing back physical barriers once thought insurmountable, beating other runners with novel tactics, and receiving invitations to race all over the world. We were national heroes. I also remember the tremendous sense of freedom running gave us. We trained on a track we had virtually to ourselves, cut off from the "outside world" by a high hedge, and we planned our own training and made our own rules. After summer workouts, we hung around for hours, eating popsicles and talking, as if we were the only people who mattered in the world. Some days, I wanted to spend the rest of my life in shorts and a tee-shirt.

But there was a social context to the self-actualization, affirmation, and pleasure that we could not ignore. Often it buoyed and encouraged us. We had a vague sense that family and ethnic background influenced our choice of sports and shaped our ambitions. As well, we were awkwardly aware that our celebrity had more to do with the resurgence of Canadian nationalism than with our particular athletic skills: some of the warmest congratulations came from people who didn't even know what distances we ran. Although our analysis was imperfect, we understood there were social limits, too. Some athletes faced poverty, yet the rules of amateurism prohibited us from receiving income from our activity, even from teaching or writing about it. Without independent means, none of us could devote all our energies to perfecting what we were best at. Others faced racial and gender prejudice and the dictates of the officials who organized competitions — we called them "badgers" because of the crested blazers they always wore — and the press barons who shaped the standards for athletic behaviour. We could test these limits, just as we pushed against the physiological and psychological barriers to better performance, but they could spring back and haunt us. If one spoke out against them, for instance, the once-adoring media treated one like an ingrate.

All Canadian athletes in the Olympic sports have trained and competed under specific material and ideological conditions. These conditions will now be examined, utilizing the political economy approach (Kidd, 1979).

Patriarchal Amateurism

It is necessary to begin with the century-old era of amateur sport. As others in this publication have shown, modern sport in Canada — and the first opportunities for high-performance sport — was fashioned in the nineteenth century by urban middle- and upper-class males of British background. They agreed upon and codified rules, and formed clubs and sports-governing bodies to enforce them. Taking advantage of the technological and managerial innovations in transportation and communications developed in the National Policy economy, they spread their new sports across the country, encouraging other men of their class to establish clubs and programs in schools, public playgrounds, businesses and factories, churches, and service clubs. They increasingly sought to triumph in the major competitions they held, by building specialized facilities and hiring successful trainers as coaches. They also sought to recruit non-British and working-class men and boys to these activities as athletes and paying spectators. While some of them were prepared to hire outstanding athletes to perform in the sports spectacles they staged — what is now known as professional sport — the majority held to the ideology of amateurism developed in this period and required adherence to the amateur code as a condition of participation. After the turn of the century, many of them embraced the modern Olympic Games project of Pierre de Coubertin, where amateurism was also a condition of eligibility, and affiliated their organizations with the international federations associated with Coubertin's International Olympic Committee (IOC). By and large, the amateur sports became the Olympic sports. The amateur era lasted until the mid-1970s, when the IOC abolished amateurism as a requirement for Olympic eligibility (Killanin, 1976) and Sport Canada began to pay athletes a stipend.

The nature of, and access to, opportunities for males during the amateur era varied considerably from sport to sport, place to place, and period to period. The age, class, gender, and ethnic composition of the area's population, the climate, the local economy, the local government, and the nature of sports traditions all influenced developments. The best facilities, coaching, and competitions tended to be in the private clubs, universities, and YMCAs in Montreal, southern Ontario, Winnipeg, and Vancouver, where the surplus from Canadian economic activity tended to accumulate and where there were commercial and professional classes of sufficient size and wealth to invest in highly competitive sport.

To be sure, working-class men and some immigrant communities created sports organizations of their own and sometimes successfully entered the amateur competitions under the control of the business and professional elites (Metcalfe, 1978; Palmer, 1979). In ice hockey, there were successful teams from rural areas and the single-industry towns of the resource hinterland, the latter often being sponsored by mining companies (Pagnucco, 1982). But on the whole, the best programs were located in the most prosperous areas. The best athletes came from middle-class and upwardly mobile working-class families. Although Gruneau's now classic profile of the socio-economic background of competitors in the 1971 Canada Winter Games was compiled in the waning hours of amateurism, after a decade of public funding, it confirms this conclusion (Gruneau, 1978).

Where the uneven development of the Canadian economy and its class and gender structure did not skew participation in favour of middle- and upper-class males, the ideology and practices of patriarchal amateurism did. In terms of class, from the beginning, the men who organized Canadian sports employed amateurism to limit participation and public acclaim to members of their own classes. In the earliest codes, the exclusions were explicit. The definition framed by the Montreal Pedestrian Club in 1873 stated:

> [An amateur] is one who has never competed in any open
> competition or for public money, or for admission

money, or with professionals for a prize, public money or admission money, nor has ever, at any period of his life taught or assisted in the pursuit of athletic exercises as a means of livelihood or is a *labourer or an Indian*. (author's emphasis)

Subsequent rule-makers dropped the ascriptive and racist proscriptions against workers and natives, but retained the prohibition against the receipt of athletic income. Although concerted challenges to amateurism were mounted in the early years of the century and during the 1930s, the majority of Canadian sports leaders voted to retain a strict definition (Morrow, 1985). As late as 1971, the Canadian Olympic Association stated:

Among others, the following are not eligible for competitions:

Those who have participated for money, for prizes exceeding $50 in value. . . .

Those who have capitalized in any way on their athletic fame or success, or those who have secured employment or promotion by reason of their sport performances rather than their ability. . . .

Those who are paid for teaching or coaching others for competition in sport. . . .

Those who have neglected their usual vocation or employment for competitive sport whether at home or abroad.

If an athlete is paid for the use of his name or picture or for a radio or television appearance, it is capitalization of athletic fame as described above. Even if no payment is made, such practices are to be deplored, since in the minds of many, particularly the young, they undermine the exalted position rightly held by amateur champions.

Such rules excluded many people by reason of circumstance, requiring competitors to have the leisure to pursue sport on a systematic basis and the funds to pay for club memberships, equipment, and, at the highest levels of performance, travel to out-of-town competitions. Many potentially outstanding athletes simply did not have these resources. As historian Roy Rosenzweig (1979:43) has written, "the most fundamental constraint on working class recreation . . . was work itself," and the same could be said for competitive sport.

It was not always easy for working people to train after a long, physically demanding day. While some employers gave athletes on company teams easier working conditions and time off for games, they rarely were so generous with those in the individual Olympic sports. Few working-class athletes ever attended the universities, nor could they easily afford private clubs and frequent out-of-town travel. Prior to the Fitness and Amateur Sport travel grants, begun in 1962, even national champions in many sports had to pay their own way, sometimes to the Olympics. In 1932, 115 of 127 Canadian Olympic Team members paid their own way to the Games in Los Angeles. At the 1936 Olympic trials, the track and field selectors picked six athletes who would be sent to Berlin all expenses paid, and ten others who would be sent if they could pay their own way. If one could not afford the necessary costs, one had to decline. Even for those who could afford it, top-level sport was expensive, and both athletes and coaches, most of whom were amateur as well, frequently engaged in fund-raising. Admittedly, there was not much of a market for athletic entrepreneurship in most sports, but the code prevented coaches and athletes from trying to expand it and share in its revenues.

The development and maintenance of amateurism can only be understood in the context of inter-class and inter-regional tensions and struggles in the developing industrial capitalist economy (Gruneau, 1983; Mott, 1983). It served not only to exclude, but to impose the values and control of the central Canadian middle class upon an increasingly popular sphere of social activity, by appealing to aspirations shared by members of all classes and both genders. Amateurism was championed in the language of civility, social harmony, self-improvement, and nationalism. According to its supporters, participation "for its own sake," without the possibility of material reward, encouraged fair play and good citizenship and, as such, represented the antithesis of the "win-at-all-costs" rule violations and brutality which were said to result from the financial incentives of professional sport. Amateurism was also believed to be broadly educational because, through the postponement of material rewards, it encouraged the development of self-discipline, mental and physical courage, and the habits of self-improvement.

Embedded as they were in the classes which had developed and stood to gain most from Confederation and the National Policy, the first organizers of Canadian sports blended amateurism with national ambition. They carved out "national" jurisdictions, held "national" championships, and selected "national" teams long before their activities extended to the boundaries of the Canadian state. With the development of international championships on a national-team basis, they increasingly gave top-level

training and competition the character of national sacrifice and
appealed to athletes to "stay amateur" to represent their country.
When the Onondaga runner Tom Longboat was offered a professional contract before the 1908 Olympics in London, for example, the *Montreal Star* publisher Hugh Graham telegraphed him:

> Sir:
>
> The world admires your track success. Cana-
> dians are proud of what you have done in the field of
> sport. With Canada's hopes of glory in the athletic field
> in the future, you have responsibilities. Your own vic-
> tories may gratify your personal ambition, but that should
> not be the end of it. Your country cannot be a little served
> by a continued example of clean sport.
>
> Most athletes of fame are exposed to extra-
> ordinary congratulations at the hands of friends and pre-
> tended friends. Remember, too, that there are always a
> lot of people jealous of a winner. Enemies will ever be
> on the watch to trap you into doing a wrong act. An ath-
> lete cannot do his best unless he is tempered and honest.
>
> When you are tempted, think of Canada. You
> have been instrumental in bringing her fame. Don't be
> misled or she will lose it. Aim high and then you will
> do the best that is in you.

The leaders of amateurism also appropriated the idealism
of the Coubertin Olympic Games, and its aspirations for international understanding and universal peace through competitive
sport. Clothed in these values, amateurism meant that sport was
undertaken as part of a noble mission. Such belief strengthened
the power of amateur officials, who had the responsibility of guard-
ing the moral purity of sport and ensuring that athletes adhered
to the proper spirit of self-discipline and sacrifice. Athletes were
often severely punished for minor infringements of the rules. At
the same time, some corrupt officials "helped" athletes with under-
the-table payments, but these only forced the athletes into hy-
pocrisy and made them vulnerable to officials' goodwill. To be
sure, the amateur sports system had its critics, especially among
the publicists of professional sport in the mass media, but criticism tended to focus on the abuses of rules and the power of officials, not the middle-class privilege which the sport protected or
the capitalist ideology it conveyed.

Amateur sport was also heavily influenced by patriarchal
ideas and practices. The first organizers made no attempt to take
the needs and experiences of females into account in any way.
On the contrary, as many scholars have shown, they tried to make

sport a male preserve, associating the skills and values involved with traditional norms of masculinity (and labelling the most popular activities "the manly sports"), excluding girls and women from participation, and, when that was not successful, discouraging them by ridicule, scientifically invalid assumptions, and the denial of adequate facilities and public programs (Hall, 1970; Lenskyj, 1980; Howell, 1982).

As a predominantly "male practice," the new sports served to ensure effective socialization for traditional masculinity and validate the existing — and male privileging — sexual division of labour at a time of rapid feminization of teaching and growing feminist challenge to male economic and political power. Working-class men generally shared these prejudices and contributed to exclusionary practices, suggesting that sports participation helped males strengthen and extend cross-class masculine bonds. Economic and social conditions — long hours of domestic labour, different and generally less adequate diets, restrictive dress, and so on — also deterred many girls and women from participation.

Despite these barriers, after the turn of the century a growing number of females engaged in competitive sport, albeit on a sex-segregated basis. This increased involvement was the result of initiatives by middle-class women in private clubs and universities, support by the organized women's movement, pressure by other girls and women for opportunities, and changing views among male doctors and physical educators about the benefits of physical activity for females. In the 1920s and 1930s, national, North American, and international events were started, and Canadian women competed with great success, validated by extensive if usually condescending mass media coverage. The nature of opportunities varied considerably. Here, too, they were highly dependent on class and region: generally the best were to be found in private clubs, high schools and universities, and business-sponsored leagues in the urban centres. Facilities and other resources were never equal to those enjoyed by males in comparable programs in the same communities. The sports available to females were fewer, and in those like track and field and swimming where events for both sexes were offered, the number of male events always outnumbered those for females (Hall, 1982).

Wherever they were conducted, female sports were pervaded by restrictive patriarchal ideologies. Despite the available examples from agriculture and industry of women performing heavy "men's work," it was widely believed that a woman's biology prevented her from competing in the men's realm and it was taken for granted that she would play on a female-only basis. In addition, organizers eliminated events that were considered too strenuous for females, or devised "girls' rules" which discouraged vigorous and aggressive play. Atkinson (1978) and Lenskyj (1986) have argued that, in part, "girls' rules" represented a tactically necessary defence against male control of women's institutions and a creative attempt to avoid some of the brutalizing features of male sports, but nonetheless they confined most females interested in sport to a ghetto of inequality which left unchallenged the existing stereotypes concerning female frailty. At the same time, female athletes faced inordinate pressures to be traditionally "feminine" and to conform to the heterosexual expectations of the dominant culture. No women's team or female athlete ever travelled to an out-of-town competition without a chaperone.

Until the Second World War, the best Canadian opportunities were comparable to those in the other industrial capitalist countries represented in international competition, and many Canadians competed with success. By today's standards, training was much less demanding — until the 1960s, very few athletes trained more than four to six times a week in one- to two-hour sessions, and often they stopped training several months a year. Competitions were fewer. Amateurism encouraged the simultaneous pursuit of other avocations, academic study, or professional careers; thus, those who could afford it often led well-rounded lives. There was a much greater emphasis on the pleasures of competition, travel, and fraternizing with athletes from other clubs and countries. As most coaches and officials were volunteers who had to administer the programs they conducted in their own time with their own resources, the effective control they enjoyed was often limited; athletes and clubs were able to conduct their activities with a considerable amount of autonomy. The amateur, "kitchen-table" era of Olympic sports in Canada should not be romanticized, but for those who were able to pursue these amateur sports, they provided many rewarding experiences.

State-directed Expansion

In the short period of time that has elapsed since the passage of the federal Fitness and Amateur Sport Act (1961), the conditions for training and competing in the Olympic sports have been dramatically changed. The state has transformed the once autonomous, voluntary, and largely regulatory sports-governing bodies into professionally administered non-profit corporations which conduct ambitious national and provincial training and developmental programs under strict governmental direction. The number of opportunities has significantly increased as the state has subsidized travel to national and international championships, and the number of summer and winter Olympic events has grown from 175 (in 1960) to 259 (in 1984). Additional new opportunities have been created by schools, community colleges, and universities, by new events such as the Canada Games and provincial equivalents, and by private entrepreneurs. Facilities have been greatly expanded and improved, the result of increased public spending at all three levels of government and special events such as the Olympic and Canada Games. Coaching has been professionalized and strengthened by the dissemination of up-to-date scientific and technical information. These improvements were made, for the most part, by sports leaders who wanted Canadians to "compete, not just participate" in international sport, and were facilitated by the long post-Second World War wave of expansion in the Canadian economy, which buoyed public revenues. At the same time, the state began to assume responsibilities in the areas of health, culture, and recreation. Finally, it was now feasible to present individual athletes and national teams as symbols of physical fitness and of the pan-Canadian nationalism of Pierre Trudeau.

The state has also provided financial incentives — stipends based on performance — to offset the best athletes' living, training, and competition expenses. In most parts of Canada, athletes first qualify when they earn a provincial ranking. The Ontario Government, for example, annually awards about 750 Gold Cards and about 250 Silver Cards to top-ranked athletes. Each Gold Card is worth $1000, free tuition in a college or university, and other benefits. A Silver Card is worth $500. The largest stipends are awarded by the federal Athlete Assistance Program, which rewards about 750 athletes annually. Under this scheme, athletes are remunerated according to established criteria as outlined in Table 1. C and D cards are awarded to athletes who "have demonstrated the potential to achieve A or B card status." An A card entitles the holder to support for two years; B, C, and D cards must be renewed annually. The base allowance at present is $650 per month for A cards, $550 for B cards, $450 for C cards, and $300 for D cards.

In addition to these stipends, a monthly supplement, granted on the basis of demonstrated need, may be paid for extra-

Table 1
Sport Canada Athlete Assistance Program 1986–87

Olympic Sports

Ranking Level	Period of Ranking	Remuneration	Criteria for Ranking
A Card	Two Years	$650/month	1. Results achieved at Olympic Games or World Championships according to the following: • Events limited to one entry per country — Top 4 • Events limited to two entries per country — Top 6 • Events with three or more entries per country — Top 8 2. Athletes must finish in the top third of the field.
B Card	Usually One Year	$550/month	1. As above criteria: • One entry — Top 8 • Two entries — Top 12 • Three or more — Top 16 2. Athletes must finish in the top half of the field.
C Card C-1	One Year	$450/month $350/month	Potential to earn A or B Cards. Probationary Support in first year of C Status.
D Card	One Year	$300/month	Young athletes who have not reached C Card Status.

ordinary training costs, child care, special equipment, moving and travel expenses, and facility rentals. As well, the program pays for university and college tuition, books, and supplies. Some athletes receive $1500 a month in total awards. After they retire, athletes who have been carded for at least three years are eligible for a final payment of $450 a month for eight months. Between 1972 and 1985, 2548 athletes in 51 sports received a total of 7182 athlete-years of assistance under this program. Ninety per cent of the 1984 Winter and Summer Canadian Olympic Teams were federally carded. If the provincial and federal assistance plans are combined, about 5000 Canadian athletes are now assisted annually. In

Non-Olympic Sports

C	One Year	$450/month ($350 in first year of ranking)	1. Finish in top six with minimum of 20 countries participating. 2. Top three — 10–19 countries participating with 10 entries for team sports and 15 entries for individual events. 3. First with minimum of 5 countries participating and a minimum of 10 entries in the event. 4. Must compete in a minimum of two international-level competitions annually.
Note		Women who compete in Olympic sports for which there is no female Olympic event (e.g. road walking, judo, 10 000 metre run) are eligible for a C card ranking as long as they meet non-Olympic sports criteria.	

Adapted from Ministry of State, Fitness and Amateur Sport, *Sport Canada: Athlete Assistance Program Policies and Guidelines, 1986–87*, Ministry of Supply and Services, July, 1986.

addition, some athletes have been able to earn appearance fees, win prize money, and negotiate endorsement contracts; these sources of income were legalized by the IOC in 1982.

These changes have greatly improved the facilities, coaching, technical and medical support, and competitive opportunities available to Canadian athletes in the Olympic sports. The Athlete Assistance Program has relieved some of the financial burden of training and competition and enabled many athletes to enjoy long and successful careers. Some athletes have received carding for more than a decade. In a 1985 survey of carded athletes commissioned by Sport Canada, 59 per cent said their funding was "adequate to help meet high performance needs," compared to just 42 per cent in a 1975 survey conducted by an athletes' group. The incentives tend to equalize opportunities on a sport-by-sport basis, for they are paid to everyone who makes the standards, not just those in sports patronized by the upper classes or where a mass market for equipment and clothing induces manufacturers to pay endorsement and appearance fees. As one result, Canadian performances in many sports have steadily improved. In 1984 in track and field, for example, 71 Canadians equalled or bettered the Olympic standard, compared to only fourteen athletes twenty years earlier. Canadians brought home more medals from the 1984 Olympic Games than ever before. Thirty-five per cent of those surveyed in 1985 reported that "to a great extent" they had met their performance goals.

Sweat-suited Philanthropists

In spite of improvements in assistance, the new programs have increased the pressures on the athlete, by requiring virtually a full-time commitment, submission to the directive of the national program, and allegiance to the nationalist, neo-conservative ideology of the state and the corporations. Perhaps the most dramatic change since the amateur era has been the increase in time commitment. Most athletes are now expected to curtail other activities and commit themselves full-time. By hiring full-time coaches and technical directors, establishing "teams-in-being" (such as the men's and women's national volleyball squads stationed at the universities of Calgary and Regina respectively), and centralizing training at national training centres (55 in 1986), Sport Canada and the national sports organizations (NSOs) have created the conditions for full-time involvement. By rewarding athletes and coaches financially for winning, Sport Canada and the NSOs encourage such specialization.

Another common practice — scheduling special training and major competitions out of the country — has accelerated this process. In 1982–83, for example, members of the national women's field hockey team were away from home a total of 142 days, while some members of the junior team were away for 172 days. Such absences make it virtually impossible to sustain other activities. The growth of national training centres seems to have reduced the athlete's time away from home, yet such absences are still significant. Only 10 per cent of the athletes carded in 1985 said they were employed full-time. Of the 56 per cent who said they were full-time students, 78 per cent reported some delay in their educational progress, 62 per cent said they had been prevented from taking certain courses or programs, and 54 per cent said their grades had suffered — all as a result of their sport (Macintosh and Albinson, 1985).

Lest the carded athlete has any doubt about his or her obligations, Sport Canada now requires that he or she sign a standard contract. If the athlete fails to maintain satisfactory training or to honour the commitments of the contract, the NSO may recommend withdrawal of card status and benefits. Coaches have used the threat of withdrawal to discourage athletes from taking part-time jobs, travelling and sightseeing after major competitions abroad, and getting married (Kidd and Eberts, 1982: 74–76). Although the "NSO/athlete agreement" now requires national sports organizations to provide the athlete with the procedural protections of "natural justice," very few have put it into practice. In addition, the agreement still gives enormous discretionary power to the coaches and the NSOs; athletes are still losing prestigious competitive opportunities because of minor "off-field" rule violations (Kidd and Eberts, 1982).

Long hours of training, the increasing use of mechanical aids such as feradic stimulation, segmented technique drills, and the routinized repetitions of interval and circuit training have given high-performance sport the character of assembly-line work (Brohm, 1978; Cantelon, 1981; Rigauer, 1981). It can also be shown that the controls surrendered to the NSO in return for carded athlete assistance have rendered the athlete a worker. When the coach or official exhorted the amateur to devote more time to training, or elicited conformity by suggesting the athlete was "letting the team down," he or she was appealing to normative controls, values, and norms that were deeply internalized. Such appeals usually had a telling effect, because most athletes shared their coach's ambition and expectations about appropriate behaviour, but if the athlete was not convinced, he or she could have ended the relationship and moved to another club. In an individual sport, he or she could have competed as a self-trained "unattached" athlete. He or she had no material interest in sport and pursued it as a form of leisure. But under carded athlete assistance, national coaches have recourse to the utilitarian and instrumental types of control characteristic of work. Of course, they will use normative controls as much as possible, especially if they have any training in human relations, but when all else fails, they can enforce behaviour by invoking the "NSO/athlete agreement" and the power to penalize the athlete and withdraw benefits. If, as in most sports, the national team has a monopoly on the specialized resources necessary for high performance, especially the allocation of stipends, the athlete has little choice other than to quit. Instrumental control utilizes material rewards and punishments that are intimately bound up with the pragmatic concerns of making a living (Sack and Kidd, 1985).

Under Canadian law, there are four main indicators of the presence of an employment relationship: (a) the employer's power of selection of the employee, (b) the payment of wages or other remuneration, (c) the employer's right to control the method of doing the work, and (d) the employer's right of suspension or dismissal. All of these indicators are present in the case of carded athletes. NSOs have the power to select athletes or suspend or dismiss them. As well, NSOs control their athletic activity, through training requirements set down by the national coach, the requirement that they attend specified camps and competitions, and the general instruction that they conduct themselves for the benefit of the team.

The only point at issue is whether the payments under the Athlete Assistance Program constitute remuneration and therefore whether athletes should fall under the jurisdiction of the Public Servant Staff Relations Act (1976). I suggest that these payments do constitute remuneration. They are made on the basis of performance, not need. Both coaches and athletes understand them as a quid pro quo. "We're paying them, so we have every right to demand a rigorous training commitment from them," national field hockey coach Marina van der Merve has said (personal communication, April 28, 1984). According to the 1985 Sport Canada survey, the program provides the sole income for 65 per cent of active performers. Only 35 per cent said they could continue current levels of training if funding were withdrawn. But those responsible assert that athlete assistance is essentially philanthropic. John Brooks, Athlete Assistance Program administrator, recently said: "This is an assistance program. It was never intended to support the full cost of the athletes' lifestyle." Sport Canada director Abby Hoffman has said: "I don't . . . think we want to get into a situation where we are employing an athlete at $25,000 a year to perform for us." Although stipends approximate the minimum wage (for a 40-hour week) in most provinces, Sport Canada has obtained an understanding from Revenue Canada that, as an employer, it will not be taxed.

As underpaid professionals, athletes are "sweat-suited philanthropists," subsidizing the careers of hundreds of fully paid coaches, sports scientists, and bureaucrats, not to mention the ambitions of the federal state and the products and ideology of the corporations which sponsor teams and competitions. In this respect, too, the elite athlete of today labours under conditions radically different from those of the amateur of yesterday. While

Sport Canada claims to be only "assisting" athletes, it does not hesitate to claim credit for their victories. On the eve of the 1978 Commonwealth Games in Edmonton, for instance, Sports Minister Iona Campagnolo announced medal quotas for athletes in every event and, when they surpassed all expectations, she marched with them in the closing ceremony parade. When Canadians fell short of predictions four years later in Brisbane, it was Sport Canada director Abby Hoffman, not team officials, who publicly took responsibility for the "disappointments." After the brilliant successes in Los Angeles in 1984, Sport Canada printed and distributed a poster of the Canadian Team marching into Olympic Stadium, with the headline, "Bravo Canada!" No mention was made of the Canadian Olympic Association and the NSOs nominally responsible for selecting and fielding the team. The expectation that elite athletes are performing for the federal state is elaborated by the bi-monthly magazine *Champion*. Published and distributed to every carded athlete and national coach by Sport Canada's Athlete Information Bureau, it regularly compares Canadian performances with those of other nations.

Corporations have also begun to set expectations for the elite athlete and have long sought to improve sales and image through a favourable association with sport. Despite the amateurism required of athletes, the Olympic Games were sponsored as early as 1908. The process has accelerated in recent years. The new leisure industries, increasingly taking control of activities once carried out by households and community groups, seek to capture the "fitness market"; polluters and producers of socially undesirable products like tobacco seek to "cleanse" their image; and the state seeks funding from the corporate sector to reduce its own costs.

In February 1986, Sports Minister Otto Jelinek established a Sport Marketing Council in the National Sport and Recreation Centre in Ottawa to encourage the NSOs to step up their attempts to sell a corporate sector association with a particular sport (such as the traditional association of beer and baseball). Most of this new revenue goes to the NSO in the form of sponsorship fees; despite the liberalization of the rules, very few individual athletes have benefitted directly. Nevertheless, sponsorship has intensified the pressure on the athlete to win and conform to behaviour codes. In addition, since few in the sports community oppose these moves, athletes unwittingly lend their labour to the whole strategy of privatization. These state-corporate expectations have become so commanding that they, in effect, have blocked expressions of the older, humanistic, amateur-based aspirations of Olympism and other values.

For the most part, the expansion of state and corporate programs over the last twenty-five years has been limited to the high-performance sector; the redistributive effect has been negligible. In only a few sports do the accessible public institutions, the school, and the community centre provide opportunities of such quality that athletes can use them to get to the top. The best opportunities remain in private clubs and universities. Most athletes must bear all their training and competition expenses until that point where they can qualify for provincial or federal aid, a requirement which has the effect of eliminating most children and adolescents from low-income households. Even carded athletes incur costs which cannot be met from Athlete Assistance: in 1985, 32 per cent were not maintaining financial equilibrium, and 27 per cent of recently retired males gave financial difficulty as a major reason for dropping out.

A study of registered swimmers in Ontario suggests that household income and class background are still major determinants of opportunity. It found that more than one-half of the athletes' fathers had annual salaries in excess of $25 000 and that one-half of the athletes' mothers worked, making family incomes in the $35 000 – $40 000 range the norm, well above the median income of $19 847 for Ontario households at the time (Eynon and Kitchener, 1977). An indirect measure of the upper-class background of Olympic athletes is the extent of university attendance. About three-quarters of current athletes were either attending or had graduated from university, while only 11.5 per cent of those in the same age group within the population as a whole attended university in 1983–84. It is not only a question of dollars. Upper-income families tend to believe in the values of intense competition because they can afford the special opportunities which enable them to experience success and because it legitimates their class position. Such an outlook gives their children the appetite and role models necessary for high-performance sport.

Nor has there been a significant equalizing of the opportunities for females. Although Sport Canada encourages increased participation by girls and women at all levels, it tends to limit program supports to those events sanctioned by the male-dominated and heavily patriarchal IOC. Between 1960 and 1984, the IOC added four winter and forty-two summer Olympic events for women, but they also added ten winter and twenty-nine summer events for men. There are still more than twice as many Olympic events for males as females and, as a result, females receive only thirty to forty per cent of the benefits of the Canada Games, federal and provincial carded athlete assistance, and so on (Hall and Richardson, 1982). Patriarchal ideologies still pervade the system and there is little pressure from the male-dominated leadership of either the sports organizations or the state to overcome this imbalance.

Another imbalance — that of geographical representation — remains virtually unchanged. Despite the redistributive intentions of the Canada Games and the special Atlantic Provinces Athlete Assistance Program, positions on national teams are still monopolized by British Columbia, Ontario, and Quebec athletes. In 1976, for example, the four Atlantic provinces, with 9.5 per cent of the population, sent only ten athletes (2.4 per cent) to the Canadian Olympic Team competing in Montreal, while British Columbia, with 10.3 per cent of the population, placed ninety athletes (22 per cent) on the team. In 1984 in Los Angeles, the breakdown was similar, except that Ontario's contribution represented 51 per cent of the team, largely at the expense of athletes from the prairie provinces. Francophones remain under-represented as well. In Los Angeles, they made up 12 per cent of the Canadian team, about half their percentage of the Canadian population as a whole (Boileau et al., 1976).

Proposals for Change

Proposals for change fall into two categories: improvements to and expansion of existing opportunities, and increased athletes' rights. Most coaches and sports administrators focus on improvements to existing opportunities. Finding that the average age of current athletes was 22 and that 57 per cent of these athletes had three or fewer years of international experience, the authors of the 1985 Sport Canada survey, Macintosh and Albinson, concluded that "retention" was a major problem of the system and recommended that greater financial incentives be provided for proven performers, that greater effort be made to meet individual athletes' special financial needs, and that subsidized housing or "athletes' villages" be developed adjacent to national training centres. They also recommended that a greater effort be made to provide

Canadian athletes with competitive experiences abroad, and that Sport Canada establish a sports training and residential centre at one of the Canadian Armed Forces bases in Germany.

More systematic application of the insights of sports science to training and competition has also been considered. Coaches and athletes have called for a significant increase in the number of C cards offered, so that the pool of well-prepared athletes from which national teams are drawn can be expanded (the instrumentalist justification) and that the quality of life, as measured by the number of enriched opportunities for Canadians to pursue culturally validated skills, can be enhanced (the intrinsic justification). Advocates of gender equality have argued that carding should be available to the top female competitors in any event in which there is a national championship, even if that event is not in the Olympic Games.

Advocates of athletes' rights argue that Canadian athletes should be paid more for their efforts, and enjoy much greater control over the planning and conduct of their athletic activity. They contend that elected athletes' representatives should sit on all major decision-making bodies and that athletes should enjoy the substantive and procedural protections of Canadian law in questions of team selection and discipline. As an alternative to the unilaterally dictated "NSO/athlete agreement," they propose that athletes' training and competitive obligations be determined by individual and collective bargaining, possibly within the structure of trade unions and federal and provincial labour law (Kidd and Eberts, 1982). They argue that the bargaining strategy must take not only the NSOs and Sport Canada into consideration, but the sponsoring corporations, competition organizers (such as Calgary's OCO 88), and the television networks. As one who supports this approach, I firmly believe that athletes can only regain control over their own lives and take advantage of the legal gains won by workers in other fields by taking collective action.

What remains to be seen is whether today's athletes will act to effect change. There is some precedent. In 1975, a group training for the Montreal Olympics won $1.7 million in additional living and training grants and the appointment of two fellow athletes to administer the money in a brief, highly publicized campaign, during which they threatened political action, up to and including a strike, against the Montreal Games. In 1980, Canadian athletes mounted considerable opposition to the boycott of the Moscow Games. Canadian artists in several disciplines, and graduate students on many campuses, groups whose means of livelihood and working conditions are similar to those of elite athletes, have formed associations and trade unions to represent their interests and bargain on their behalf. By comparison, elite athletes are very poorly organized. They enjoy representation on only seventeen of sixty national sports bodies recently surveyed by Sport Canada (1986) and most of these "representatives" are appointed by coaches and administrators, not elected. Only a small number of the members of the Canadian Olympic Association's Athlete Advisory Council are elected by fellow athletes. Two of the most recent efforts by athletes to increase their influence — the attempt by track and field competitors to form a union and that of women field hockey players to obtain the appointment of a coach more to their liking — ended in failure. It also remains to be seen whether athletes will act for reasons other than their own interests. None of the above proposals and strategies will significantly expand the class base of participation in the Olympic sports. That would require a major attack on inequality throughout society and a concerted effort to improve the quantity and quality of public opportunities for sport and recreation.

Most observers argue that few athletes will ever act aggressively in their own self-interest, let alone against the widespread inequality of Canadian society. They point out that most are young and inexperienced, that the intense competition they face for the few cards or jobs in their sport discourages them from taking collective action, and that the very structure of sport induces submission to authority and limits occasions for the expression of critical, transformative ideas (Hargreaves, 1975). They argue that, since most come from middle- and upper-class families and manage to obtain a university education during their competitive careers, they can afford to endure the relative deprivation of their years in sport, confident that they will find well-paying jobs upon retirement.

Sport Canada's retirement assistance plan and the Canadian Olympic Association's newly created Olympic Athlete Career Centre reinforce this approach. Sceptics also contend that, since athletes embrace the goals of high-performance sport, they are unlikely to question the way the vocabulary of "excellence," with which it is associated, has been employed to justify the whole neoconservative project of authoritarian controls, cutbacks in public spending, and the further redistribution of income to the already privileged. There is much to recommend these views, especially at a time when the North American student movement, the inspiration for earlier athlete mobilizations, is quiescent and conservative. It may well be that, during the next decade, few athletes will attempt to change their material conditions or struggle to effect greater control over the meanings of their performances.

On the other hand, the pressure on athletes to perform and conform is likely to intensify, while the funds available for living and training costs are not likely to increase and may even decline with inflation. The federal government seems intent on freezing or even reducing the amount of public funds to be spent on high-performance sport and there is little evidence that privatization can make up the difference. It may simply widen the gap between opportunities in different sports. At the same time, the headlong rush by both the state and the sports bodies to commodify the Olympic sports and open them up to full professionals strips away the last veneer of the amateur appeal to self-sacrifice. As these contradictions sharpen, as athletes watch millions being spent on every aspect of the Olympic project but their well-being, they may well turn to collective action to seek larger rewards and fewer controls. The task would be formidable, but not impossible. The public and private investment in major games like the Olympics gives them enormous potential for "job action."

If negotiation was unsuccessful and athletes had to go public with their demands for better living and working conditions, it is unclear how much support they would enjoy. During the last decade of increased and highly visible public investment in high-performance sport, other public programs in the broad area of fitness and amateur sport — physical education in the schools, municipal recreation, and provincially funded parks and recreation — have been cut back, so for some, the term "elite athlete" means economic privilege and brings resentment. If past campaigns are any indication, the mass media are not likely to be supportive. Yet some possibility for coalition-building exists. Athletes would have to clarify their reasons for participation and their relationship to the state and the corporations, but they could widen public support by linking their demands to those for improved opportunities for physical education and sport which would benefit the entire population. There is also a wide network of artists, labour organizations, women's associations, and consumer and community groups mobilized against the neo-conservative strategy of cutbacks and privatization which they could join.

Sports scholars cannot expect to be impartial in these struggles; their analyses contribute to the elaboration and justification of, and contestation over, the different positions. The development of elite athletes has had both its positive and negative consequences. Subsequent research must consider these consequences and suggest possible avenues of change to the current training programs of elite athletes.

Suggested Readings

To a considerable extent, the scholarly analysis of athletic labour has been inspired by the "jockraker" literature written in the late 1960s and early 1970s. While theoretically primitive, these largely autobiographical indictments of North American sport, such as Paul Hoch's (1972), *Rip Off the Big Game*, New York, Doubleday, and Jack Scott's (1971), *The Athletic Revolution*, New York, Free Press, laid bare the increasing alienation of athletes as the commodification of high-performance sport intensified. Jean-Marie Brohm's (1978), *Sport — A Prison of Measured Time*, London, Ink Links, and Bero Rigauer's (1981), *Sport and Work*, New York, Columbia University Press, are written from more explicit political perspectives. If read alongside Rob Beamish (1982), "Sport and the Logic of Capitalism," in Hart Cantelon and Richard S. Gruneau (Eds.) (1982), *Sport, Culture and the Modern State*, Toronto, University of Toronto Press, these earlier works would prove most informative.

Selected Bibliography

Not all citations are listed in the bibliography. Unpublished documents or those that are not readily available in libraries have not been included. Readers who desire additional information about such entries may contact the editors.

Books or articles which appear in translation have been cited in the appropriate bibliography. For example, Jean Marie Brohm's *Critique du sport* (1976) which appears in the French text is listed as *Sport: A Prison of Measured Time* (1978) in the English text.

Adelman, M. L. (1986), *A Sporting Time: New York City and the Rise of Modern Athletics*, Urbana, University of Illinois Press.

Ansart, P. (1972), "L'occultation idéologique," in *Cahiers internationaux de sociologie*, LII.

Apollonia, L. d' (1941), "La gloire du corps chrétien," in *Relations*, August 1941.

Association canadienne d'hygiène publique (1984), *Rapport sur le projet condition physique et mode de vie au travail 1983*, Condition physique et sport amateur, Canada.

Atkinson, P. (1978), "Fitness, Feminism and Schooling," in Sara Delamond and Lorna Duffin (Eds.), *The Nineteenth Century Woman: Her Cultural and Physical World*, London, Croom Helm.

Auger, C. (CSN) (1981), "L'activité physique et les travailleurs," Paper presented at the Conference on Physical Activity and Workers, Montréal, U.Q.A.M.

Bailey, P. (1978), *Leisure and Class in Victorian England*, London, Routledge & Kegan Paul.

Barrett, M. (1979), *Ideology and Cultural Production*, London, Croom Helm.

Baudrillard, J. (1969), "La genèse idéologique des besoins," in *Cahiers internationaux de sociologie*, XLVII.

Beamish, R. (1981a), "The Materialist Approach to Sport Study: An Alternative Prescription to the Discipline's Methodological Malaise," in *Quest*, XXXI, 1.

Beamish, R. (1981b), "Central Issues in the Materialist Study of Sport as a Cultural Practice," in S. Greendorfer and A. Yiannakis (Eds.), *Sociology of Sport: Diverse Perspectives*, West Point, Leisure Press.

Beamish, R. (1982a), "Sport and the Logic of Capitalism," in H. Cantelon and R. S. Gruneau (Eds.), *Sport, Culture, and the Modern State*, Toronto, University of Toronto Press.

Beamish, R. (1982b), *Some Neglected Political Themes in Sport Study*, Paper presented at the 77th meeting of the American Sociological Association, San Francisco.

Bélisle, R. (1964), *Rapport du Comité d'étude sur les loisirs, l'éducation physique et les sports*, Québec.

Bellefleur, M. (1983), "Loisir et pouvoir clérical au Québec (1930–1960)," in *Loisir et Société*, VI, 1.

Bellefleur, M. (1986), *L'Église et le loisir au Québec avant la révolution tranquille*, Sillery, Presses de l'Université du Québec.

Benzécri, J., et al. (1973), *L'analyse des données*, 2 tomes, Paris, Dunod.

Betts, J. (1974), *America's Sporting Heritage, 1850–1950*, Reading, Addison-Wesley.

Birrell, S. and J. Loy (1979), "Media Sport: Hot and Cool," in *International Review of Sport Sociology*, I, 14.

Black, E. and T. Black (1983), "The Making of the East End Community Club," in *Labour/Le Travailleur*, XII, Autumn.

Bliss, M. (1974), *A Living Profit: Studies in the Social History of Canadian Business, 1883–1911*, Toronto, McClelland and Stewart.

Boileau, R. (1982), "Rôle et statut du professionnel de l'activité physique," in *L'éducation physique, où va la profession?*, Montréal, Bellarmin-Desport.

Boileau, R., et al. (1976), "Les Canadiens français et les Grands Jeux internationaux 1908–74," in R. S. Gruneau and J. Albinson (Eds.), *Canadian Sport: Sociological Perspectives*, Don Mills, Addison-Wesley.

Boltanski, L. (1971), "Les usages sociaux du corps," in *Annales: Économies, Sociétés, Civilisations*, XVII.

Bourdieu, P. (1962), "Célibat et condition paysanne," in *Études Rurales*, 5–6.

Bourdieu, P. (1978), "Sport and Social Class," in *Social Science Information*, XVII, 6.

Bourdieu, P. (1984), *Distinction. A Social Critique of the Judgement of Taste*, Harvard, Routledge & Kegan Paul.

Bourdieu, P., J.-C. Chamboredon and J.-C. Passeron (1972), *Le métier de sociologue*, Paris, Mouton.

Boutilier, M. and L. SanGiovanni (1983), *The Sporting Woman*, Illinois, Human Kinetics.

Brandes, S. (1970), *American Welfare Capitalism, 1880–1940*, Chicago, University of Chicago Press.

Bratton, R. (1971), "Demographic Characteristics of Executive Members of Two Canadian Sports Associations," in *CAHPER Journal*, XXXVII, 3.

Brodeur, P. (1980), "Conditionnement individuel pour une santé collective: une autre mystification," in *Le Desport*, September–October.

Brohm, J.-M. (1976), *Critiques du sport*, Paris, Christian Bourgeois Éditeur.

Brohm, J.-M. (1978), *Sport — A Prison of Measured Time*, Translated by Ian Fraser, London, Ink Links.

Broom E. F. and R. S. Baka (1978), *Canadian Government and Sport*, Vanier, CAHPER Sociology of Sport Monographs.

Buscombe, E. (Ed.) (1975), *Football on Television*, London, The British Film Institute Educational Advisory Service.

Caillé, M. (1941), "L'action catholique, agent de rechristianisation," in *Semaines Sociales du Canada*, 18.

Campagnolo, I. (1977), *Toward a National Policy on Amateur Sport: A Working Paper*, Ottawa, Ministry of State, Fitness and Amateur Sport.

Campagnolo, I. (1979a), *Toward a National Policy on Fitness and Recreation*, Ottawa, Government of Canada.

Campagnolo, I. (1979b), *Partners in Pursuit of Excellence*, Ottawa, Government of Canada.

Cantelon, H. (1981), "High Performance Sport and the Child Athlete: Learning to Labour," in A. Ingham and E. Broom (Eds.), *Career Patterns and Career Contingencies in Sport*, Vancouver, University of British Columbia Press.

Cantelon, H. and R. S. Gruneau (1982), *Sport, Culture and the Modern State*, Toronto, University of Toronto Press.

Cantelon, H. and R. S. Gruneau (1984), *Images of Canadian Sport and English Language Television*, Interim and Final Reports, Ottawa, Social Sciences and Humanities Research Council.

Cappon, P. (1978), *In Our Own House: Social Perspectives on Canadian Literature*, Toronto, McClelland and Stewart.

Carroll, J. D. and J. J. Chang (1970), "Analysis of Individual Differences in Multidimensional Scaling via N-way Generalization of Eckart-Young Decomposition," in *Psychometrika*, XXXV.

Chambat, P. (1980), "Les muscles de Marianne: Gymnastique et bataillons scolaires dans la France des années 1880," in *Recherches*, 43.

Charland, R. (1941), "La YMCA," in *Revue Dominicaine*, XLVII, 1.

Charron, C. (1979), *On a un monde à recréer: Livre blanc sur le loisir au Québec*, Québec, Gouvernement du Québec.

Chauvier, R. (1979), "Science(s) et éducation physique: quel savoir?," in *Travaux et recherches en EPS*, Paris, INSEP, 4.

Childerhose, R. J. (1968), *Winter Racehorse*, Toronto, Peter Martin.

Childerhose, R. J. (1973), *Hockey Fever in Goganne Falls*, Toronto, Macmillan.

Clarke, A. and J. Clarke (1982), "Highlights and Action Replays — Ideology,

Sport and the Media," in J. Hargreaves (Ed.), *Sport, Culture and Ideology*, London, Routledge & Kegan Paul.

Cliff, H. G. (1981), "The National Sport and Recreation Centre," Unpublished Student Paper, University of Ottawa.

CNTU (Confederation of National Trade Unions) (1984), *Nos loisirs et nos vacances c'est pas du luxe*, Plate-forme de revendications de la CSN, Montréal.

Cochrane, J., A. Hoffman and P. Kincaid (1977), *Women in Canadian Life: Sports*, Toronto, Fitzhenry and Whiteside.

Cockburn, C. (1977), *The Local State: Management of Cities and People*, London, Pluto.

Colley, I. and G. Davies (1981), "Kissed by History: Football as Drama," in C. Jenkins and M. Green (Eds.), *Sporting Fictions*, Birmingham Centre for Contemporary Cultural Studies, University of Birmingham.

Cominsky, P., J. Bryant and D. Zillman (1977), "Commentary as a Substitute to Action," in *Journal of Communication*, XXVII, Summer.

Consentino, F. and M. L. Howell (1971), *A History of Physical Education in Canada*, Toronto, General Publishing.

Cooper, K. H. (1970), *The New Aerobics*, New York, Bantam Books.

Coriat, B. (1979), *L'atelier et le chronomètre*, Paris, Christian Bourgeois Éditeur.

Corner, J. (1983), "Textuality, Communication and Media Power," in H. Davies and P. Walton (Eds.), *Language, Media, Power*, Oxford, Basil Blackwell.

Coulson, M. A. and C. Riddell (Eds.) (1980), *Approaching Sociology*, Second Edition, Boston, Routledge & Kegan Paul.

Coulson, M. A. and C. Riddell (1981), *Devenir sociologue*, Montréal, Éditions coopératives Albert Saint-Martin.

Craig, J. (1973), *Power Play*, New York, Dodd Mead.

Crawford, R. (1981), "You are Dangerous to Your Health: the Ideology of Victim-Blaming," in *International Journal of Health Services*, VII, 4.

Cunningham, H. (1980), *Leisure in the Industrial Revolution, 1780–1880*, New York, St. Martin's Press.

David, R. and R. Gagnon (1983), *Le loisir au Québec 1981. Étude auprès de la population*, Québec, Ministère du Loisir de la Chasse et de la Pêche.

De Grazia, V. (1978), "La Taylorisation des loisirs ouvriers: les institutions sociales de l'industrie dans l'Italie fasciste," in *Recherches*, 32/33.

DeLottinville, P. (1981–82), "Joe Beef of Montreal: Working Class Culture and the Tavern, 1869–1889," in *Labour/Le Travailleur*, 8–9, Autumn/Spring.

Demers, P. J. (1979), "L'humanisation de l'éducation physique québécoise: vers une ré-hiérarchisation des valeurs," in *Intracom*, 3.

Demers, P. J. (1980), "La formation universitaire en éducation physique: une analyse critique," in *Intracom*, 4.

Demers, P. J. (1981), "La formation universitaire: la clef d'une ré-orientation de l'éducation physique québécoise," in *Intracom*, 6.

Demers, P. J. (1982), "L'éducation physique québécoise replacée dans une perspective d'éducation permanente," in *Intracom*, 8.

Demers, P. J. (1984), "La base conceptuelle en éducation physique: de l'opposition à la complémentarité," in *CAHPER Journal*, L, 3.

Deschênes, L. (1984), *La formation en éducation physique au Canada*, Ph.D. dissertation in comparative education, Université de Montréal.

Dion, G. (1943), *L'Oeuvre des terrains de Jeux de Québec*, Québec, Éditions du Cap Diamant.

Direction générale de la santé et du sport amateur (1975), *Santé et condition physique*, Ottawa, Information Canada, brochure.

Donnelly, P. (forthcoming), "Sport as a Form of Popular Resistance," in R. S. Gruneau (Ed.), *Popular Cultures and Political Practices*, Toronto, Garamond.

Drache, D. (1984), "The Formation and Fragmentation of the Canadian Class: 1820–1920," in *Studies in Political Economy*, XV, Fall.

Dubois (1855), *Rapports sur le service de santé des mines de Blany et du Montceau*, Paris, Bailly, Divry et Cie.

Dumazedier, J. (1977), *Sociologie empirique du loisir*, Paris, Seuil.

Dunning, E. (1973), "The Structural-Functional Properties of Folk Games and Modern Sport," in *Sportwissenschaft*, III, 1.

Dunning, E. and K. Sheard (1979), *Barbarians, Gentlemen and Players: A Sociological Study of the Development of Rugby Football*, Oxford, M. Robertson.

Duquin, M. (1978), "The Androgynous Advantage," in C. Oglesby (Ed.), *Women in Sport: From Myth to Reality*, Philadelphia, Lea & Febiger.

Eagleton, T. (1976), *Marxism and Literary Criticism*, Berkeley, University of California Press.

Evan, W. (1972), "The All-American Boys: A Study of Boys Sports Fiction," in *The Journal of Popular Culture*, VI, 1.

Eynon, B. and P. Kitchener (1977), "Socio-Economic Analysis of Parents of Competitive Swimmers in Ontario," University of Western Ontario.

Farber, M. (1984), "Canada Has High Hopes for Winter Games," in *The Gazette*, Montreal, January 28.

Fawcett, M. J. (1977), *The Corpus Almanac's Canadian Sports Annual*, Toronto, Corpus.

Featherstone, M. (1985), "The Fate of Modernity: An Introduction," in *Theory, Culture and Society*, II, 2.

Fitness and Amateur Sport (1982), "Women in Sport Leadership: Summary of National Survey," Ottawa, Fitness and Amateur Sport Women's Program.

Forest, M.-C. (1936), "Notre américanisation par les sports," in *Revue Dominicaine*, XLII, 1.

Fox, R. (1945), *The Novel and the People*, New York, International Publishers.

Franks, C.E.S. and D. Macintosh (1984), "Evolution of Federal Government Policy Towards Sport and Culture in Canada: A Comparison," in N. Theberge and P. Donnelly (Eds.), *Sport and the Sociological Imagination*, Fort Worth, Texas Christian University Press.

Gagnon, E. (1954), "Travail et repos," in *Nos Cours*, XII, 26.

Galasso, P. J. (1973), "The Involvement of the Canadian Federal Government in Sports and Fitness," in *Canadian Journal of History of Sport and Physical Education*, XIV, 2.

Gear, J. L. (1973), "Factors Influencing the Development of Government Sponsored Fitness Programmes in Canada from 1850 to 1972," in *Canadian Journal of History of Sport and Physical Education*, XIV, 2.

Giard, L. (1977), "Contre-image de la science," in *Esprit: Changer la culture et la politique*, I, 11.

Giddens, A. (1976), *New Rules for Sociological Method*, New York, Basic Books.

Giddens, A. (1977), *Studies in Social and Political Theory*, New York, Basic Books.

Giddens, A. (1979), *Central Problems in Social Theory*, Berkeley, University of California Press.

Giddens, A. (1982), *Sociology: A Brief but Critical Introduction*, New York, Harcourt Brace Jovanovich.

Gingras, J.-F. and N. Nevitte (1984), "The Evolution of Quebec Nationalism," in A. C. Gagnon (Ed.), *Quebec: State and Society*, Toronto, Methuen.

Gitlin, T. (1979), "News as Ideology and Contested Area: Towards a Theory of Hegemony, Crisis and Opposition," in *Socialist Review*, IX, 6.

Glasgow University Media Group (1976), *Bad News*, London, Routledge & Kegan Paul.

Glasgow University Media Group (1980), *More Bad News*, London, Routledge & Kegan Paul.

Glasgow University Media Group (1985), *War and Peace News*, Milton Keynes, Open University Press.

Goldstein, J. H. and R. Arms (1971), "Effects of Observing Athletic Contests and Hostility," in *Sociometry*, XXXIV, 1.

Goodman, C. (1979), *Choosing Sides: Playground and Street Life on the Lower East Side*, New York, Schocken.

Government of Quebec (1978), *A Cultural Development Policy for Quebec*, Quebec, Government of Quebec.

Government of Quebec (1984), *Le temps de l'excellence: un défi québécois*, Québec, Loisir, Chasse et Pêche.

Gramsci, A (1957), "Américanisme et Fordisme," in *Cahiers Internationaux*, September–October.

Gramsci, A. (1971), *Selections From the Prison Notebooks*, London, Lawrence and Wishart.

Gramsci, A. (1977), *Gramsci dans le texte*, Paris, Éditions sociales.

Gritti, G. (1975), *Sport à la une*, Paris, Armand Colin.

Gruneau, R. S. (1976a), "Class or Mass: Notes on the Democratization of Canadian Amateur Sport," in R. S. Gruneau and J. Albinson (Eds.), *Canadian Sport: Sociological Perspectives*, Don Mills, Addison-Wesley.

Gruneau, R. S. (1976b), "Sport as an Area of Sociological Study," in R. S. Gruneau and J. Albinson (Eds.), *Canadian Sport: Sociological Perspectives*, Don Mills, Addison-Wesley.

Gruneau, R. S. (1978), "Elites, Class and Corporate Power in Canadian Sport," in F. Landry and W. Orban (Eds.), *Sociology of Sport*, Miami, Symposia Specialists.

Gruneau, R. S. (1982), "Sport and the Debate on the State," in H. Cantelon and R. S. Gruneau (Eds.), *Sport, Culture and the Modern State*, Toronto, University of Toronto Press.

Gruneau, R. S. (1983), *Class, Sports, and Social Development*, Amherst, University of Massachusetts Press.

Gruneau, R. S. and R. G. Hollands (1979), "Demographic and Socio-economic Characteristics of Canadian National Sports Executives," *Working Papers in the Sociological Study of Sport and Leisure*, II, 5, Kingston, Queen's University Press.

Guay, D. (1973), "Problèmes de l'intégration du sport dans la société canadienne 1830–1865: le cas des courses de chevaux," in *Revue canadienne de l'histoire des sports*, IV, 2.

Guay, D. (1981), *L'histoire de l'éducation physique au Québec: conceptions et événements (1830–1980)*, Chicoutimi, Gaétan Morin.

Guay, D. (1985), *Histoire des courses de chevaux au Québec*, Montréal, VLB.

Gurevitch, M., et al. (Eds.) (1982), *Culture, Society and the Media*, London, Methuen.

Guttmann, A. (1978), *From Ritual to Record: The Nature of Modern Sports*, New York, Columbia University Press.

Gyarmati, G. K. (1975), "La doctrine des professions: fondement d'un pouvoir," in *Revue Internationale des sciences sociales*, XXVII, 4.

Hall, A. (1970), "Women's Sport in Canada prior to 1914," Paper presented at the First Canadian Symposium on the History of Sport and Physical Education, Edmonton.

Hall, A. (1981), *Sport and Gender*, Vanier, CAHPER Sociology of Sport Monographs.

Hall, A. (1982), "Sport and Sex/Gender Role Socialization," Paper presented at the Annual Meeting of the Canadian Sociological and Anthropological Association.

Hall, A. (1984), "Towards a Feminist Analysis of Gender Inequality in Sport," in N. Theberge and P. Donnelly (Eds.), *Sport and the Sociological Imagination*, Fort Worth, Texas Christian University Press.

Hall, A. and D. Richardson (1982), *Fair Ball*, Ottawa, Canadian Advisory Council on the Status of Women.

Hall, S. (1981), "Notes on Deconstructing the Popular," in R. Samuel (Ed.), *People's History and Socialist Theory*, London, Routledge & Kegan Paul.

Hall, S., et al. (Eds.) (1976), *Resistance Through Rituals*, London, Hutchinson.

Hall, S., et al. (1980), *Culture, Media, Language*, London, Hutchinson.

Hallett, W. D. (1981), *A History of Federal Government Involvement in the Development of Sport in Canada: 1943–1979*, Ph.D. dissertation, University of Alberta.

Hamelin, J. (1984), *Le catholicisme québécois: Le XXᵉ siècle*, tome 2, *De 1940 à nos jours*, Montréal, Boréal Express.

Hamelin, J. and N. Gagnon (1984), *Le catholicisme québécois: Le XXᵉ siècle*, tome 1, *1898–1940*, Montréal, Boréal Express.

Hargreaves, J. (1975), "The Political Economy of Mass Sport," in S. Parker et al. (Eds.), *Sport and Leisure in Contemporary Society*, London, School of the Environment, Polytechnic of Central London.

Hargreaves, J. (1982a), "Sport, Culture and Ideology," in J. Hargreaves (Ed.), *Sport, Culture and Ideology*, London, Routledge & Kegan Paul.

Hargreaves, J. (1982b), "Sport and Hegemony: Some Theoretical Problems," in H. Cantelon and R. S. Gruneau (Eds.), *Sport, Culture and the Modern State*, Toronto, University of Toronto Press.

Harnecker, M. (1974), *Les concepts élémentaires du matérialisme historique*, Bruxelles, Éditions contradictions.

Harvey, D. (1973), *Social Justice and the City*, London, Arnold.

Harvey, J. (1982), "La mise en condition du corps: Kino-Québec et le discours professionnel sur la condition physique," in *Loisir et Société*, V, 1.

Harvey, J. (1983), *Le corps programmé ou La rhétorique de Kino-Québec*, Montréal, Éditions coopératives Albert Saint-Martin.

HCJLS (Haut-Commissariat à la jeunesse, aux loisirs et aux sports) (1977), *Etude sur les programmes d'activités sportives et de conditionnement physique au niveau des entreprises*, First interim report, HCJLS.

Higgs, R. J. and R. D. Isaacs (1977), *The Sporting Athlete: Athletes in Literature and Life*, New York, Harcourt Brace Jovanovich.

Hoch, P. (1972), *Rip Off the Big Game*, New York, Doubleday.

Hoggart, R. (1958), *The Uses of Literacy*, New York, Pelican Books.

Hollands, R. G. (1984a), "Images of Women in Canadian Sports Fiction," in N. Theberge and P. Donnelly (Eds.), *Sport and the Sociological Imagination*, Fort Worth, Texas Christian University Press.

Hollands, R. G. (1984b), "The Role of Cultural Studies and Social Criticism in the Sociological Study of Sport," in *Quest*, XXXVI, 1.

Horowitz, I. (1974), "Sports Broadcasting," in R. Noll (Ed.), *Government and the Sports Business*, Washington, The Brookings Institution.

Howell, R. (Ed.) (1982), *Her Story in Sport*, West Point, New York, Leisure Press.

Hrycaiko, D., et al. (1978), *Sport, Physical Activity and TV Role Models*, Vanier, CAHPER Sociology of Sport Monographs.

Humber, W. (1982), "Cheering for the Home Team: Baseball and Town Life in 19th Century Ontario, 1854–1869," in *Proceedings of the 5th Canadian Symposium on the History of Sport and Physical Education*, University of Toronto.

Illich, I. (1977), *Le chômage créateur*, Paris, Seuil.
Ilowite, S. H. (1972), *Centerman from Quebec: A Hockey Story*, New York, Hastings House.
Jamet, M. (1980), *Les sports et l'État au Québec*, Montréal, Éditions coopératives Albert Saint-Martin.
Jamieson, S. (1968), *Times of Trouble: Labour Unrest and Industrial Conflict in Canada, 1900–1966*, Ottawa, Queen's Printer.
Jenkins C. and M. Green (Eds.) (1981), *Sporting Fictions*, Birmingham Centre for Contemporary Cultural Studies, University of Birmingham.
Jhally, S. (1984), "The Spectacle of Accumulation: Material and Cultural Factors in the Evolution of the Sport/Media Complex," in *Insurgent Sociologist*, XII, 3.
Jones, J. C. (1976), "The Economics of the National Hockey League," and "The Economics of the N.H.L. Revisited: A Postscript on Structural Change," in R. S. Gruneau and J. Albinson (Eds.), *Canadian Sport: Sociological Perspectives*, Don Mills, Addison-Wesley.
Kenyon, G. S. (1967), "Do We Really Know What We are Doing?," Paper presented at New York State University at Brockport, New York, November 16.
Kidd, B. (1978), "Canadian Opposition to the 1936 Olympics in Germany," in *Canadian Journal of the History of Sport and Physical Education*, IX, 2.
Kidd, B. (1979), *The Political Economy of Sport*, Vanier, CAHPER Sociology of Sport Monographs.
Kidd, B. (1981), "The Canadian State and Sport: The Dilemma of Intervention," in *Annual Conference Proceedings of the National Association for Physical Education in Higher Education*, Champlain, Human Kinetics.
Kidd, B. (1982), "Sport, Dependency and the Canadian State," in H. Cantelon and R. S. Gruneau (Eds.), *Sport, Culture and the Modern State*, Toronto, University of Toronto Press.
Kidd, B. and M. Eberts (1982), *Athletes Rights in Canada*, Toronto, Ministry of Tourism and Recreation.
Kidd, B. and J. MacFarlane (1972), *The Death of Hockey*, Toronto, New Press.
Killanin, M. (1976), "Eligibility and Amateurism," in M. Killanin and J. Rodda (Eds.), *The Olympic Games: 80 Years of People, Events and Records*, Don Mills, Collier-Macmillan Canada.
Kirsh, C., B. Dixon and M. Bond (1973), *Les loisirs au Canada 1972*, Toronto, A. E. Desing et Éditions Culturcan.
Laberge, S. (1983), "L'activité physique chez les femmes: des conditions d'existence qui font la différence," in *Canadian Woman Studies*, IV, 3.
Labonté, R. (1982), "Half Truths About Health," in *Policy Options*, III, 1.
Labonté, R. and S. Penford (1981), "Analyse critique des perspectives canadiennes en promotion de la santé," in *Education sanitaire*, April.
Lalive d'Epinay, C., M. Bassand, E. Christe and D. Gros (1982), *Temps libre. Culture de masse et cultures de classes aujourd'hui*, Lausanne, Éditions Pierre-Marcel Favre.

Lalonde, M. (1974), *A New Perspective on the Health of Canadians*, Ottawa, Ministry of National Health and Welfare.

Landry, F. (1979), *Kino-Québec et le mouvement international sport pour tous*, Meeting of the Coordinators of Modules, Québec, Kino-Québec.

Lansley, K. (1971), *The Amateur Athletic Union of Canada and Changing Concept of Amateurism*, Ph.D. dissertation, University of Alberta.

Larouche, R. (1982), "La situation occupationnelle en éducation physique et les diverses possibilités de réorientation de carrière," in *L'éducation physique, où va la profession?*, Montréal, Bellarmin-Desport.

Larouche, R. (1984), "La socialisation professionnelle des éducateurs physiques," in *Revue des Sciences de l'Education*, X, 3.

Lawson, H. A. (1985), "Knowledge for Work in the Physical Education Profession," in *Sociology of Sport Journal*, II, 1.

Lenskyj, H. (1980), "Moral Physiology in Physical Education for Girls in Ontario, 1800–1930," in *Proceedings of the 5th Canadian Symposium on the History of Sport*, Toronto.

Lenskyj, H. (1986), *Out of Bounds: Women, Sport and Sexuality*, Toronto, Women's Press.

Le Pogam, Y. (1979), *Démocratisation du sport: mythe ou réalité?*, Paris, Jean-Pierre Delarge Éditeur.

Levasseur, R. (1980), "Contribution à une sociologie de l'action culturelle," in *Loisir et Société*, III, 1.

Levasseur, R. (1982), *Loisir et culture au Québec*, Montréal, Boréal Express.

Levasseur, R. (1983), "Le loisir et l'État au Québec, 1960–1980," in *Loisir et Société*, VI, 1.

Lindsay, P. (1969), *A History of Sport in Canada 1807–1867*, Ph.D. dissertation, University of Alberta.

Linteau, P.-A., R. Durocher and J.-C. Robert (1979), *Histoire du Québec contemporain: De la confédération à la crise*, Montréal, Boréal Express.

Longstreth, T. M. (1962), *The Calgary Challengers*, Toronto, Macmillan.

Loy, J., et al. (1978), *Sport and Social Systems*, Reading, Addison-Wesley.

Lukacs, G. (1964), *Realism in Our Time*, New York, Harper Torchbooks.

Lukes, S. (1977), *Essays in Social Theory*, New York, Columbia University Press.

Macintosh, D. (1984), "The Interface Between School Sports and the National Coaching Certification Program in Canada," in *Proceedings of the 7th Commonwealth and International Conference on Sport, Physical Education, Recreation and Dance*, Brisbane, Australia.

Macintosh, D. (1985), "Sport and the Wider Goals of Government," in *CAHPER Journal*, LI, 7.

Macintosh, D. and J. Albinson (1985), *An Evaluation of the Athlete Program*, Ottawa, Sport Canada.

Macintosh, D. and T. Bedecki (1984), *Federal Government Sport Policy-Making Since 1961*, Parts 1 to 5, Report, Ottawa, Social Sciences and Humanities Research Council.

Macintosh, D. and C.E.S. Franks (1982), "Evolution of Federal Government Sport Policy in Canada, 1961–1968," Paper presented at the World Congress of Sociology, Mexico City.

Macintosh, D., T. Bedecki and C.E.S. Franks (1987), *Sport and Politics in Canada*, Kingston and Montreal, McGill-Queen's University Press.

Mackenzie King, W. L. (1918), *Industry and Humanity*, Toronto, Thomas Allen.

Magnussen, W. (1985), "The Local State," in *Studies in Political Economy*, 16.

Malo, A. (1941), "L'Action catholique et le clergé," in *Semaines sociales du Canada*, 18.

Mandel, E. (1970), *Marxist Economic Theory*, New York, Modern Reader.

Marx, K. (1965), *Oeuvres*, Paris, Gallimard, "La Pléiade."

Marx, K. and F. Engels (1977), *L'idéologie allemande*, Paris, Éditions sociales.

Mathews, R. (1969), *The Struggle for Canadian Universities*, Toronto, New Press.

Mauss, M. (1966), *Sociologie et anthropologie*, Paris, PUF.

McCabe, M. (1978), "Give It Another Try, Athletes Tell Ottawa," *The Globe and Mail*, January 16, Toronto.

McFarlane, L. (1975), *The Dynamite Flynns*, Toronto, Methuen.

McFarlane, L. (1976), *Breakaway*, Toronto, Methuen.

McMurtry, W. (1974), *Investigation and Inquiry into Violence in Amateur Hockey*, Toronto, Queen's Printer.

McRoberts, K. and D. Postgate (1980), *Quebec: Social Change and Political Crisis*, Toronto, McClelland and Stewart.

Meisel, J. and V. Lemieux (1972), *Ethnic Relations in Canadian Voluntary Associations*, Ottawa, Documents of the Royal Commission on Bilingualism and Biculturalism, 13.

Melchers, R. F. (1984), *La vieillesse ouvrière, 1836–1914*, Ph.D. dissertation, Université d'Aix-Marseille II.

Mercier, C. (1931), "La culture exagérée du sport," in *L'enseignement secondaire au Canada*, XII, December.

Merwin, D. J. and B. A. Northrop (1982), "Health Action in the Work Place: Complex Issues — No Simple Answers," in *Health Education Quarterly*, IX.

Metcalfe, A. (1978), "Working Class Recreation in Montreal, 1860–1895," in *Working Papers in the Sociological Study of Sport and Leisure*, I, 2.

Metcalfe, A. (1983), "Le sport au Canada français au XIXe siècle: le cas de Montréal, 1800–1914," in *Loisir et Société*, VI, 1.

Meynaud, J. (1966), *Sport et politique*, Paris, Payot.

Miliband, R. (1969), *The State in Capitalist Society*, London, Quartet.

Miliband, R. (1977), *Marxism and Politics*, Oxford, Oxford University Press.

Mills, C. Wright (1959), *The Sociological Imagination*, New York, Oxford University Press.

Morrow, D. (1985), "The Athletic War in Canada: Conflict and Sisyphian Resolution," Paper presented to the North American Society for Sport History, University of Wisconsin-Lacrosse.

Mott, M. (1983), "One Solution to the Urban Crisis: Manly Sports and Winnipeggers, 1900–1914," in *Urban History Review*, XII, 2.

Mouffe, C. (1979), *Gramsci and Marxist Theory*, London, Routledge & Kegan Paul.

Munro, J. (1970), *A Proposed Sport Policy for Canadians*, Ottawa, Queen's Printer.

Naylor, T. (1975), *The History of Canadian Business 1867–1914*, Toronto, Lorimer.

Néron, G. (1975), *Final Report of the Study Committee on Violence in Amateur Hockey in Quebec*, Government of Quebec.

Nichols, B. (1981), *Ideology and the Image: Social Representation in the Cinema and Other Media*, Bloomington, Indiana University Press.

O'Brien, A. (1967), *Hockey Wingman*, Toronto, George J. McLeod Limited.

O'Neill, J. (Ed.) (1973), *Modes of Individualism and Collectivism*, London, Heinemann.

Orr, F. (1966), *Buck Martin in World Hockey*, Toronto, Musson Book Company.

Pagnucco, F. (1982), *Home Grown Heroes: Sports History of Sudbury*, Sudbury, Miller Publishing.

Palmer, B. (1979), *A Culture in Conflict: Skilled Workers and Industrial Capitalism in Hamilton, Ontario, 1860–1914*, Kingston and Montreal, McGill-Queen's University Press.

Palmer, B. (1985), *Working-Class Experience*, Toronto, Butterworths.

Panitch, L. (Ed.) (1977), *The Canadian State: Political Economy and Political Power*, Toronto, University of Toronto Press.

Paplauskas-Ramunas, A. (1954), *L'éducation physique dans l'humanisme intégral*, Ottawa, Presses de l'Université d'Ottawa.

Paplauskas-Ramunas, A. (1968), *Development of the Whole Man through Physical Education: An Interdisciplinary Comparative Exploration and Appraisal*, Ottawa, University of Ottawa Press.

Peters, R. (1976), *Television Coverage of Sport*, Occasional Stencilled Papers, Birmingham Centre for Contemporary Cultural Studies, University of Birmingham.

Pius XII (1945), "Les formations sportives," in *Nos Cours*, XII, 26.

Pius XII (1952), "Sport et conscience morale," in *Nos Cours*, XIV, 18.

Plante, J. R. (1975), "Crime et châtiment au forum (un mythe à l'oeuvre et à l'épreuve)," in *Stratégie*.

Pociello, C. (1981), *Sports et société*, Paris, Vigot.

Pronovost, G. (1983), *Temps, culture et société*, Sillery, Presses de l'Université du Québec.

Racicot, C. (1949), "Les loisirs: Nature et but," in *Semaines sociales du Canada*, 26.

Rea, H., P. DesRuisseaux and N. Green (1969), *Report of the Task Force on Sports for Canadians*, Ottawa, Queen's Printer.

Redmond, G. (1982), *The Sporting Scots of Nineteenth-Century Canada*, Rutherford, New Jersey, Fairleigh Dickinson University Press.

Regan, G. A. (1981), *A Challenge to the Nation*, Ottawa, Government of Canada.

Reynolds, B. (1985), "Mary Roberts: Toronto Comeback," in *Muscle and Fitness Magazine*, September.

Rigauer, B. (1981), *Sport and Work*, Translated by Allen Guttmann, New York, Columbia University Press.

Robin, M. (1968), *Radical Politics and Canadian Labour 1880–1930*, Kingston, Queen's Industrial Relations Centre.

Rosenzweig, R. (1979), "Middle-Class Parks and Working-Class Play: The Struggle over Recreational Space in Worcester, Massachusetts, 1870–1910," in *Radical History Review*, XXI, 43.

Ross, M. G. (1951), *The Y.M.C.A. in Canada: the Chronicle of a Century (1851–1951)*, Toronto, Ryerson.

Ross, S. (1978), "A Critique of the Undergraduate Curriculum in Physical Education in Canadian Universities," in *Proceedings of the 6th Commonwealth Conference on Sport, Education and Recreation*, Edmonton.

Ross, S. (1981), "The Epistemic Geography of Physical Education: Addressing the Problem of Theory and Practice," in *Quest*, XXXIII, 1.

Sack, A. L. and B. Kidd (1985), "The Amateur Athlete as Employee," in A. T. Johnson and J. H. Frey (Eds.), *Government and Sport: the Public Policy Issues*, Totowa, New Jersey, Rowman and Allenheld.

Saint-Arnaud, F. X. (1946), "Loisirs des jeunes," in *Semaines sociales du Canada*, XXIII.

Sattel, J. (1977), "Heroes on the Right," in *The Journal of Popular Culture*, XI, 1.

Sawula, L. W. (1973), "Why 1970, Why Not Before?," in *Canadian Journal of History of Sport and Physical Education*, XIV, 2.

Schrodt, B. (1984), "Federal Programmes of Physical Recreation and Fitness: The Contributions of Ian Eisenhart and B.C.'s PRO-REC," in *Canadian Journal of History of Sport*, XV, 2.

Sennet, R. (1980), *La famille contre la ville: les classes moyennes de Chicago à l'ère industrielle 1872–1890*, Paris, Encres.

Sheedy, A. (1976), "Une philosophie de l'éducation physique: un embarras, un luxe ou une nécessité?," in *Canadian Journal of Applied Sport Sciences*, I, 4.

Sheedy, A. (1982), "Les pratiques d'intervention professionnelle en éducation physique: un exercice de réflexion critique," in *La Revue québécoise de l'activité physique*, 1.

Slack, T. (1981), "Volunteers in Amateur Sports Organizations: Biographic and Demographic Characteristics and Patterns of Involvement," in A. Ingham and E. Broom (Eds.), *Career Patterns and Career Contingencies in Sport*, Vancouver, University of British Columbia Press.

Smith, G. (1975), "A View from the Play Pen: A Study of the Sports Journalist," Faculty of Physical Education, University of Alberta.

Sopinka, J. (1984), *Can I play?*, The Report of the Task Force on Equal Opportunity in Athletics, Ontario, Ministry of Labour.

Soucie, D. and A. Brodeur (1979), "Le profil de carrière des diplômés en éducation physique à l'Université d'Ottawa (1968–1975)," in *CAHPER Journal*, XLV, 4.

Sport Canada (1986), *Athletes' Representation on Board of Directors*, Ottawa.

Statistics Canada (1978), *Culture Statistics: Recreational Activities 1976*, Ottawa.

Stevick, P. (Ed.) (1967), *The Theory of the Novel*, New York, The Free Press.

Swingewood, A. (1975), *The Novel and Revolution*, London, Macmillan.

Taylor, B. M. (1976), *The Unification of Sport Report*, Ottawa, National Centre of Sport and Recreation.

Taylor, B. M. (1984), "Flextime," in *Toronto Star Magazine*, August.

Theberge, N. (1980), "A Comparison of Men and Women in Leadership Roles in Ontario Amateur Sport," a Report submitted to the Ontario Ministry of Culture and Recreation.

Thériault, Y. J. (1985), *La société civile*, Montréal, Québec/Amérique.

Thompson, E. P. (1968), *The Making of the English Working Class*, Harmondsworth, Middlesex, Penguin Books.

Tolman, W. H. (1909), *Social Engineering*, New York, Macmillan.

Touraine, A. (1971), *The Post-Industrial Society*, New York, Random House.

Trottier, C., P. Lavergne and A. Juneau (1967), *L'organisation des loisirs: Étude sur la Fédération des Loisirs de la région de Québec*, Québec, Fédération des Loisirs de la région de Québec.

Vickers, J. (1984), *A Comparative Study: Relative Opportunities for Women in the CIAU: 1978–1982*, Prepared by the CIAU Women's Committee, Ottawa.

Villeneuve, Cardinal R. (1934), "Culture physique au regard de l'Église," in *Tracts de l'Action catholique*, 5.

Weinstein, J. (1968), *The Corporate Ideal in the Liberal State*, Boston, Beacon Press.

West, T. J. (1973), "Physical Fitness, Sport and the Federal Government, 1909 to 1954," in *Canadian Journal of History of Sport and Physical Education*, XIV, 2.

Westland, C. (1979), *Fitness and Amateur Sport in Canada: the Federal Government's Programme: An Historical Perspective*, Vanier, Canadian Association of Parks and Recreation.

Whannel, G. (1981), "Narrative and Television Sport: the Coe and Ovett Story," in C. Jenkins and M. Green (Eds.), *Sporting Fictions*, Birmingham Centre for Contemporary Cultural Studies, University of Birmingham.

Whannel, G. (1984), "Fields in Vision: Sport and Representation," in *Screen*, XXV, 3.

Williams, R. (1958), *Culture and Society*, London, Chatto and Windus.

Williams, R. (1965), *The Long Revolution*, Middlesex, Penguin Books.

Williams, R. (1974), *Television: Technology and Cultural Form*, London, Collins.

Williams, R. (1976), *Keywords: A Vocabulary of Culture and Society*, Croom Helm, Fontana.

Williams, R. (1977), *Marxism and Literature*, Oxford, Oxford University Press.

Williams, R. (1980), *Problems In Materialism and Culture*, London, Verso Editions.

Willis, P. (1982), "Women in Sport in Ideology," in J. Hargreaves (Ed.), *Sport, Culture and Ideology*, London, Routledge & Kegan Paul.

Wise, S. (1974), "Sport and Class Values in Old Ontario and Quebec," in W. Heick and R. Graham (Eds.), *His Own Man: Essay in honour of Arthur Reginald Marsden Lower*, Kingston and Montreal, McGill-Queen's University Press.

Young, S. (1952), *Scrubs on Skates*, Boston, Little, Brown and Company.

Young, S. (1953), *Boy on Defence*, Toronto, McClelland and Stewart.

Young, S. (1963), *A Boy at the Leafs' Camp*, Boston, Little, Brown and Company.

Young, S. and G. Robertson (1972), *Face-Off*, Richmond Hill, Ontario, Simon and Schuster.

Zeigler, E. (1983), "A Proposal for the Reunification of our Professional and Scholarly Dimensions," in *CAHPER Journal*, L, 4.